REFERENCE GUIDE TO THE OCCUPATIONAL THERAPY

ETHICS STANDARDS

2008 EDITION

Deborah Yarett Slater
MS, OT/L, FAOTA
Editor

Foreword by
Penelope Moyers Cleveland
EdD, OTR/L, BCMH, FAOTA

AOTA
PRESS ®

The American
Occupational Therapy
Association, Inc.

Centennial Vision
We envision that occupational therapy is a powerful, widely recognized, science-driven, and evidence-based profession with a globally connected and diverse workforce meeting society's occupational needs.

Vision Statement
The American Occupational Therapy Association advances occupational therapy as the pre-eminent profession in promoting the health, productivity, and quality of life of individuals and society through the therapeutic application of occupation.

Mission Statement
The American Occupational Therapy Association advances the quality, availability, use, and support of occupational therapy through standard-setting, advocacy, education, and research on behalf of its members and the public.

AOTA Staff
Frederick P. Somers, *Executive Director*
Christopher M. Bluhm, *Chief Operating Officer*

Chris Davis, *Director, AOTA Press*
Michael N. Melletz, *Book and Journal Production Manager*
Carrie Mercadante, *Production Editor*

Beth Ledford, *Director, Marketing and Member Communications*

The American Occupational Therapy Association, Inc.
4720 Montgomery Lane
Bethesda, MD 20814
Phone: 301-652-AOTA (2682)
TDD: 800-377-8555
Fax: 301-652-7711
www.aota.org
To order: 1-877-404-AOTA (2682)

Disclaimers
This publication is designed to provide accurate and authoritative information in regard to the subject matter covered. It is sold or distributed with the understanding that the publisher is not engaged in rendering legal, accounting, or other professional services. If legal advice or other expert assistance is required, the services of a competent professional person should be sought.
—*From the Declaration of Principles jointly adopted by the American Bar Association and a Committee of Publishers and Associations*

It is the objective of the American Occupational Therapy Association to be a forum for free expression and interchange of ideas. The opinions expressed by the contributors to this work are their own and not necessarily those of the American Occupational Therapy Association.

ISBN 10: 1-56900-261-4
ISBN 13: 978-1-56900-261-2

Library of Congress Control Number: 2008924873

Design by Sarah Ely and Michael N. Melletz
Original Composition by Circle Graphics, Columbia, MD
Printed by Automated Graphic Systems, Inc., White Plains, MD

Contents

Foreword

The profession of occupational therapy is an exciting career. I am always thankful that I learned about this profession, and I am grateful for the rewards I have experienced since becoming an occupational therapist. What has been sustaining for me throughout my professional life has been the impact we have on the lives of those whom we serve. There can be no greater impact than helping people participate in meaningful and necessary daily life activities regardless of limitations due to personal capacity, task complexity, or environmental barriers. We are in a special position to assist our clients, whether persons, populations, or organizations, to achieve their best possible outcomes so they can fully engage as members of society.

We are able to influence these outcomes not only by direct intervention but also by the way we educate our students, the way we conduct science and research, how we develop and manage programs designed for populations or organizations, the way in which we represent ourselves to the public, how we carry out our commitment to leadership within communities or professional organizations, and how we use advocacy to influence public policy actions.

The broad sphere of influence which occupational therapy personnel have on the lives of individuals makes it clear that the responsibility of being a professional extends well beyond time spent on the job. Society holds high standards for professionals and their conduct. By virtue of having the *Occupational Therapy Code of Ethics*

(American Occupational Therapy Association [AOTA], 2005), professionals are given greater autonomy and privilege in their decision making but also are expected to comply with the principles, values, and conduct delineated in that Code and related ethics documents, collectively known as the "Ethics Standards." These standards apply "not only to conduct within occupational therapy roles but also to conduct that may affect the performance of occupational therapy or the reputation of the profession" (AOTA, 2007, p. 679). Therefore, an expectation exists that the interactions and performance of occupational therapy personnel will meet the intent of the Ethics Standards across all the diverse roles that they may assume. These roles are not only related to those in practice, education, and research but also are related to elected and appointed volunteer leadership positions in AOTA and in the community.

ETHICAL REASONING

The complexities of the current health care and social services environments and our professional obligation to advocate and promote benefit for our clients require knowledge and skills in ethical reasoning. Ethical reasoning begins with a thorough familiarity with and understanding of the Ethics Standards (in addition to the Code, includes *Guidelines to the Occupational Therapy Code of Ethics* [AOTA, 2006] and the *Core Values and Attitudes of Occupational Therapy* [AOTA, 1993]). Ethical reasoning is further developed through commitment to developing and maintaining a strong moral character as demonstrated through our actions to promote good on behalf of our clients. Mindful reflection is needed on our actions to promote good so that we can enhance our professional reasoning for future situations.

The Ethics Standards are the basis for critical reasoning that is well developed through ongoing experience and focused competency development where one is deliberate in identifying learning needs related to quality service provision. In fact, pursuit of high standards of competency, regardless of professional role assumed, are a core ethical concept (Principle 4 of the Code). Educators and scientists in occupational therapy are responsible for the quality of their research and educational programs, making certain that participants are involved in educational activities that lead to significant learning or in research designs that actually study what is intended. Entrepreneurs and administrators are expected to make business decisions that not only support the business but also lead to exemplary customer service. When we assume leadership roles in professional organizations or in the community, we are responsible for carrying out the duties associated with leadership in a way that is timely and effective and avoids conflicts of interest. We also must be careful to avoid conflict of commitment and only assume leadership positions to which we can devote adequate time and thoughtfulness. We are careful in our advocacy to fully understand the implications, intended and unintended, of the public policy changes we propose, ensuring that we keep our focus as client-centered as possible. In other words, occupational therapy personnel must "do" what they say they are going to "do." When all occupational therapy personnel collectively work toward attaining a high aspirational standard of ethical behavior, we can be confident that the public will value and trust in our services.

ABOUT THIS BOOK

This *Reference Guide to the Occupational Therapy Ethics Standards* was written to assist all occupational therapy personnel as they confront ethical issues throughout their careers due to the complexity of society and the systems in which we work. The content includes a broad variety of educational tools, including new advisory opinions and articles that address particularly current ethical trends. Readers will no doubt be challenged to rethink some of the situations you have encountered in the past, perhaps because of increased awareness of the ethical issues that are not always initially apparent. Ethical reasoning skills and learning are best developed by reflection on experiences, along with education or consultation, to make a thoughtful and defensible ethical decision. We thank the authors for their dedication to provide the resources and tools needed to facilitate the ethical reasoning that will positively affect those whom we serve.

—Penelope Moyers Cleveland, EdD, OTR/L, BCMH, FAOTA
President, American Occupational Therapy Association

REFERENCES

American Occupational Therapy Association. (1993). Core values and attitudes of occupational therapy practice. *American Journal of Occupational Therapy, 47*, 1085–1086.

American Occupational Therapy Association. (2005). Occupational therapy code of ethics (2005). *American Journal of Occupational Therapy, 59*, 639–642.

American Occupational Therapy Association. (2006). Guidelines to the occupational therapy code of ethics. *American Journal of Occupational Therapy, 60*, 652–658.

American Occupational Therapy Association. (2007). Enforcement procedures for the occupational therapy code of ethics. *American Journal of Occupational Therapy, 61*, 679–685.

Acknowledgments

This 2008 edition of the *Reference Guide to the Occupational Therapy Ethics Standards* was updated by the members of the AOTA Ethics Commission:

Kathlyn L. Reed, PhD, OTR, FAOTA, MLIS,
Chairperson

Lea Cheyney Brandt, OTD, OTR/L,
Member at Large

Darryl John Austin, MS, OT/L,
Practice Representative

Betsy DeBrakeleer, COTA/L, ROH,
OTA Representative

Linda Gabriel, PhD, OTR/L,
Education Representative

Donna F. Homenko, PhD, RDH,
Public Member

Craig R. Jackson, JD, MSW,
Public Member

Deborah Yarett Slater, MS, OT/L, FAOTA,
AOTA Staff Liaison

The Ethics Commission refined, organized, and made additions to the contents of this new edition to enhance its functionality and relevance as a core text for members of the occupational therapy profession and the educational community.

ETHICS STANDARDS

CHAPTER 1

Reference Guide on Ethics

AOTA ETHICS COMMISSION

The AOTA Ethics Commission (EC, formerly the Commission on Standards and Ethics) was established in 1975 by the AOTA Representative Assembly (RA) with the passage of Resolution 461-75. As stated in the AOTA Bylaws, the purpose of the EC is "to serve the Association members and public through the identification, development, review, interpretation, and education of the Ethics Standards and to provide the process whereby the ethics of the Association are enforced."

The AOTA has developed the *Ethics Standards* (*Occupational Therapy Code of Ethics, Guidelines to the Occupational Therapy Code of Ethics*, and *Core Values and Attitudes of Occupational Therapy Practice*) and *Standards of Practice for Occupational Therapy* to promote quality care and professional conduct. The EC is responsible for reviewing and enforcing ethics standards related to education, practice, and research. The contents of this edition of the *Reference Guide to the Occupational Therapy Ethics Standards* have an increased focus on all aspects of professional conduct and its application to the many roles in which occupational therapists, occupational therapy assistants, or students may find themselves. These go beyond traditional practice, education, and research and include elected and volunteer leadership roles in the profession.

The EC has no jurisdiction over certification or accreditation standards. Initial certification is the responsibility of the National Board for Certification in Occupational Therapy (NBCOT), formed in 1986. Compliance with accreditation standards for occupational therapy educational programs is the responsibility of the Accreditation Council for Occupational Therapy Education (ACOTE). Note that violations of the *Occupational Therapy Code of Ethics (2005)* also may be reported to state regulatory boards (SRBs) or NBCOT for consideration. Similarly, SRBs or NBCOT may refer cases of violation of professional conduct, licensure, or certification standards to the EC for their information and action as deemed appropriate.

RELATIONSHIP TO SRBS

States with regulatory laws governing occupational therapy personnel have the responsibility to investigate alleged violations that have caused or have the potential to cause harm to the public in that state and take disciplinary action as defined within those state laws and regulations. Disciplinary language in state regulations may reflect AOTA documents on standards of practice and ethical conduct. When informed of disciplinary action by SRBs, the EC may take further action or may take independent action if the individual is an AOTA member.

AOTA *STANDARDS OF PRACTICE*

The AOTA, through the Commission on Practice (COP) and the Commission on Continuing Competence and Professional Development (CCCPD), has developed *Standards of Practice* and related documents for occupational therapy practitioners. The AOTA RA has adopted the following standards (most recent revision is listed):

- *Standards of Practice* for Occupational Therapy. This document was mostly recently revised and approved in 2005 (see *American Journal of Occupational Therapy, 59,* 663–665).
- *Guidelines for Supervision, Roles, and Responsibilities During the Delivery of Occupational Therapy Services (2004)* (see *American Journal of Occupational Therapy, 58,* 663–667).
- *Standards for Continuing Competence (2005)* (see *American Journal of Occupational Therapy, 59,* 661–662).
- *Scope of Practice (2004)* (see *American Journal of Occupational Therapy, 58,* 673–677).

AOTA *OCCUPATIONAL THERAPY CODE OF ETHICS (2005)*

The *Occupational Therapy Code of Ethics* was initially adopted in 1977 and revised in 1979, 1988, 1994, 2000, and 2005. It is reviewed for potential revision, at a minimum, every 5 years. The AOTA RA adopted the current *Occupational Therapy Code of Ethics* in May 2005. This document replaces the 2000 *Occupational Therapy Code of Ethics* (see *American Journal of Occupational Therapy, 54,* 614–616). The *Occupational Therapy Code of Ethics (2005)* is one of three documents (with *Guidelines to the Occupational Therapy Code of Ethics* and *Core Values and Attitudes of Occupational Therapy Practice*) that are known collectively as the "Ethics Standards" and apply to AOTA members. They apply to occupational therapy personnel at all levels in professional roles such as those of practitioner, educator, fieldwork educator or coordinator, clinical supervisor, man-

ager, administrator, consultant, faculty, program director, researcher/scholar, private practice owner, entrepreneur, student, and others, including elected and appointed volunteer roles within AOTA. The *Occupational Therapy Code of Ethics (2005)* is available to AOTA members and the public on AOTA's Web site (www.aota.org) and through AOTA's Ethics Office. It also can be found in the *American Journal of Occupational Therapy* (see above). Other documents, such as *Core Values and Attitudes in Occupational Therapy Practice* and *Guidelines to the Occupational Therapy Code of Ethics,* also are available through the Ethics Office and on the AOTA Web site (www.aota.org) under both the Consumer (Consumers/Ethics Resources) and Practitioner (Practitioners/Ethics/Ethics Documents) tabs.

ENFORCEMENT PROCEDURES

To ensure maintenance of the *Occupational Therapy Code of Ethics (2005)* and compliance by AOTA members, procedures have been developed for the investigation and adjudication of alleged violations. These procedures, initially approved by the 1996 AOTA RA and most recently updated in 2007, enable the Association to act fairly in the performance of its responsibilities as a professional membership organization. Their purpose also is to safeguard the rights of individuals against whom complaints have been made. A copy of the most current *Enforcement Procedures for the Occupational Therapy Code of Ethics* is included in this *Reference Guide.*

Penny Kyler, MA, OTR/L, FAOTA
July 1998, revised March 2003

Deborah Yarett Slater, MS, OT/L, FAOTA
AOTA Staff Liaison to the Ethics Commission
Revised December 2005, January 2008

CHAPTER 2

Occupational Therapy Code of Ethics (2005)

PREAMBLE

The American Occupational Therapy Association (AOTA) *Occupational Therapy Code of Ethics (2005)* is a public statement of principles used to promote and maintain high standards of conduct within the profession and is supported by the *Core Values and Attitudes of Occupational Therapy Practice* (AOTA, 1993). Members of AOTA are committed to promoting inclusion, diversity, independence, and safety for all recipients in various stages of life, health, and illness and to empower all beneficiaries of occupational therapy. This commitment extends beyond service recipients to include professional colleagues, students, educators, businesses, and the community.

Fundamental to the mission of the occupational therapy profession is the therapeutic use of everyday life activities (occupations) with individuals or groups for the purpose of participation in roles and situations in home, school, workplace, community, and other settings. "Occupational therapy addresses the physical, cognitive, psychosocial, sensory, and other aspects of performance in a variety of contexts to support engagement in everyday life activities that affect health, well-being and quality of life" (*Definition of Occupational Therapy Practice for the AOTA Model Practice Act*, 2004). Occupational therapy personnel have an ethical responsibility first and foremost to recipients of service as well as to society.

The historical foundation of this Code is based on ethical reasoning surrounding practice and professional issues, as well as empathic reflection regarding these interactions with others. This reflection resulted in the establishment of principles that guide ethical action. Ethical action goes beyond rote following of rules or application of principles; rather, it is a manifestation of moral character and mindful reflection. It is a commitment to beneficence for the sake of others, to virtuous practice of artistry and science, to genuinely good behaviors, and to noble acts of courage. It is an empathic way of being among others, which is made every day by all occupational therapy personnel.

The AOTA *Occupational Therapy Code of Ethics (2005)* is an aspirational guide to professional conduct when ethical issues surface. Ethical decision making is a process that includes awareness regarding how the outcome will impact occupational therapy clients in all spheres. Applications of Code principles are considered situation-specific, and where a conflict exists, occupational therapy personnel will pursue responsible efforts for resolution.

The specific purpose of the AOTA *Occupational Therapy Code of Ethics (2005)* is to:

1. Identify and describe the principles supported by the occupational therapy profession
2. Educate the general public and members regarding established principles to which occupational therapy personnel are accountable
3. Socialize occupational therapy personnel new to the practice to expected standards of conduct
4. Assist occupational therapy personnel in recognition and resolution of ethical dilemmas.

The AOTA *Occupational Therapy Code of Ethics (2005)* defines the set principles that apply to occupational therapy personnel at all levels:

Principle 1.

Occupational therapy personnel shall demonstrate a concern for the safety and well-being of the recipients of their services. (BENEFICENCE)

Occupational therapy personnel shall

A. Provide services in a fair and equitable manner. They shall recognize and appreciate the cultural components of economics, geography, race, ethnicity, religious and political factors, marital status, age, sexual orientation, gender identity, and disability of all recipients of their services.
B. Strive to ensure that fees are fair and reasonable and commensurate with services performed. When occupational therapy practitioners set fees, they shall set fees considering institutional, local, state, and federal requirements, and with due regard for the service recipient's ability to pay.
C. Make every effort to advocate for recipients to obtain needed services through available means.
D. Recognize the responsibility to promote public health and the safety and well-being of individuals, groups, and/or communities.

Principle 2.

Occupational therapy personnel shall take measures to ensure a recipient's safety and avoid imposing or inflicting harm. (NONMALEFICENCE)

Occupational therapy personnel shall

A. Maintain therapeutic relationships that shall not exploit the recipient of services sexually, physically, emotionally, psychologically, financially, socially, or in any other manner.
B. Avoid relationships or activities that conflict or interfere with therapeutic professional judgment and objectivity.
C. Refrain from any undue influences that may compromise provision of service.
D. Exercise professional judgment and critically analyze directives that could result in potential harm before implementation.
E. Identify and address personal problems that may adversely impact professional judgment and duties.
F. Bring concerns regarding impairment of professional skills of a colleague to the attention of the appropriate authority when or if attempts to address concerns are unsuccessful.

Principle 3.

Occupational therapy personnel shall respect recipients to assure their rights. (AUTONOMY, CONFIDENTIALITY)

Occupational therapy personnel shall

A. Collaborate with recipients, and if they desire, families, significant others, and/or caregivers in setting goals and priorities throughout the intervention process, including full disclosure of the nature, risk, and potential outcomes of any interventions.
B. Obtain informed consent from participants involved in research activities and ensure that they understand potential risks and outcomes.

C. Respect the individual's right to refuse professional services or involvement in research or educational activities.

D. Protect all privileged confidential forms of written, verbal, and electronic communication gained from educational, practice, research, and investigational activities unless otherwise mandated by local, state, or federal regulations.

Principle 4.

Occupational therapy personnel shall achieve and continually maintain high standards of competence. (DUTY)

Occupational therapy personnel shall

A. Hold the appropriate national, state, or any other requisite credentials for the services they provide.

B. Conform to AOTA standards of practice and official documents.

C. Take responsibility for maintaining and documenting competence in practice, education, and research by participating in professional development and educational activities.

D. Be competent in all topic areas in which they provide instruction to consumers, peers, and/or students.

E. Critically examine available evidence so they may perform their duties on the basis of current information.

F. Protect service recipients by ensuring that duties assumed by or assigned to other occupational therapy personnel match credentials, qualifications, experience, and scope of practice.

G. Provide appropriate supervision to individuals for whom they have supervisory responsibility in accordance with Association official documents; local, state, and federal or national laws and regulations; and institutional policies and procedures.

H. Refer to or consult with other service providers whenever such a referral or consultation would be helpful to the care of the recipient of service. The referral or consultation process shall be done in collaboration with the recipient of service.

Principle 5.

Occupational therapy personnel shall comply with laws and Association policies guiding the profession of occupational therapy.
(PROCEDURAL JUSTICE)

Occupational therapy personnel shall

A. Familiarize themselves with and seek to understand and abide by institutional rules; applicable Association policies; and local, state, and federal/national/international laws.

B. Be familiar with revisions in those laws and Association policies that apply to the profession of occupational therapy and shall inform employers, employees, and colleagues of those changes.

C. Encourage those they supervise in occupational therapy–related activities to adhere to the Code.

D. Take reasonable steps to ensure employers are aware of occupational therapy's ethical obligations, as set forth in this Code, and of the implications of those obligations for occupational therapy practice, education, and research.

E. Record and report in an accurate and timely manner all information related to professional activities.

Principle 6.

Occupational therapy personnel shall provide accurate information when representing the profession. (VERACITY)

Occupational therapy personnel shall

A. Represent their credentials, qualifications, education, experience, training, and competence accurately. This is of particular importance for those to whom occupational therapy personnel provide their services or with whom occupational therapy personnel have a professional relationship.

B. Disclose any professional, personal, financial, business, or volunteer affiliations that may pose a conflict of interest to those with whom they may establish a professional, contractual, or other working relationship.

C. Refrain from using or participating in the use of any form of communication that contains false, fraudulent, deceptive, or unfair statements or claims.

D. Identify and fully disclose to all appropriate persons errors that compromise recipients' safety.

E. Accept responsibility for their professional actions that reduce the public's trust in occupational therapy services and those that perform those services.

Principle 7.

Occupational therapy personnel shall treat colleagues and other professionals with respect, fairness, discretion, and integrity. (FIDELITY)

Occupational therapy personnel shall

A. Preserve, respect, and safeguard confidential information about colleagues and staff, unless otherwise mandated by national, state, or local laws.

B. Accurately represent the qualifications, views, contributions, and findings of colleagues.

C. Take adequate measures to discourage, prevent, expose, and correct any breaches of the Code and report any breaches of the Code to the appropriate authority.

D. Avoid conflicts of interest and conflicts of commitment in employment and volunteer roles.

E. Use conflict resolution and/or alternative dispute resolution resources to resolve organizational and interpersonal conflicts.

F. Familiarize themselves with established policies and procedures for handling concerns about this Code, including familiarity with national, state, local, district, and territorial procedures for handling ethics complaints. These include policies and procedures created by AOTA, licensing and regulatory bodies, employers, agencies, certification boards, and other organizations having jurisdiction over occupational therapy practice.

GLOSSARY

Autonomy The right of an individual to self-determination. The ability to independently act on one's decisions for one's own well-being (Beauchamp & Childress, 2001).

Beneficence Doing good for others or bringing about good for them. The duty to confer benefits to others.

Confidentiality Not disclosing data or information that should be kept private to prevent harm and to abide by policies, regulations, and laws.

Dilemma A situation in which one moral conviction or right action conflicts with another. It exists because there is no one, clear-cut, right answer.

Duty Actions required of professionals by society or actions that are self-imposed.

Ethics A systematic study of morality (i.e., rules of conduct that are grounded in philosophical principles and theory).

Fidelity Faithfully fulfilling vows and promises, agreements, and discharging fiduciary responsibilities (Beauchamp & Childress, 2001).

Justice Three types of justice are
    Compensatory justice Making reparation for wrongs that have been done.
    Distributive justice The act of distributing goods and burdens among members of society.
    Procedural justice Assuring that processes are organized in a fair manner and policies or laws are followed.

Morality Personal beliefs regarding values, rules, and principles of what is right or wrong. Morality may be culture-based or culture-driven.

Nonmaleficence Not harming or causing harm to be done to oneself or others; the duty to ensure that no harm is done.

Veracity A duty to tell the truth; avoid deception.

REFERENCES

American Occupational Therapy Association. (1993). Core values and attitudes of occupational therapy practice. *American Journal of Occupational Therapy, 47,* 1085–1086.

American Occupational Therapy Association. (1998). Guidelines to the occupational therapy code of ethics. *American Journal of Occupational Therapy, 52,* 881–884. (*Note:* This document was updated in 2006. American Occupational Therapy Association. (2006). *American Journal of Occupational Therapy, 60,* 652–658.)

American Occupational Therapy Association. (2004). Association policies. *American Journal of Occupational Therapy, 58,* 694–695.

Beauchamp, T. L., & Childress, J. F. (2001). *Principles of biomedical ethics* (5th ed.). New York: Oxford University Press.

Definition of Occupational Therapy Practice for the AOTA Model Practice Act. (2004). Retrieved January 18, 2008, from http://www.aota.org/Practitioners/Advocacy/State/Resources/PracticeAct/36437.aspx

Authors

Commission on Standards and Ethics (SEC):

S. Maggie Reitz, PhD, OTR/L, FAOTA, Chairperson

Melba Arnold, MS, OTR/L

Linda Gabriel Franck, PhD, OTR/L

Darryl J. Austin, MS, OT/L

Diane Hill, COTA/L, AP, ROH

Lorie J. McQuade, MEd, CRC

Daryl K. Knox, MD

Deborah Yarett Slater, MS, OT/L, FAOTA, Staff Liaison

With contributions to the Preamble by Suzanne Peloquin, PhD, OTR, FAOTA

Adopted by the Representative Assembly 2005C202

Note. This document replaces the 2000 document, *Occupational Therapy Code of Ethics (2000) (American Journal of Occupational Therapy, 54,* 614–616).

Prepared 4/7/2000, revised draft 1/2005, second revision 4/2005 by SEC.

Note: Commission on Standards and Ethics (SEC) changed to Ethics Commission (EC) in September 2005 per AOTA Bylaws.

Note. This *AOTA Occupational Therapy Code of Ethics* is one of three documents that constitute the "Ethics Standards." The other two are the *Core Values and Attitudes of Occupational Therapy Practice* (1993) and the *Guidelines to the Occupational Therapy Code of Ethics.*

Core Values
and Attitudes
of Occupational
Therapy Practice

INTRODUCTION

In 1985, the American Occupational Therapy Association (AOTA) funded the Professional and Technical Role Analysis Study (PATRA). This study had two purposes: to delineate the entry-level practice of OTRs and COTAs through a role analysis and to conduct a task inventory of what practitioners actually do. Knowledge, skills, and attitude statements were to be developed to provide a basis for the role analysis. The PATRA study completed the knowledge and skills statements. The Executive Board subsequently charged the Standards and Ethics Commission (SEC) to develop a statement that would describe the attitudes and values that undergird the profession of occupational therapy. The SEC wrote this document for use by AOTA members.

The list of terms used in this statement was originally constructed by the American Association of Colleges of Nursing (AACN, 1986). The PATRA committee analyzed the knowledge statements that the committee had written and selected those terms from the AACN list that best identified the values and attitudes of our profession. This list of terms was then forwarded to the SEC by the PATRA Committee to use as the basis for the *Core Values and Attitudes* paper.

The development of this document is predicated on the assumption that the values of occupational therapy are evident in the offi-cial documents of the American Occupational Therapy Association. The official documents that were examined are (a) *Dictionary Definition of Occupational Therapy* (AOTA, 1986), (b) *The Philosophical Base of Occupational Therapy* (AOTA, 1979), (c) *Essentials and Guidelines for an Accredited Educational Program for the Occupational Therapist* (AOTA, 1991a), (d) *Essentials and Guidelines for an Accredited Educational Program for the Occupational Therapy Assistant* (AOTA, 1991b), and (e) *Occupational Therapy Code of Ethics* (AOTA, 1988). It is further assumed that these documents are representative of the values and beliefs reflected in other occupational therapy literature.

A *value* is defined as a belief or an ideal to which an individual is committed. Values are an important part of the base or foundation of a profession. Ideally, these values are embraced by all members of the profession and are reflected in the members' interactions with those persons receiving services, colleagues, and the society at large. Values have a central role in a profession and are developed and reinforced throughout an individual's life as a student and as a professional.

Actions and attitudes reflect the values of the individual. An attitude is the disposition to respond positively or negatively toward an object, person, concept, or situation. Thus, there is an assumption that all professional actions and interactions are rooted in certain core values and beliefs.

Seven Core Concepts

In this document, the *core values and attitudes* of occupational therapy are organized around seven basic concepts—altruism, equality, freedom, justice, dignity, truth, and prudence. How these core values and attitudes are expressed and implemented by occupational therapy practitioners may vary depending upon the environments and situations in which professional activity occurs.

Altruism is the unselfish concern for the welfare of others. This concept is reflected in actions and attitudes of commitment, caring, dedication, responsiveness, and understanding.

Equality requires that all individuals be perceived as having the same fundamental human rights and opportunities. This value is demonstrated by an attitude of fairness and impartiality. We believe that we should respect all individuals, keeping in mind that they may have values, beliefs, or lifestyles that are different from our own. Equality is practiced in the broad professional arena but is particularly important in day-to-day interactions with those individuals receiving occupational therapy services.

Freedom allows the individual to exercise choice and to demonstrate independence, initiative, and self-direction. There is a need for all individuals to find a balance between autonomy and societal membership that is reflected in the choice of various patterns of interdependence with the human and nonhuman environment. We believe that individuals are internally and externally motivated toward action in a continuous process of adaptation throughout the life span. Purposeful activity plays a major role in developing and exercising self-direction, initiative, interdependence, and relatedness to the world. Activities verify the individual's ability to adapt, and they establish a satisfying balance between autonomy and societal membership. As professionals, we affirm the freedom of choice for each individual to pursue goals that have personal and social meaning.

Justice places value on the upholding of such moral and legal principles as fairness, equity, truthfulness, and objectivity. This means we aspire to provide occupational therapy services for all individuals who are in need of these services and that we will maintain a goal-directed and objective relationship with all those served. Practitioners must be knowledgeable about and have respect for the legal rights of individuals receiving occupational therapy services. In addition, the occupational therapy practitioner must understand and abide by the local, state, and federal laws governing professional practice.

Dignity emphasizes the importance of valuing the inherent worth and uniqueness of each person. This value is demonstrated by an attitude of empathy and respect for self and others. We believe that each individual is a unique combination of biologic endowment, sociocultural heritage, and life experiences. We view human beings holistically, respecting the unique interaction of the mind, body, and physical and social environment. We believe that dignity is nurtured and grows from the sense of competence and self-worth that is integrally linked to the person's ability to perform valued and relevant activities. In occupational therapy we emphasize the importance of dignity by helping the individual build on his or her unique attributes and resources.

Truth requires that we be faithful to facts and reality. Truthfulness or veracity is demonstrated by being accountable, honest, forthright, accurate, and authentic in our attitudes and actions. There is an obligation to be truthful with ourselves, those who receive services, colleagues, and society. One way that this is exhibited is through maintaining and upgrading professional competence. This happens, in part, through an unfaltering commitment to inquiry and learning, to self-understanding, and to the development of an interpersonal competence.

Prudence is the ability to govern and discipline oneself through the use of reason. To be prudent is to value judiciousness, discretion, vigilance, moderation, care, and circumspection in the management of one's affairs, to temper extremes, make judgments, and respond on the basis of intelligent reflection and rational thought.

SUMMARY

Beliefs and values are those intrinsic concepts that underlie the core of the profession and the professional interactions of each practitioner. These values describe the profession's philosophy and provide the basis for defining purpose. The emphasis or priority that is given to each value may change as one's professional career evolves and as the unique characteristics of a situation unfold. This evolution of values is developmental in nature. Although we have basic values that cannot be violated, the degree to which certain values will take priority at a given time is influenced by the specifics of a situation and the environment in which it occurs. In one instance dignity may be a higher priority than truth; in another, prudence may be chosen over freedom. As we process information and make decisions, the weight of the values that we hold may change. The practitioner faces dilemmas because of conflicting values and is required to engage in thoughtful deliberation to determine where the priority lies in a given situation.

The challenge for us all is to know our values, be able to make reasoned choices in situations of conflict, and be able to clearly articulate and defend our choices. At the same time, it is important that all members of the profession be committed to a set of common values. This mutual commitment to a set of beliefs and principles that govern our practice can provide a basis for clarifying expectations between the recipient and the provider of services. Shared values empower the profession and, in addition, build trust among ourselves and with others.

REFERENCES

American Association of Colleges of Nursing. (1986). *Essentials of college and university education for professional nursing.* (Final report). Washington, DC: Author.

American Occupational Therapy Association. (1979). Resolution C, 531–79. The philosophical base of occupational therapy. *American Journal of Occupational Therapy, 33,* 785.

American Occupational Therapy Association. (1986, April). *Dictionary definition of occupational therapy.* Adopted and approved by the Representative Assembly to fulfill Resolution 596-83. (Available from AOTA, 4720 Montgomery Lane, Bethesda, MD 20814.)

American Occupational Therapy Association. (1988). Occupational therapy code of ethics. *American Journal of Occupational Therapy, 42,* 795–796. (*Note:* This document has been updated. American Occupational Therapy Association. (2005). *American Journal of Occupational Therapy, 59,* 639–642.)

American Occupational Therapy Association. (1991a). Essentials and guidelines for an accredited educational program for the occupational therapist. *American Journal of Occupational Therapy, 45,* 1077–1084.

American Occupational Therapy Association. (1991b). Essentials and guidelines for an accredited educational program for the occupational therapy assistant. *American Journal of Occupational Therapy, 45,* 1085–1092.

Prepared by

Elizabeth Kanny, MA, OTR
Education Representative (1990–1996) for the Standards and Ethics Commission

Ruth A. Hansen, PhD, OTR, FAOTA
Chairperson (1988–1994)

Approved by the Representative Assembly June 1993

Originally published and copyrighted in 1993 by the American Occupational Therapy Association in the *American Journal of Occupational Therapy, 47,* 1085–1086.

Guidelines to the Occupational Therapy Code of Ethics

PROFESSIONAL BEHAVIORS	PRINCIPLES FROM CODE
1. HONESTY: *Professionals must be honest with themselves, must be honest with all whom they come in contact with, and must know their strengths and limitations.*	
1.1. In education, research, practice, and leadership roles, individuals must be honest in receiving and disseminating information by providing opportunities for informed consent and for discussion of available options.	Veracity
1.2. Occupational therapy practitioners must be certain that informed consent has been obtained prior to the initiation of services, including evaluation. If the service recipient cannot give informed consent, the practitioner must be sure that consent has been obtained from the person who is legally responsible for the service recipient.	Autonomy, Veracity
1.3. Occupational therapy practitioners must be truthful about their individual competencies as well as the competence of those under their supervision. In some cases the therapist may need to refer the client to another professional to assure that the most appropriate services are provided.	Duty, Veracity
1.4. Referrals to other health care specialists shall be based exclusively on the other provider's competence and ability to provide the needed service.	Beneficence
1.5. All documentation must accurately reflect the nature and quantity of services provided.	Veracity
1.6. Occupational therapy practitioners terminate services when they do not meet the needs and goals of the recipient or when services no longer produce a measurable outcome.	Procedural Justice, Beneficence
1.7. All marketing and advertising must be truthful and carefully presented to avoid misleading the client or the public.	Veracity

(continued on next page)

1.8.	All occupational therapy personnel shall accurately represent their credentials and roles.	Veracity
1.9.	Occupational therapy personnel shall not use funds for unintended purposes or misappropriate funds.	Duty, Veracity

2. COMMUNICATION: *Communication is important in all aspects of occupational therapy. Individuals must be conscientious and truthful in all facets of written, verbal, and electronic communication.*

2.1.	Occupational therapy personnel do not make deceptive, fraudulent, or misleading statements about the nature of the services they provide or the outcomes that can be expected.	Veracity
2.2.	Professional contracts for occupational therapy services shall explicitly describe the type and duration of services as well as the duties and responsibilities of all involved parties.	Veracity, Procedural Justice
2.3.	Documentation for reimbursement purposes shall be done in accordance with applicable laws, guidelines, and regulations.	Veracity, Procedural Justice
2.4.	Documentation shall accurately reflect the services delivered and the outcomes. It shall be of the kind and quality that satisfies the scrutiny of peer reviews, legal proceedings, payers, regulatory bodies, and accrediting agencies.	Veracity, Procedural Justice, Duties
2.5.	Occupational therapy personnel must be honest in gathering and giving fact-based information regarding job performance and fieldwork performance. Information given shall be timely and truthful, accurate, and respectful of all parties involved.	Veracity, Fidelity
2.6.	Documentation for supervisory purposes shall accurately reflect the factual components of the interactions and the expected outcomes.	Veracity
2.7.	Occupational therapy personnel must give credit and recognition when using the work of others.	Veracity, Procedural Justice
2.8.	Occupational therapy personnel do not fabricate data, falsify information, or plagiarize.	Veracity, Procedural Justice
2.9.	Occupational therapy personnel refrain from using biased or derogatory language in written, verbal, and electronic communication about clients, students, research participants, and colleagues.	Nonmaleficence, Fidelity
2.10.	Occupational therapy personnel who provide information through oral and written means shall emphasize that ethical and appropriate service delivery for clients cannot be done without proper individualized evaluations and plans of care.	Beneficence

3. **ENSURING THE COMMON GOOD:** *Occupational therapy personnel are expected to increase awareness of the profession's social responsibilities to help ensure the common good.*

3.1.	Occupational therapy personnel take steps to make sure that employers are aware of the ethical principles of the profession and occupational therapy personnel's obligation to adhere to those ethical principles.	Duty
3.2.	Occupational therapy personnel shall be diligent stewards of human, financial, and material resources of their employers. They shall refrain from exploiting these resources for personal gain.	Fidelity
3.3.	Occupational therapy personnel should actively work with their employer to prevent discrimination and unfair labor practices. They should also advocate for employees with disabilities to ensure the provision of reasonable accommodations.	Procedural Justice
3.4.	Occupational therapy personnel should actively participate with their employer in the formulation of policies and procedures. They should do this to ensure that these policies and procedures are legal, in accordance with regulations governing aspects of practice, and consistent with the AOTA *Occupational Therapy Code of Ethics*.	Procedural Justice
3.5.	Occupational therapy personnel in educational settings are responsible for promoting ethical conduct by students, faculty, and fieldwork colleagues.	Duty, Fidelity
3.6.	Occupational therapy personnel involved in or preparing to be involved in research, including education and policy research, need to obtain all necessary approvals prior to initiating research.	Procedural Justice

4. **COMPETENCE:** *Occupational therapy personnel are expected to work within their areas of competence and to pursue opportunities to update, increase, and expand their competence.*

4.1.	Occupational therapy personnel developing new areas of competence (skills, techniques, approaches) must engage in appropriate study and training, under appropriate supervision, before incorporating new areas into their practice.	Duty
4.2.	When generally recognized standards do not exist in emerging areas of practice, occupational therapy personnel must take responsible steps to ensure their own competence.	Duty

(continued on next page)

4.3.	Occupational therapy personnel shall develop an understanding and appreciation for different cultures in order to be able to provide culturally competent service. Culturally competent practitioners are aware of how service delivery can be affected by economic, age, ethnic, racial, geographic, gender, gender identity, religious, and political factors, as well as marital status, sexual orientation, and disability.	Beneficence, Duty
4.4.	In areas where the ability to communicate with the client is limited (e.g., aphasia, different language, literacy), occupational therapy personnel shall take appropriate steps to facilitate meaningful communication and comprehension.	Autonomy
4.5.	Occupational therapy personnel must ensure that skilled occupational therapy interventions or techniques are performed only by qualified persons.	Duty, Beneficence, Nonmaleficence
4.6.	Occupational therapy administrators (academic, research, and clinical) are responsible for ensuring the competence and qualifications of personnel in their employment.	Beneficence, Nonmaleficence
5.	**CONFIDENTIAL AND PROTECTED INFORMATION:** *Information that is confidential must remain confidential. This information cannot be shared verbally, electronically, or in writing without appropriate consent. Information must be shared on a need-to-know basis only with those having primary responsibilities for decision making.*	
5.1.	All occupational therapy personnel shall respect the confidential nature of information gained in any occupational therapy interaction. The only exceptions are when a practitioner or staff member believes that an individual is in serious, foreseeable, or imminent harm. In this instance, laws and regulations require disclosure to appropriate authorities without consent.	Confidentiality
5.2.	Occupational therapy personnel shall respect the clients' and colleagues' right to privacy.	Confidentiality
5.3.	Occupational therapy personnel shall maintain the confidentiality of all verbal, written, electronic, augmentative, and non-verbal communications (as required by HIPAA).	Confidentiality
6.	**CONFLICT OF INTEREST:** *Avoidance of real or perceived conflict of interest is imperative to maintaining the integrity of interactions.*	
6.1.	Occupational therapy personnel shall be alert to and avoid any action that would interfere with the exercise of impartial professional judgment during the delivery of occupational therapy services.	Nonmaleficence
6.2.	Occupational therapy personnel shall not take advantage of or exploit anyone to further their own personal interests.	Nonmaleficence

6.3.	Gifts and remuneration from individuals, agencies, or companies must be reported in accordance with employer policies as well as state and federal guidelines.	Veracity, Procedural Justice
6.4.	Occupational therapy personnel shall not accept obligations or duties that may compete with or be in conflict with their duties to their employers.	Veracity, Fidelity
6.5.	Occupational therapy personnel shall not use their position or the knowledge gained from their position in such a way that knowingly gives rise to real or perceived conflict of interest between themselves and their employers, other association members or bodies, and/or other organizations.	Veracity, Fidelity

7. IMPAIRED PRACTITIONER: *Occupational therapy personnel who cannot competently perform their duties after reasonable accommodation are considered to be impaired. The occupational therapy practitioner's basic duty to students, patients, colleagues, and research subjects is to ensure that no harm is done. It is difficult to report a professional colleague who is impaired. The motive for this action must be to provide for the protection and safety of all, including the person who is impaired.*

7.1.	Occupational therapy personnel shall be aware of their own personal problems and limitations that may interfere with their ability to perform their job competently. They should know when these problems have the potential to cause harm to clients, colleagues, students, research participants, or others.	Nonmaleficence
7.2.	The individual should seek the appropriate professional help and take steps to remedy personal problems and limitations that interfere with job performance.	Nonmaleficence
7.3.	Occupational therapy personnel who believe that a colleague's impairment interferes with safe and effective practice should, when possible, discuss their questions and concerns with the individual and assist their colleague in seeking appropriate help or treatment.	Nonmaleficence
7.4.	When efforts to assist an impaired colleague fail, the occupational therapy practitioner is responsible for reporting the individual to the appropriate authority (e.g., employer, agency, licensing or regulatory board, certification body, professional organization).	Nonmaleficence

8. SEXUAL RELATIONSHIPS: *Sexual relationships that occur during any professional interaction are forms of misconduct.*

8.1.	Because of potential coercion or harm to former clients, students, or research participants, occupational therapy practitioners are responsible for ensuring that the individual with whom they enter into a romantic/sexual relationship has not been coerced or exploited in any way.	Nonmaleficence

(continued on next page)

8.2.	Sexual relationships with current clients, employees, students, or research participants are not permissible, even if the relationship is consensual.	Nonmaleficence
8.3.	Occupational therapy personnel must not sexually harass any persons.	Nonmaleficence
8.4.	Occupational therapy personnel have full responsibility to set clear and appropriate boundaries in their professional interactions.	Nonmaleficence

9. **PAYMENT FOR SERVICES AND OTHER FINANCIAL ARRANGEMENTS:** *Occupational therapy personnel shall not guarantee or promise specific outcomes for occupational therapy services. Payment for occupational therapy services shall not be contingent on successful outcomes.*

9.1.	Occupational therapy personnel shall only collect fees legally. Fees shall be fair and reasonable and commensurate with services delivered.	Procedural Justice
9.2.	Occupational therapy personnel do not ordinarily participate in bartering for services because of potential exploitation and conflict of interest. However, such an arrangement may be appropriate if it is not clinically contraindicated, if the relationship is not exploitative, and if bartering is a culturally appropriate custom.	Beneficence
9.3.	Occupational therapy practitioners can render pro bono ("for the good," free of charge) or reduced-fee occupational therapy services for selected individuals only when consistent with guidelines of the business/facility, third-party payer, or government agency.	Beneficence, Procedural Justice
9.4.	Occupational therapy personnel may engage in volunteer activities to improve access to occupational therapy or by providing individual service and expertise to charitable organizations.	Beneficence
9.5.	Occupational therapy personnel who participate in a business arrangement as owner, stockholder, partner, or employee have an obligation to maintain the ethical principles and standards of the profession. They also shall refrain from working for or doing business with organizations that engage in illegal or unethical business practices (e.g., fraudulent billing).	Procedural Justice

10. RESOLVING ETHICAL ISSUES: *Occupational therapy personnel should utilize any and all resources available to them to identify and resolve conflicts and/or ethical dilemmas.*

10.1.	Occupational therapy personnel are obligated to be familiar with the Code and its application to their respective work environments. Occupational therapy practitioners are expected to share the Code with their employer and other employees and colleagues. Lack of familiarity with and knowledge of the Code is not an excuse or a defense against a charge of ethical misconduct.	Duty
10.2.	Occupational therapy personnel who are uncertain of whether a specific action would violate the Code have a responsibility to consult with knowledgeable individuals, ethics committees, or other appropriate authorities.	Duty
10.3.	When conflicts occur in professional organizations, members must clarify the nature of the conflict and, where possible, seek to resolve the conflict in a way that permits the fullest adherence to the Code.	Fidelity
10.4.	Occupational therapy personnel shall attempt to resolve perceived violations of the Code within institutions by utilizing internal resources.	Fidelity
10.5.	If the informal resolution is not appropriate or is not effective, the next step is to take action by consultation with or referral to institutional, local, district, territorial, state, or national groups who have jurisdiction over occupational therapy practice.	Fidelity
10.6.	Occupational therapy personnel shall cooperate with ethics committee proceedings and comply with resulting requirements. Failure to cooperate is, in itself, an ethical violation.	Procedural Justice
10.7.	Occupational therapy personnel shall file only formal ethics complaints aimed at protecting the public or promoting professional conduct rather than harming or discrediting a colleague.	Fidelity

Originally published in 1998 and revised and copyrighted in 2006 by the American Occupational Therapy Association in *American Journal of Occupational Therapy, 60*, 652–658.

ENFORCEMENT

CHAPTER 5

Overview to Enforcement Procedures for the Occupational Therapy Code of Ethics

The *Enforcement Procedures for the Occupational Therapy Code of Ethics* were revised by AOTA's Ethics Commission (EC) several times in the past few years, most recently in 2007 and were adopted by the Representative Assembly in May of that year. This public document articulates the procedures that are followed by the EC as it carries out its duties to enforce the *Occupational Therapy Code of Ethics (2005)*. A major goal of these procedures is to ensure objectivity and fundamental fairness to all individuals who may be parties in an ethics complaint.

The Code is a public statement of the values and principles used as a guide in promoting and maintaining high standards of professional conduct in occupational therapy. The Code applies to occupational therapy personnel at all levels and in the diverse roles in which they may find themselves. These include not only professional behavior in our roles as researchers, educators, clinicians, and students but also in our elected and voluntary leadership roles, whether they are within the Association or in the community where the occupational therapy perspective can provide a valuable benefit. The *Enforcement Procedures* are used to help ensure compliance with the values and principles that members of the profession have identified as important. A series of revisions were made to this document since they were published in the 2006 edition of this *Reference Guide* to provide more delineation of procedures and clarified language. This was an effort to address ambiguous situations that arose during the application of the *Procedures* in recent years. However, the disciplinary actions enforceable by the EC and its jurisdiction remain unchanged.

The *Enforcement Procedures* are composed of an "Introduction," which discusses the jurisdiction of the Code, disciplinary actions, or the circumstances under which complaints may be dismissed, and educational options such as advisory opinions or educative letters. Recent revisions have included more explicit language about expectations related to confidentiality and the scope of information that may be obtained by the EC. Specifically, Sections 1.7 and 1.7.1 ("Confidentiality and Disclosure") were modified to expand the expectations related to confidentiality by all parties to a complaint and the penalties for violating them while also identifying situations (e.g., legal) in which the EC may be required to disclose confidential information. Section 2, "Complaints," identifies the different types of complaints, how they may be received, the initial process for handling complaints initiated by the EC, and how evidence is considered. New language is included in Section 2.1.2 provides a process for handling conflict resolution in the event the EC determines that the complaint does not rise to the level of an ethical violation.

This also applies to complaints related to elected/volunteer leadership of AOTA in their official roles and directs the parties to utilize *Roberts Rules* and/or other conflict resolution resources.

Section 3 "EC Review and Investigations," establishes the procedures used by the Ethics Office and the EC to evaluate and investigate cases as well as criteria for dismissal. This section also includes the investigation timeline and the circumstances under which a complaint may be referred to another jurisdiction or stayed. Section 3.4.4 was modified to include the sharing of evidence received by the EC as a result of their investigation with both respondent and complainant. The "EC Review and Decision" process is presented in Section 4.

Discussion of the role of "The Disciplinary Council" occurs in Section 5. The purpose of this section is to outline a procedure for selecting members and convening a hearing in which the respondent can refute the decision of a formal charge or sanction by the EC. The hearing is also held to allow the EC, represented by its chair, to present evidence to support the charge or sanction. The timelines for the Council's hearing and decision also are presented.

If the respondent chooses to appeal the Council's decision, the final step is to request an Appeal Panel. The process for this is described in Section 6, "Appeal Process." As with other procedures delineated in this document, information is presented that includes the timelines and process for convening the panel, case review and issuing a decision. Section 6.3 is now designated as "Composition and Leadership of Appeal Panel" and a process for selecting the Chair of the Appeal Panel from among its members was identified.

The final sections of the *Enforcement Procedures* are "Notifications" (Section 7), "Records and Reports" (Section 8), Publication (Section 9), and "Modification" (Section 10).

The EC and AOTA's Ethics Office make the *Enforcement Procedures for the Occupational Therapy Code of Ethics* public and available to members of the profession, state regulatory boards, consumers, and others for their use. When questions arise concerning the AOTA *Occupational Therapy Code of Ethics* and its *Enforcement Procedures*, the Ethics Office at AOTA is available for assistance.

Author

Janie B. Scott, MA, OTR/L, FAOTA
AOTA Ethics Officer
March 2003

Deborah Yarett Slater, MS, OT/L, FAOTA
AOTA Staff Liaison to the Ethics Commission
Revised December 2005, February 2008

Enforcement Procedures for the Occupational Therapy Code of Ethics (edited 2007)

1. INTRODUCTION

The American Occupational Therapy Association (AOTA) and its members are committed to furthering each individual's ability to function fully within his or her total environment. To this end, the occupational therapist and occupational therapy assistant render services to clients in all phases of health and illness, to institutions, to organizations, to other professionals and colleagues, to students, and to the public.

The AOTA's *Occupational Therapy Code of Ethics*, its *Guidelines*, and its *Core Values* (hereinafter jointly referred to as "Ethics Standards") are public statements of values and principles to use as a guide in promoting and maintaining high standards of behavior in occupational therapy.

The Ethics Standards apply to occupational therapy personnel at all levels. They apply to professional roles such as those of practitioner, educator, fieldwork educator or coordinator, clinical supervisor, manager, administrator, consultant, faculty, program director, researcher/scholar, private practice owner, entrepreneur, student, and other professional roles, including elective and appointed volunteer roles within the AOTA. More broadly, these Ethics Standards apply not only to conduct within occupational therapy roles but also to conduct that may affect the performance of occupational therapy or the reputation of the profession. The principal purposes of the Ethics Standards are to help protect the public and to reinforce its confidence in the occupa-

tional therapy profession rather than to resolve private business, legal, or other disputes for which there are other more appropriate forums.

To ensure compliance with the Ethics Standards, these *Enforcement Procedures* are established and maintained by the Ethics Commission and (hereinafter referred to as the "EC"). Acceptance of membership in the AOTA commits members to adherence to the Ethics Standards and cooperation with its *Enforcement Procedures*. The EC urges particular attention to the following issues.

1.1. Professional Responsibility, Other Processes

All occupational therapy personnel have an obligation to maintain the standards of ethics of their profession and to promote and support these standards among their colleagues. Each member must be alert to practices that undermine these standards and is obligated to take action that is appropriate in the circumstances. At the same time, members must carefully weigh their judgments as to potentially unethical practice to ensure that they are based on objective evaluation and not on personal bias or prejudice, inadequate information, or simply differences of professional viewpoint. It is recognized that individual occupational therapy personnel may not have the authority or ability to address or correct all situations of concern. Whenever feasible and appropriate, members should first pursue other corrective steps within the relevant institution or setting before resorting to the AOTA ethics complaint process.

1.2. Jurisdiction

The Code of Ethics (hereinafter referred to as the "Code") applies to persons who are or were members of the AOTA at the time of the conduct in question. Later nonrenewal or relinquishment of membership does not affect AOTA jurisdiction. The Code that is applicable to any complaint shall be the Code in force at the time the alleged act or omission occurred, unless the date of the alleged act or omission cannot be precisely determined. In that case, the conduct shall be judged by the Code in force on the date of the complaint.

1.3. Disciplinary Actions/Sanctions (Pursuing a Complaint)

If the EC determines that unethical conduct has occurred, it may impose sanctions, including reprimand, censure, probation, suspension, or permanent revocation of membership in the AOTA. In all cases, except those involving only reprimand, the AOTA will report the conclusions and sanctions in its official publications and will also communicate to any appropriate persons or entities. The potential sanctions are defined as follows:

- *1.3.1. Reprimand*—A formal expression of disapproval of conduct communicated privately by letter from the Chairperson of the EC that is nondisclosable and noncommunicative to other bodies (e.g., state regulatory boards [SRBs]; National Board for Certification in Occupational Therapy, hereinafter known as "NBCOT®").

- *1.3.2. Censure*—A formal expression of disapproval that is public.

- *1.3.3. Probation of membership subject to terms*—Failure to meet terms will subject a member to any of the disciplinary actions or sanctions.

- *1.3.4. Suspension*—Removal of membership for a specified period of time.

- *1.3.5. Revocation*—Permanent denial of membership.
    - *1.3.5.1.* If an individual is on either the Roster of Fellows (ROF) or the Roster of Honor (ROH), the chairperson of the EC (via the EC staff liaison) shall notify the Chairperson of the Recognitions Committee (and Executive Director) of their membership revocation. That individual shall have their name removed from either the ROF or the ROH and no longer has the right to use the designated credential of FAOTA or ROH.

1.4. Educative Letters

If the EC determines that the alleged conduct, even if proven, does not appear to be unethical but may not be completely in keeping with the aspirational nature of the Code or within the prevailing standards of practice or good professionalism, the EC may send a letter to educate the Respondent only regarding standards of practice and/or good professionalism. In addition, a different educative letter, if appropriate, may be sent to the Complainant.

1.5. Advisory Opinions

The EC may issue general advisory opinions on ethical issues to inform and educate the membership. These opinions shall be publicized to the membership.

1.6. Rules of Evidence

The EC proceedings shall be conducted in accordance with fundamental fairness. However, formal rules of evidence that are employed in legal proceedings do not apply to these *Enforcement Procedures*. The Disciplinary Council (see Section 5) and the Appeal Panel (see Section 6) can consider any evidence that they deem appropriate and pertinent.

1.7. Confidentiality and Disclosure

The EC develops and adheres to strict rules of confidentiality in every aspect of its work. Maintaining confidentiality throughout the investigation and enforcement process of a formal ethics complaint is essential in order to ensure fairness to all parties involved. These rules of confidentiality pertain not only to the EC but also apply to others involved in the complaint process. Beginning with the EC staff liaison and support staff, strict rules of confidentiality are followed. These same rules of confidentiality apply to complainants, respondents and their attorneys, and witnesses involved with the EC's investigatory process. Due diligence must be exercised by everyone involved in the investigation to avoid compromising the confidential nature of the process. Any AOTA member who breaches these rules of confidentiality may become subject to an ethics complaint/investigatory process himself or herself. Non–AOTA members may lodge an ethics complaint against an AOTA member, and these individuals are still expected to adhere to AOTA's confidentiality rules. The AOTA reserves the right to take appropriate action against non–AOTA members who violate confidentiality rules, including notification of their appropriate licensure boards, etc.

- *1.7.1. Disclosure*—When the EC investigates a complaint, it may request information from a variety of sources. The process of obtaining additional information is carefully executed in order to maintain confidentiality. The EC may request information from a variety of sources, including state licensing agencies, academic councils, courts, employers, and other persons and entities. It is within the EC's purview to determine what disclosures are appropriate for particular parties in order to effectively implement its investigatory obligations. Public sanctions by the EC, Disciplinary Council, or Appeal Panel will be publicized as provided in these Procedures. Normally, the EC does not disclose information or documentation reviewed in the course of an investigation unless the EC determines that disclosure is necessary to obtain additional, relevant evidence or to administer the ethics process or is legally required.

Individuals who file a complaint (i.e., complainant) and those who are the subject of one (i.e., respondent) must not disclose to anyone their role in an ethics complaint. Disclosing this information in and of itself may jeopardize the ethics process and violate the rules of fundamental fairness by which all parties are protected. Disclosure of information related to any case under investigation by the EC is prohibited and, if done, will lead to repercussions as outlined in these Procedures (see Section 2.2.3.).

2. COMPLAINTS

2.1. Interested Party Complaints

- *2.1.1.* Complaints stating an alleged violation of the Code may originate from any individual, group, or entity within or outside the Association. All complaints must be in writing, signed by the complainant(s), and submitted to the Chairperson of the EC at the address of the AOTA's headquarters. Complainants must complete the Formal Statement of Complaint Form at the end of this document. All complaints shall identify the person against whom the complaint is directed (the respondent), the ethical principles that the complainant believes have been violated, and the key facts of the alleged violations. If lawfully available, supporting documentation should be attached.

- *2.1.2.* Within 90 days of receipt of a complaint, the EC shall make a preliminary assessment of the complaint and decide whether it presents sufficient questions as to a potential ethics violation that an investigation is warranted. Commencing an investigation does not imply a conclusion that an ethical violation has in fact occurred or any judgment as to the ultimate sanction, if any, which may be appropriate. In the event the EC determines that the complaint does not rise to the level of an ethical violation, the EC may direct the parties to utilize *Roberts Rules* and/or other conflict resolution resources via an educative letter. This applies to all complaints, including those involving elected/volunteer leadership of the Association related to their official roles.

2.2. Complaints Initiated by the EC

- *2.2.1.* The EC itself may initiate a complaint (a "sua sponte" complaint) when it receives information from a governmental body, certification or similar body, public media, or other source indicating that a person subject to its jurisdiction may have committed acts that violate the Code. AOTA will ordinarily act promptly after learning of the basis of a sua sponte complaint, but there is no specified time limit.

  If the EC passes a motion to initiate a sua sponte complaint, the members of the EC will complete the Formal Statement of Complaint Form (at the end of this document) and will describe the nature of the factual allegations that led to the complaint and the manner in which the EC learned of the matter. The Complaint Form will be signed by the Chairperson of the EC on behalf of the EC. The form will be given to the EC staff liaison.

- *2.2.2. De Jure Complaints*—De jure sua sponte complaints will proceed as follows:
  a. The EC staff liaison will present to the EC any findings from external sources (as described above) pertaining to members of AOTA that come to his or her attention and that may warrant sua sponte complaints.
  b. Since *de jure* complaints are based upon the findings of fact or conclusions of another official body, the EC will decide whether or not to act based on such findings or conclusions and will not ordinarily initiate another investigation, absent clear and convincing evidence that such findings and conclusions were erroneous or not supported by substantial evidence. Based upon the information presented by the EC staff liaison, the EC will determine whether the findings of the public

body also are sufficient to demonstrate an egregious violation of the Code and therefore warrant an ethics charge.
  c. If the EC decides that a formal charge is warranted, the Chairperson of the EC will notify the respondent in writing of the formal charge and the proposed education and/or disciplinary action. In response to the *de jure* sua sponte charge by the EC, the respondent may either
  1. Accept the decision of the EC (as to both the ethics violation and the sanction) based solely upon the findings of fact and conclusions of the EC or the public body, or
  2. Accept the charge that the respondent committed unethical conduct but within 30 days submit to the EC a statement setting forth the reasons why any sanction should not be imposed or reasons why the sanction should be mitigated or reduced, or
  3. Within 30 days, present information showing the findings of fact of the official body relied upon by the EC to initiate the charge is clearly erroneous and request reconsideration by the EC. The EC may have the option of opening an investigation or modifying the sanction in the event they find clear and convincing evidence that the findings and the conclusions of the other body are erroneous.
  d. In cases of de jure complaints, a Disciplinary Council hearing can later be requested (pursuant to Section 5 below) only if the respondent has first exercised Option 2 or 3.

- *2.2.3.* The EC shall have the jurisdiction to investigate, charge, or sanction any matter or person for violations based on information learned in the course of investigating a complaint under Section 2.2.2.

2.3. Continuation of Complaint Process

If a member relinquishes membership, fails to renew membership, or fails to cooperate with the ethics investigation, the EC shall nevertheless continue to process the complaint, noting in its report the circumstances of the respondent's action. Such actions shall not deprive the EC of jurisdiction.

3. EC REVIEW AND INVESTIGATIONS

3.1. Initial Action

The purpose of the preliminary review is to decide whether or not the information submitted with the complaint warrants opening the case. If in its preliminary review of the complaint the EC determines that an investigation is not warranted, the complainant will be so notified.

3.2. Dismissal of Complaints

The EC may at any time dismiss a complaint for any of the following reasons:

- *3.2.1. Lack of Jurisdiction*—The EC determines that it has no jurisdiction over the respondent (e.g., a complaint against a person who is or was not a member at the time of the alleged incident or who has never been a member).

- *3.2.2. Absolute Time Limit/Not Timely Filed*— The EC determines that the violation of the Code is alleged to have occurred more than 7 years prior to the filing of the complaint.

- *3.2.3. Subject to Jurisdiction of Another Authority*—The EC determines that the complaint is based on matters that are within the authority of and are more properly dealt with by another governmental or nongovernmental body, such as an SRB, NBCOT, an AOTA component other than the EC, an employer, or a court (e.g., accusing a superior of sexual harassment at work, accusing someone of anticompetitive practices subject to the antitrust laws).

- *3.2.4. No Ethics Violation*—The EC finds that the complaint, even if proven, does not state a basis for action under the Code (e.g., simply accusing someone of being unpleasant or rude on an occasion).

- *3.2.5. Insufficient Evidence*—The EC determines that there clearly would not be sufficient factual evidence to support a finding of an ethics violation.

- *3.2.6. Corrected Violation*—The EC determines that any violation it might find already has been or is being corrected, and that this is an adequate result in the given case.

- *3.2.7. Other good cause.*

3.3. Investigator (Avoidance of Conflict of Interest)

The investigator chosen shall not have a conflict of interest (i.e., shall never have had a substantial professional, personal, financial, business, or volunteer relationship with either the complainant or the respondent). In the event that the EC staff liaison has such a conflict, the EC Chairperson shall appoint an alternate investigator who has no conflict of interest.

3.4. Investigation

If an investigation is deemed warranted, the EC Chairperson shall do the following within 15 days: Appoint the EC staff liaison at the AOTA headquarters to investigate the complaint and notify the respondent (by certified, return-receipt mail) that a complaint has been received and an investigation is being conducted. A copy of the complaint and supporting documentation shall be enclosed with this notification. The complainant will also receive notification by certified, return-receipt mail that the complaint is being investigated.

- *3.4.1.* Ordinarily, the investigator will send questions formulated by the EC to be answered by the complainant and/or the respondent.

- *3.4.2.* The complainant shall be given 30 days from receipt of the questions to respond in writing to the investigator.

- *3.4.3.* The respondent shall be given 30 days from receipt of the questions to respond in writing to the investigator.

- *3.4.4.* The EC ordinarily will notify the complainant of any substantive new evidence adverse to the complainant's initial complaint that is discovered in the course of the ethics investigation and allow the complainant to respond to such adverse evidence. In such cases, the complainant will be given a copy of such evidence and will have 14 days in which to submit a written response. If the new evidence clearly shows that there has been no ethics violation, the EC may terminate the proceeding. In addition, if the investigation includes questions for both the respondent and the complainant, the evidence submitted by each party in response to the investigatory questions shall be available to the other party upon their request. The EC may request reasonable payment for copying expenses depending on the volume of material to be sent.

- *3.4.5.* The investigator, in consultation with the EC, may obtain evidence directly from third parties.

3.5. Investigation Timeline

The investigation will be completed within 90 days after receipt of notification by the respondent or his/her designee that an investigation is being conducted, unless the EC determines that special circumstances warrant additional time for the investigation. All timelines noted here can be extended for good cause at the discretion of the EC, including the EC's schedule and additional requests of the respondent. The respondent and the complainant shall be notified in writing if a delay occurs or if the investigational process requires more time.

3.6. Report

The investigator's report shall include the complaint and any documentation on which the EC relied in initiating the investigation and shall state findings without recommendations.

3.7. Cooperation by Member

Every AOTA member has a duty to cooperate reasonably with enforcement processes under the Code. Failure of the respondent to participate and/or cooperate with the investigative process of the EC shall not prevent continuation of the ethics process, and this behavior itself may constitute a violation of the Code.

3.8. Referral of Complaint

The EC may at any time refer a matter to NBCOT, SRB, or other recognized authorities for appropriate action. Despite such referral to an appropriate authority, the EC shall retain jurisdiction. EC action may be stayed for a reasonable period pending notification of a decision by that authority, at the discretion of the EC (and such delays will extend the time periods under these Procedures). A stay in conducting an investigation shall not constitute a waiver by the EC of jurisdiction over the matters. The EC shall provide written notice by mail (requiring signature and proof of date of receipt) to the respondent and the complainant of any such stay of action.

4. EC REVIEW AND DECISION

4.1. Charges

The EC shall review the investigator's report and shall render a decision on whether a charge by the EC is warranted within 90 days of receipt of the report. The EC may, in the conduct of its review, take whatever further investigatory actions it deems necessary. If the EC determines that an ethics complaint warrants a charge, the EC shall proceed with a disciplinary proceeding by promptly sending a notice of the charge(s) to the respondent and complainant by mail with signature and proof of date received. The notice of the charge(s) shall describe the alleged conduct that, if proven in accordance with these *Procedures,* would constitute a violation of the Code. The notice of charge(s) shall describe the conduct in sufficient detail to inform the respondent of the nature of the unethical behavior that is alleged. The EC may indicate in the notice its preliminary view (absent contrary facts or mitigating circumstances) as to what sanction would be warranted if the violation is proven in accordance with these *Procedures*.

4.2. Respondent's Response

Within 30 days of notification of the EC's decision to charge, and proposed sanction, if any, the respondent shall either

- *4.2.1.* Advise the EC Chairperson in writing that he or she accepts the EC's charge of an ethics violation and the proposed sanction and waives any right to a Disciplinary Council hearing, or

- *4.2.2.* Advise the EC Chairperson in writing that he or she accepts the EC's charge of an ethics violation but believes the sanction is not justified and requests a hearing before the Council on that matter alone, or

- *4.2.3.* Advise the EC Chairperson in writing that he or she contests the EC's charge and the proposed sanction and requests a hearing before the Disciplinary Council.

Failure of the respondent to take one of these actions within the time specified will be deemed to constitute acceptance of the charge and proposed sanction. If the respondent requests a Disciplinary Council hearing, it will be scheduled. If the respondent does not request a Disciplinary Council hearing but accepts the decision, the EC will notify all relevant parties and implement the sanction.

5. THE DISCIPLINARY COUNCIL

5.1. Purpose

The purpose of the Disciplinary Council (hereinafter to be known as "the Council") hearing is to provide the respondent an opportunity to present evidence and witnesses to answer and refute the charge and/or the proposed sanction and to permit the EC Chairperson or designee (the "EC Chair") to present evidence and witnesses in support of his or her charge. The Council shall consider the matters alleged in the complaint; the matters raised in defense; and other relevant facts, ethical principles, and

federal or state law, if applicable. The Council may question the parties concerned and determine ethical issues arising from the factual matters in the case even if those specific ethical issues were not raised by the complainant. The Council also may choose to apply Principles (from the AOTA *Occupational Therapy Code of Ethics*) and Guidelines not originally identified by the EC. The Council may affirm the decision of the EC or reverse or modify it if it finds that the decision was clearly erroneous or a material departure from its written procedure.

5.2. Parties

The parties to a Council Hearing are the respondent and the EC Chairperson.

5.3. Criteria and Process for Selection of Council Chairperson

- *5.3.1. Criteria*
  - *5.3.1.1.* Must currently be a member of a Disciplinary Council or a former EC member who has been off the EC for at least 3 years.
  - *5.3.1.2.* Must have experience in analyzing/reviewing cases.
  - *5.3.1.3.* May be selected from the pool of candidates for the Council.
  - *5.3.1.4.* The EC Chairperson shall not serve as the Council chairperson.

- *5.3.2. Process*
  - *5.3.2.1.* The Assembly Speaker (in consultation with EC staff liaison) will select the Council chairperson.
  - *5.3.2.2.* If the Assembly Speaker needs to be recused from this duty the Vice Speaker will select the chairperson.

5.4. Criteria and Process for Selection of Council Members:

- *5.4.1. Criteria:*
  - *5.4.1.1.* Association Administrative SOP guidelines in Policy 2.6 shall be considered in the selection of qualified potential candidates for the Council, and it shall be composed of qualified individuals and

AOTA members drawn from a pool of candidates who meet the criteria outlined below.

– *5.4.1.2.* Members ideally will have some knowledge or experience in the areas of activity that are at issue in the case. They will also have experience in disciplinary hearings and/or general knowledge about ethics as demonstrated by education, presentations, and/or publications.

– *5.4.1.3.* No conflict of interest may exist with either the complainant or the respondent (refer to AOTA Policy 1.22–Conflict of Interest for guidance).

– *5.4.1.4.* No individual may serve on the Disciplinary Council who is currently a member of the EC or the Board of Directors.

– *5.4.1.5.* No individual may serve on the Disciplinary Council who has previously been the subject of an ethics complaint that resulted in a specific EC disciplinary action.

– *5.4.1.6.* The public member on the Disciplinary Council shall have knowledge of the profession and ethical issues.

– *5.4.1.7.* The public member shall not be an occupational therapy practitioner.

• *5.4.2. Process:*

– *5.4.2.1.* Potential candidates for the Disciplinary Council pool will be recruited through public postings in Association publications and via the listservs, etc. AOTA leadership will be encouraged to recruit qualified candidates. Potential members of the Council shall be interviewed to ascertain:

(a) Willingness to serve on the Council and availability for a period of 3 years

(b) Qualifications per criteria outlined in section 5.3.1.

– *5.4.2.2.* The President and EC staff liaison will maintain a pool of no less than six (6) and no more than twelve (12) qualified individuals.

– *5.4.2.3.* The President and EC staff liaison will select from the pool the members

of each Council within 30 days of notification by a respondent that a Council is being requested.

– *5.4.2.4.* Each Council shall be composed of three (3) AOTA members in good standing and a public member.

– *5.4.2.5.* The EC staff liaison will remove anyone with a potential conflict of interest in a particular case from the potential Disciplinary Council pool.

5.5. Notification of Parties (EC Chairperson, Complainant, Respondent, Council Members)

• *5.5.1.* The Council Chairperson shall schedule a hearing date in coordination with the EC staff liaison.

• *5.5.2.* The Council (via the EC staff liaison) shall notify all parties at least forty-five (45) days prior to the hearing of the date, time, and place of hearing.

• *5.5.3.* Case material will be sent to all parties and the Council members by national delivery service or mail with signature required and proof of date received with return receipt.

5.6. Hearing Witnesses, Materials, and Evidence

• *5.6.1.* Within 30 days of notification of the hearing, the respondent shall submit to the Council a written response to the charges, including a detailed statement as to the reasons that he or she is appealing the decision and a list of potential witnesses (if any) with a statement indicating the subject matter they will be addressing.

• *5.6.2.* The complainant before the Council also will submit a list of potential witnesses (if any) to the Council with a statement indicating the subject matter they will be addressing. Only under limited circumstances may the Council consider additional material evidence from the Respondent or the Complainant not presented or available prior to the issuance of their proposed sanction. Such new or additional evidence may be considered by the Council if the Council is satisfied that the Respondent or the Complainant has demonstrated the new evidence was previously unavailable and provided it is submitted to all parties in writing no later than 15 days prior to the hearing.

- 5.6.3. The Council Chairperson may permit testimony by conference call (at no expense to the participant), limit participation of witnesses in order to curtail repetitive testimony, or prescribe other reasonable arrangements or limitations. The Respondent may elect to appear (at Respondent's own expense) and present testimony.

5.7. Counsel

The Respondent may be represented by legal counsel at his or her own expense. The AOTA legal counsel shall advise and represent the Association at the hearing. The AOTA legal counsel also may advise the Council regarding procedural matters to ensure fairness to all parties. All parties and legal counsel (at the request of the EC or the Council) shall have the opportunity to question witnesses.

5.8. Hearing

- 5.8.1. The Disciplinary Council hearing shall be recorded by a professional transcription service and shall be limited to two (2) hours.

- 5.8.2. The Council Chairperson will conduct the hearing and does not vote except in the case of a tie.

- 5.8.3. Each person present shall be identified for the record and the Chairperson will describe the procedures for the Council hearing. An oral affirmation of truthfulness will be requested from each participant who gives factual testimony in the Council hearing.

- 5.8.4. The Council Chairperson shall allow for questions.

- 5.8.5. The EC Chairperson shall present the ethics charge, a summary of the evidence re-

sulting from the investigation, and the EC recommendation(s) for disciplinary action against the respondent.

- 5.8.6. The respondent may present a defense to the charges(s) after the EC presents its case.

- 5.8.7. Each party and/or their legal representative shall have the opportunity to call witnesses to present testimony and to question any witnesses, including the EC Chairperson or their designee. The Council chairperson shall be entitled to provide reasonable limits on the extent of any witnesses' testimony or any questioning.

- 5.8.8. The Chairperson may recess the hearing at any time.

- 5.8.9. The Council Chairperson shall call for final statements from each party before concluding the hearing.

- 5.8.10. Decisions of the Council will be by majority vote.

5.9. Disciplinary Council Decision

- 5.9.1. An official copy of the transcript shall be sent to each Council member, the EC Chairperson, AOTA legal counsel, the EC staff liaison, and the respondent and his/her counsel as soon as it is available from the transcription company.

- 5.9.2. The Chairperson of the Disciplinary Council shall work with the EC staff liaison and the AOTA legal counsel in preparing the text of the final decision.

- 5.9.3. The Council shall issue a decision in writing to the AOTA Executive Director within thirty (30) days of receiving the written transcription of the hearing (unless special circumstances warrant additional time). The Council decision shall be based on the record and evidence presented and may affirm, modify, or reverse the decision of the EC, including increasing or decreasing the level of sanction or determining that no disciplinary action is warranted.

5.10. Action, Notification, and Timeline Adjustments

- *5.10.1.* A copy of the Disciplinary Council's official decision and appeal process (Section 6) is sent to the respondent, the EC Chairperson, and other appropriate parties within fifteen (15) working days via mail (with signature and proof of date received) after notification of the AOTA Executive Director.

- *5.10.2.* The time limits specified in the *Enforcement Procedures for the Occupational Therapy Code of Ethics* may be extended by mutual consent of the respondent, complainant, and Disciplinary Council Chairperson for good cause by the Chairperson.

- *5.10.3.* Other features of the preceding *Procedures* may be adjusted in particular cases in light of extraordinary circumstances, consistent with fundamental fairness.

5.11. Appeal

Within 30 days after notification of the Council's decision, a respondent upon whom a sanction was imposed may appeal the decision as provided in Section 6. Within 30 days after notification of the Council's decision, the EC may also appeal the decision as provided in Section 6. If no appeal is filed within that time, the Executive Director shall notify appropriate bodies within the Association and make any other notifications deemed necessary.

6. APPEAL PROCESS

6.1. Appeals

Either the EC or the respondent may appeal. Appeals shall be written, signed by the appealing party, and sent by certified mail to the Executive Director c/o the Ethics Office of AOTA. The grounds for the appeal shall be fully explained in this document. When an appeal is requested, the other party will be notified.

6.2. Grounds for Appeal

Appeals shall generally address only the issues, procedures, or sanctions that are part of the record before the Disciplinary Council. However, in the interest of fairness, the Appeal Panel may consider newly available evidence relating to the original charge only under extraordinary circumstances.

6.3. Composition and Leadership of Appeal Panel

The Vice-President, Secretary, and Treasurer of the Association shall constitute the Appeal Panel. In the event of vacancies in these positions or the existence of a conflict of interest, the Vice President shall appoint replacements drawn from among the other Board members. If the entire Board of Directors has a conflict of interest (e.g., the Complainant or Respondent is or was recently a member of the Board of Directors), the Board Appeal process shall be followed. The President shall not serve on the Appeal Panel. No individual may serve on the Council who has previously been the subject of an ethics complaint that resulted in a specific EC disciplinary action.

The chair of the Appeal Panel will be selected by its members from among themselves.

6.4. Appeal Process

The Executive Director shall forward any letter of appeal to the Appeal Panel within 15 days of receipt. Within 45 days after the Appeal Panel receives the appeal, the Panel shall determine whether a hearing is warranted according to the Board of Directors policy on appeals (unless it is an EC appeal). If the Panel decides that a hearing is warranted, timely notice for such hearing shall be given to the parties. Participants at the hearing shall be limited to the Respondent and legal counsel (if so desired), the EC Chairperson, Disciplinary Council Chairperson, AOTA legal counsel, or others approved in advance by the Appeal Panel as necessary to the proceedings.

6.5. Decision

- *6.5.1.* The Appeal Panel shall have the power to (a) affirm the decision, or (b) modify the decision, or (c) reverse or remand to the EC, but only if there were procedural errors materially prejudicial to the outcome of the proceeding or if the Disciplinary Council decision was against the clear weight of the evidence.

- *6.5.2.* Within 45 days after receipt of the appeal if no hearing was granted, or within 30 days after receipt of the transcript if a hearing was held, the Appeal Panel shall notify the AOTA Executive Director of its decision. The Executive Director shall promptly notify the respondent, the original complainant, appropriate bodies of the Association, and any other parties deemed appropriate. For Association purposes, the decision of the Appeal Panel shall be final.

7. NOTIFICATIONS

All notifications referred to in these *Procedures* shall be in writing and shall be delivered by national delivery service or mail with signature and proof of date of receipt required.

8. RECORDS AND REPORTS

At the completion of the Ethics process, the written records and reports that state the initial basis for the complaint, material evidence, and the disposition of the complaint shall be retained in the Ethics Office for a period of 5 years. Electronic files will be kept indefinitely.

9. PUBLICATION

Final decisions will be publicized only after any Appeal Panel process has been completed.

10. MODIFICATION

AOTA reserves the right to (a) modify the time periods, procedures, or application of these Procedures for good cause consistent with fundamental fairness in a given case and (b) modify its Code of Ethics and/or these Procedures, with such modifications to be applied only prospectively.

Adopted by the Representative Assembly 2006C0458 as Attachment A of the Standard Operating Procedures (SOPs) of the Commission on Standards and Ethics (SEC).

Reviewed by BPPC 1/04, 1/05, 9/06, 1/07

Adopted by RA 4/96, 5/04, 5/05, 11/06, 4/07

Revised by SEC 4/98, 4/00, 1/02, 1/04, 12/04, 9/06

Revised by EC 12/06, 2/07

Note: The Commission on Standards and Ethics (SEC) changed to Ethics Commission (EC) in September 2005 as per *AOTA Bylaws.*

AMERICAN OCCUPATIONAL THERAPY ASSOCIATION ETHICS COMMISSION
Formal Complaint of Alleged Violation of the
Occupational Therapy Code of Ethics

If an investigation is deemed necessary, a copy of this form will be provided to the individual against whom the complaint is filed.

Date _____

COMPLAINANT (Information regarding individual filing the complaint)

Name _____ Signature _____

Address _____ Telephone (_____)_____

_____ E-mail Address _____

RESPONDENT (Information regarding individual against whom the complaint is directed)

Name _____

Address _____ Telephone (_____)_____

_____

1. **Indicate the Ethical Principle(s) you believe have been violated:**

2. **Summarize in an attachment the facts and circumstances, including dates and events, warranting the complaint. Attach documentation that you think would help the Ethics Commission in its assessment of this complaint. Please sign and date all documents you have written and are submitting. *Do not include confidential documents such as patient or employment records.*** (Statements from witnesses are not necessary at this time.)

3. **If you have filed a complaint about this same matter to any other agency (e.g., NBCOT; SRB; academic institution; any federal, state, or local official), indicate to whom it was submitted and the approximate date(s).**

4. **What steps have been taken to resolve this complaint?**

I CERTIFY THAT THE STATEMENTS/INFORMATION WITHIN THIS COMPLAINT ARE CORRRECT AND TRUTHFUL TO THE BEST OF MY KNOWLEDGE.

_____
Signature

Send completed form, with accompanying documentation, IN AN ENVELOPE MARKED <u>CONFIDENTIAL</u> to:

Ethics Commission
American Occupational Therapy Association, Inc.
Attn: Staff Liaison to the EC/Ethics Office
4720 Montgomery Lane, PO Box 31220
Bethesda, MD 20824-1220

| **Office Use Only:** |
| Membership verified? ☐ Yes ☐ No |
| By: _____ |

Ec/forms/complaint form, revised 1/04

FIGURE 6.1. AOTA Ethics Commission Statement of Formal Complaint of Alleged Violation of the *Occupational Therapy Code of Ethics*

JURISDICTION

CHAPTER 7

Disciplinary Action: Whose Responsibility?

JURISDICTION

NBCOT All certified individuals (OTs and OTAs) and persons who are currently applicants to sit for the OT and OTA examinations.

SRBs All individuals regulated in that state (varies from state to state), e.g., OTs, OTAs, OT aides, and students.

AOTA All members of AOTA. Includes all membership categories, i.e., OTs, OTAs, students, and associates.

Author

Ruth A. Hansen, PhD, OTR, FAOTA
Chairperson, Commission on Standards and Ethics (1988–1994)

September 15, 1994, Revised May 1999, Edited July 2000

QUESTION	JURISDICTION		
	NBCOT	SRB	AOTA
1. Who should I call if I have questions about the following?			
a. Ethical violations that could cause harm or have potential to cause harm to a consumer/the public	X	X	X
b. Violations that do not cause harm or have a limited potential of causing harm to a consumer/the public			X
c. Violations of professional values that do not relate directly to potential harm to the public			X
2. Where did the alleged violation occur, and who was involved in the alleged incident?			
a. Took place in a state with rules, regulations, and disciplinary procedures in place	X	X	X
b. Took place in an unregulated state	X		X
c. Was committed by an AOTA member	X	X	X
d. Was committed by a person who is not an AOTA member	X	X	
3. What is the disciplinary action that you wish as a consequence of filing a complaint?			
a. Restrict or revoke licensure		X	
b. Restrict or revoke certification	X		
c. Restrict or prohibit membership in AOTA			X

FIGURE 7.1. Disciplinary Responsibility.

CHAPTER 8

Overview of the Ethical Jurisdictions of AOTA, NBCOT, and SRBs

Three entities have jurisdiction and concerns about the ethical conduct of occupational therapy personnel: the American Occupational Therapy Association (AOTA), the National Certification Board for Occupational Therapy (NBCOT), and state regulatory boards (SRBs).

AOTA

AOTA is a voluntary membership organization that represents and promotes the profession and the interests of individuals who choose to become members. Because membership is voluntary, AOTA has no direct authority over occupational therapists and occupational therapy assistants who are not members. AOTA has no direct legal mechanism for preventing nonmembers who are incompetent, unethical, or unqualified from practicing.

It is important to remember that AOTA is concerned about ethical conduct across the multiple roles that occupational therapists and occupational therapy assistants can play—student, researcher, educator, manager, practitioner, entrepreneur, elected or appointed volunteer leader, and so forth. The Ethics Commission (EC) is the volunteer sector component of AOTA that is responsible for writing, revising, and enforcing the *Ethics Standards* (AOTA, 1993, 2005, 2006). The EC also is responsible for informing and educating members about current ethical trends and issues and for reviewing allegations of unethical conduct by AOTA members.

There are five types of potential disciplinary action:

1. *Reprimand* is a formal expression of disapproval of conduct communicated privately by letter from the chairperson of the EC.
2. *Censure* is a formal expression of disapproval that is public (e.g., published in *OT Practice,* in the *American Journal of Occupational Therapy,* and at www.aota.org).
3. *Probation of membership* subject to certain terms—membership is conditional depending on compliance with specific requirements (e.g., continuing education). Failure to meet these terms will subject a member to any of the disciplinary actions or sanctions.
4. *Suspension* requires removal of membership for a specified time.
5. *Revocation* prohibits a person from being a member of AOTA indefinitely (AOTA, 2007).

NBCOT

NBCOT is a private, not-for-profit, non-governmental credentialing organization that oversees and administers the entry-level certification examination for occupational therapists and occupational therapy assistants. This examination is what the SRBs use as one of the criteria for licensure (or other forms of regulation). NBCOT uses the examination as one of the criteria for initial NBCOT certification.

NBCOT certifies eligible individuals as Occupational Therapist Registered (OTR®) or Certified Occupational Therapy Assistant (COTA®). The OTR® and COTA® credentials are registered certification marks owned by NBCOT. Certification by NBCOT indicates to the public that the OTR or the COTA has met all of NBCOT's educational, fieldwork, and examination requirements (NBCOT, 2002, as cited in Smith & Willmarth, 2003). Maintaining NBCOT certification entitles individuals to the continued use of NBCOT's registered certification marks OTR® or COTA®. Individuals who choose not to renew this certification are required by NBCOT to no longer use its certification marks.

States or jurisdictions commonly require occupational therapists and occupational therapy assistants to be initially certified (i.e., pass the NBCOT entry-level certification exam) before they can qualify for a license. Most states or jurisdictions, however, do not require practitioners to renew this certification to maintain their licenses to practice.[1]

NBCOT does not use the AOTA *Occupational Therapy Code of Ethics* as its guide in reviewing complaints about incompetent or impaired practitioners but has its own set of procedures for disciplinary action. NBCOT will take action when there is a clear violation of its *Candidate/Certificant Code of Conduct* (NBCOT, 2003). The three main categories of violations that warrant disciplinary action are incompetence, unethical behavior, and impairment.

When NBCOT receives a complaint, it initiates an intensive, confidential review process to determine whether the allegations are warranted. If so, the Qualifications and Compliance Review Committee (QCRC) may recommend one of several sanctions, depending on the seriousness of the misconduct. Below is a listing of the available options, all

of which are made public, except for reprimand and ineligibility (NBCOT, 2004). NBCOT has six types of disciplinary action:

1. *Ineligibility for certification* can be either indefinite or for a certain duration.
2. *Reprimand* is a formal, written expression of disapproval that is retained in an individual's certification file but is not announced publicly.
3. *Censure* is a formal expression of disapproval that is announced publicly (on the NBCOT Web site and in its newsletter, *Report to the Profession*).
4. *Probation* requires that an individual fulfill certain conditions, such as monitoring, education, supervision, or counseling for a specified time. An individual must meet these conditions to remain certified.
5. *Suspension* is the loss of certification for a specified time after which an individual may need to apply for reinstatement. The QCRC may use suspension when it determines that a person must complete specific amounts of public service or participate in a rehabilitation program.
6. *Revocation* means that an individual loses certification permanently.

SRBs

SRBs are public bodies created by state legislatures to ensure the health and safety of the citizens of that state. Their responsibility is to protect the public from potential harm caused by incompetent or unqualified practitioners. The primary concern of each state is to protect the people living in that state, and there is a process for reviewing and handling any complaint that may be filed with the board.

When an SRB determines that an individual has violated the law, it can elect several

---

[1]Exceptions include the following: Occupational therapy assistants are not regulated in Hawaii or Colorado and are not required to take the exam in New York. Occupational therapists and occupational therapy assistants in Puerto Rico are not required to take the exam for licensure and may instead take a test developed by the Puerto Rico Occupational Therapy Board. South Carolina is the only state requiring current certification for licensure renewal at this time.

sanctions as a disciplinary measure. Examples of disciplinary actions are *public censure, temporary or permanent suspension of a license* to practice in that state, *monetary fine,* and *imprisonment.*

State regulation may be in the form of licensure, registration, certification, or title protection. Only those states with licensure, registration, or certification laws have regulatory boards (or advisory councils) to enforce the law. States with title protection (or trademark law) do not have SRBs. In these states, the attorney general or a state agency has the authority to enforce the law. The legal guidelines of states with licensure specify the scope of practice for the profession and the qualifications that professionals must meet to practice.

In several states, SRBs have adopted the AOTA *Occupational Therapy Code of Ethics* for this purpose. The majority of those states use this Code as their template for reviewing complaints about harm to the public by a practitioner who is licensed in that state. States often adopt the Code at a point in time. Regulations are updated only occasionally, which means that the adopted Code can stay on the books for a while, sometimes leading to outdated AOTA documents existing as the standard in a particular state. Other states have language describing professional conduct as a standard.

Each SRB has direct jurisdiction over those practitioners who are licensed or regulated in that state. By the very nature of this limited jurisdiction, each state can monitor the practitioners in that state more closely than can national organizations such as AOTA and NBCOT. In addition, they have the authority by state law to discipline members of a profession practicing in that state if they have caused harm to citizens of that state. This gives them legal authority to conduct investigations, including the subpoena of witnesses, as well as imposing fines or recommending imprisonment. Violations of the law at this level may be referred to the attorney general's office for potential prosecution. By virtue of their authority to suspend or revoke a license, SRBs control an indi-

vidual's ability to practice occupational therapy, thereby having the strongest impact on practitioners. SRBs also can intervene in situations in which it is made aware of actions through the judicial system that may affect professional practice (e.g., misappropriation of funds through false billing practices) or in which behaviors were not directly related to practice but demonstrate potential harm to the consumer in some way (e.g., poor decision making as evidenced by multiple drunk driving convictions).

WHERE TO GO FIRST

As one can see, AOTA, NBCOT, and SRBs have specific jurisdictions over occupational therapy practitioners (see Figure 7.1). Some areas of concern overlap among the three entities; others are separate and distinct. Individuals who need information or want to file a complaint must know which of the three is the most appropriate to contact. The following questions may assist in clarifying where to file:

1. In what state did the alleged violation take place, and what level of regulation does that state have for occupational therapy?
2. Is the individual a member of AOTA? Is the individual currently certified by NBCOT?
3. What consequences are considered appropriate if the complaint is determined to be justified (Hansen, 2000)?

Certainly in some instances, an individual may feel that it is appropriate to file a complaint with any or all of the three entities. For example, all three have concerns if there has been harm or potential harm to a consumer. On the other hand, ethical violations of professional values that have no potential to cause harm would likely be of interest to only AOTA. For example, AOTA would be concerned about plagiarism of a colleague's professional work, but NBCOT and the SRB would not.

Individuals also should consider what disciplinary action they would consider appropriate for a particular violation: Revoking or restricting the person's state license to practice? Suspending or revoking the individual's certification? Restricting or prohibiting the person's ability to be a member of AOTA? An individual considering an action should seek advice before filing a complaint to be sure that he or she has selected the agency with the jurisdiction to achieve the consequences commensurate to the violation (Hansen, 2000).

Conclusion

Three primary organizations have ethical oversight of the occupational therapy profession. In some cases, their jurisdictions may overlap, but each focuses on particular areas of ethical behavior and has procedures for enforcing appropriate professional conduct. Occupational therapists and occupational therapy assistants have a responsibility to be aware of and comply with the policies and procedures of these organizations.

References

American Occupational Therapy Association. (1993). Core values and attitudes for occupational therapy. *American Journal of Occupational Therapy, 47,* 1085–1086.

American Occupational Therapy Association. (2005). Occupational therapy code of ethics (2005). *American Journal of Occupational Therapy, 59,* 639–642.

American Occupational Therapy Association. (2006). Guidelines to the occupational therapy code of ethics. *American Journal of Occupational Therapy, 60,* 652–658.

American Occupational Therapy Association. (2007). Enforcement procedures for occupational therapy code of ethics. *American Journal of Occupational Therapy, 61,* 679–685.

Hansen, R. A. (2000). Ethical jurisdiction of occupational therapy: The role of AOTA, NBCOT, and state regulatory boards. In P. Kyler (Ed.), *Reference guide to the occupational therapy code of ethics* (pp. 22–24). Bethesda, MD: American Occupational Therapy Association.

National Board for Certification in Occupational Therapy. (2002). *Certification renewal.* Retrieved April 11, 2002, from http://www.nbcot.org/programs/cert_renewal.htm

National Board for Certification in Occupational Therapy. (2003). *Candidate/certificant code of conduct.* Retrieved December 14, 2005, from http://www.nbcot.org/webarticles/anmviewer.asp?a=76

National Board for Certification in Occupational Therapy. (2004). *Enforcement procedures for the candidate/certificant code of conduct.* Retrieved December 14, 2005, from http://www.nbcot.org/WebArticles/articlefiles/121-enforcement_procedures.pdf

Smith, K. C., & Willmarth, C. (2003). State regulation of occupational therapists and occupational therapy assistants. In G. L. McCormack, E. G. Jaffe, & M. Goodman-Lavey (Eds.), *The occupational therapy manager* (4th ed., pp. 439–459). Bethesda, MD: AOTA Press.

Author

Ruth A. Hansen, PhD, OTR, FAOTA
Excerpted/adapted from Hansen, R. A. (1998). Ethics in occupational therapy.
In M. E. Neistadt & E. B. Crepeau (Eds.), *Willard and Spackman's occupational therapy* (9th ed., pp. 819–827). Philadelphia: Lippincott.

Deborah Yarett Slater, MS, OT/L, FAOTA
Revised December 2005

ADVISORY OPINIONS

The Ethics Commission issues advisory opinions on ethical issues and trends to inform and educate the membership of the American Occupational Therapy Association (AOTA). Advisory opinions evolve from multiple sources. They respond to questions frequently posed through member inquiries, changes in occupational therapy practice, and unprofessional conduct, which may have led to disciplinary actions taken by state regulatory boards and other bodies.

The following opinions have been included in this book:
- Ethical Issues Around Payment for Services
- Patient Abandonment
- Plagiarism
- State Licensure, Professionalism, and the AOTA Occupational Therapy Code of Ethics
- Ethical Considerations When Occupational Therapists Engage in Business Transactions With Clients
- Cultural Competency and Ethical Practice
- Ethical Considerations for Professional Education of Students with Disabilities
- Balancing Patient Rights and Practitioner Values
- Ethics in Governance
- Organizational Ethics.

Several of these opinions can be accessed in the "Members" section of the AOTA Web site at www.aota.org (click "Practice/Ethics/ Advisory Opinions"). Readers are encouraged to check periodically for updates and additions.

CHAPTER 9

Ethical Issues Around Payment for Services

THE ISSUES

The current health care environment has created the potential for ethical issues regarding payment for occupational therapy services that may have appeared minimal or nonexistent to occupational therapy practitioners prior to the past 15 years. Central questions include, How do occupational therapy practitioners ethically apply rules for payment? Provide quality care to achieve desired outcomes? Manage resources? Additional concerns may arise from administrative decisions based on maximizing reimbursement (perhaps to offset escalating health care costs) rather than based on clinical judgment. These have the potential to erode trust and respect for the dignity of the client, both of which are the foundation of a therapeutic relationship and place clinicians in a quandary, trying to balance professional ethics with business ethics (Povar et al., 2004).

For example, in the clinical practice arena, payment for services is governed by a variety of federal and private payment guidelines. Clinicians may be confronted with providing treatment to several recipients of service with the same diagnosis but who are "entitled" by differing insurance plans to different levels of care (e.g., number of visits, coverage of equipment/splints, span of treatment) at different levels of reimbursement. For example, some plans provide for a 90% payment and 10% copay by the recipient of service, some plans provide an 80%/20% split, and some have larger out-of pocket costs. Different insurance plans provide certain levels and types of health care coverage, so in some instances, inevitable differences in care may result in the clinic.

Sometimes, recipients of services are limited to designated facilities because of payer contract restrictions. In some cases, the facilities in the provider network may not necessarily be those best suited by competence of staff and equipment to address the client's specific medical needs. This raises ethical issues based on the concepts of *beneficence, autonomy, and justice.* Within the arena of payment for services are ethical concerns about who makes the decisions regarding length and duration of clinical services. Determination of approved services may be done by a third-party case manager without full regard for the complexity of the clinical aspects of a specific case. In the managed care model (including, in many cases, Medicare and Medicaid), the clinical decisions regarding treatment often are made by non-clinical personnel on what may appear to be arbitrary and rigid guidelines (Slater & Kyler, 1999).

For clinical practitioners whose altruism is usually the primary motivating force for seeking a career in occupational therapy and whose guiding principle of ethical practice is *beneficence,* or "doing good" for the recipient of services, these payment and clinical service issues can present frequent dilemmas. At the heart of these dilemmas may be the overriding question

49

of professional autonomy based on who is most competent to direct medical care and the duty to advocate for the good of the patient within the system (Povar et al., 2004). The perception that conflicting motives (business vs. altruism) underlie this decision process has the inevitable potential to put the occupational therapy practitioner, the employer, and the insurance entity in conflict.

Ethical allocation of finite resources is yet another related and critical issue. Constraints have always existed in health care, as in other aspects of daily life. Material and human resources have never been unlimited. Yet the tremendous advances in medical technology and health care costs over the past few decades have brought the issue of allocating health care resources responsibly and fairly to the forefront (Povar et al., 2004). Managed care and other payer attempts to control spiraling health care costs have resulted in a swing in the pendulum to what many feel are excessive constraints on treatment that could potentially lead to blatant denial of care. Occupational therapists have faced arbitrary discharges or terminations of treatment due to limitations in health insurance coverage. Occupational therapy treatment may be cut short prematurely or never initiated because of policy limits or restrictions in services. However, occupational therapy practitioners also have ethical obligations to see that resources are most appropriately allocated according to the principle of distributive justice. The allocation of occupational therapy resources should weigh the skill level of the practitioner, the treatment intensity, the type of intervention needed, and the appropriate timing of that intervention so that consumers can achieve optimal outcome. It is unethical to waste resources.

The prevalence of capitated payment systems in skilled-nursing facilities as well as most traditional medical settings may promote efforts by management to dictate frequency and duration of therapy to ensure maximal reimbursement resulting in pressure on clinicians to comply. If clinicians are not making these decisions based on their professional judgment, resources may be misallocated based on payer source with some patients getting unnecessary therapy and others receiving less benefit. Likewise, in these situations, practitioners may be tempted to modify their documentation of intervention needs to support increased reimbursement, which also is an ethical issue.

Finally, the growth in emerging or nontraditional practice areas (e.g., use of alternative or complementary interventions as an adjunct to more usual occupational therapy practice) presents its own potential ethical issues. In these cases, third-party payment is likely to be very limited or nonexistent. Practitioners need to be clear on whether the services they provide fall within the scope of occupational therapy and legitimately can be billed as such. They also need to understand ethical considerations in developing fee schedules for a client group that may include private payment from individuals as well as by third-party payers. In addition, they need to ensure that their provider contracts do not violate ethical or professional standards.

Discussion

All these issues (e.g., payment rules that may present arbitrary limitations to care, quality of treatment to achieve outcomes, appropriate application of limited resources) can present awkward dilemmas between recipients of services and providers. They also are ethical concerns for clinicians. In this environment, the concepts of *beneficence, competence, informed consent, autonomy*, and *education* are paramount. Familiarity with and reference to several documents from AOTA can provide a useful framework for making ethical decisions, which are effective in daily practice. In addition, facility-based ethics committees, supervisors with ethics knowledge, as well as AOTA ethics staff and Ethics Commission (EC) members can assist in analyzing issues and identifying strategies to deal with ethical dilemmas. In many cases, these complex issues do not have clear-cut resolutions, so it is not in the client's best interest for clinicians to attempt to handle them on their own. As stated in Section 10.2 of the *Guidelines to the Occupational Therapy Code of Ethics*, "occupational therapy personnel who are uncertain of whether a specific action would violate the Code have a responsibility to consult with knowledgeable individuals, ethics committees, or other appropriate authorities" (AOTA, 2006).

Level of Care and Informed Consent

With respect to loss of autonomy in determining appropriate skill level, treatment intensity, and interventions needed to achieve optimal outcome or the greatest good for recipients of services, both managers and clinicians must rethink service delivery models and educate themselves about cost-effective methods of rendering care. A focus should be on increased collaboration when setting goals with recipients of services so that treatment time is used for the most direct benefit. This is consistent with a client-centered approach to care and with Principle 3A of the *Occupational Therapy Code of Ethics (2005)* (AOTA, 2005), which states that "occupational therapy personnel shall collaborate with recipients, and if they desire, families, significant others, and/or caregivers in setting goals and priorities throughout the intervention process, including full disclosure of the nature, risk, and potential outcomes of any interventions" (p. 640).

The concept of informed consent in any health care environment is particularly important. Clinicians must be able to discuss all treatment options with a patient and significant others so that they can be fully informed and make appropriate decisions about their care. Recommendations for care also must be free from influence by contractual or other arrangements the insurer may have with the provider (Povar et al., 2004). That does not, however, ensure that all interventions will be reimbursed. In some cases, providing services

on a pro bono or private-pay basis may be appropriate and viable options to improve access to care. Again, clients must be educated as to risks, benefits, and alternatives in an understandable manner (considering, e.g., language, culture, literacy) so that they can make an informed decision whether to consent or refuse services (Povar et al., 2004).

Section 9.3 of the *Guidelines to the Occupational Therapy Code of Ethics* supports this principle by providing an option for rendering pro bono services with certain parameters: "Occupational therapy practitioners can render *pro bono* (meaning 'for the good' or free of charge) or reduced-fee occupational therapy services for selected individuals only when consistent with guidelines of the business/facility, third-party payer, or government agency" (AOTA, 2006, italics added). Although it is not universally possible, within the boundaries of the employer's policy and financial resources, pro bono services can improve access to occupational therapy.

Competence

Practitioner competence is another way to help ensure that, irrespective of external payment limits, treatment sessions are focused on the goals established by the occupational therapy practitioner and the recipient of services. This is addressed directly in Section 4 of the *Guidelines to the Occupational Therapy Code of Ethics* (AOTA, 2006): "Occupational therapy personnel are expected to work within their areas of competence and to pursue opportunities to update, increase, and expand their competence." Regardless of length of treatment, the recipient of service will gain the greatest good through clinicians that are highly competent to provide specific care, thus ensuring that the ethical concept of beneficence is central to the scope of occupational therapy services.

The concepts of *competence* in today's health care environment are broad. They include not only clinical competence but also knowledge and ongoing education about financial realities and reimbursement/regulatory guidelines, as well as how to meet them. In addition, competence includes an occupational therapy practitioner's ability to advise recipients of alternative strategies to reach their goals of decreased impairment and increased occupational performance and participation. This is consistent with Principles 4C and 4E of the *Occupational Therapy Code of Ethics* (2005): "Occupational therapy personnel shall take responsibility for maintaining and documenting competence by participating in professional development and educational activities" (AOTA, 2005, p. 640), and "occupational therapy personnel shall critically examine available evidence so they may perform their duties on the basis of current information" (p. 640). This will assist occupational therapy practitioners in providing interventions that are most clinically appropriate and effective at the most appropriate point in the continuum of care.

Education and Advocacy

Education and advocacy are additional realms of knowledge that aid occupational therapy practitioners in negotiating the potential minefield of payment guidelines. Section 3.2 in the *Guidelines to the Occupational Therapy Code of Ethics* supports the development of these skills to allow occupational therapy personnel to be "diligent stewards of human, financial, and material resources of their employers" (AOTA, 2006). The trust so critical to the therapeutic relationship also includes "a responsibility to practice effective and efficient health care and to use... resources responsibly" (Povar et al., 2004, p. 133). Likewise, it also is a patient's responsibility to be knowledgeable about and share with his or her therapist the details about his or her insurance plan and reimbursement as it relates to occupational therapy services.

In cases in which there is lack of or limited coverage and the service is essential, there should be a clear and fair procedure for appeal. A clinician's ability to educate clients on advocacy strategies, rights, and options in the health care system is another way of "doing good" for recipients of services and resolving ethical dilemmas resulting from limitations to care. Advocacy on behalf of clients can include documentation of objective data and relevant evidence to support the positive outcomes of occupational therapy intervention.

It is not unusual for occupational therapy practitioners to treat several clients with the same diagnosis but whom, by virtue of different insurance plans, are entitled to different parameters of care. It is important to remember that recipients of services have chosen a health plan that entitles them to benefits that may not be the same across all payers (Kyler, 1996). It is also important to distinguish between recipients' perceived right to have services and the obligation of occupational therapy practitioners to their role as an employee of a health care facility to provide more services than are covered. This is not in conflict with the core concept of justice (AOTA, 1993), which states that we "aspire to provide occupational therapy services for all individuals who are in need of these services" (p. 1086), as these services do not need to be provided in the same way, only in a "goal directed and objective" manner to the extent possible. However, this situation again emphasizes the importance of occupational therapy practitioners' competence and presents an opportunity for clinicians to educate recipients of their services about advocacy skills in the greater health care system. It also facilitates a collaborative educational process as occupational therapy practitioners and clients may discuss treatment options, strategies, expected outcomes, and alternative methods of reaching goals.

This collaboration has the potential to make recipients of occupational therapy services more active participants in their own care, thereby increasing the likelihood of a positive outcome. Consistent with Principle 3A of the *Occupational Therapy Code of Ethics (2005)*, "occupational therapy personnel shall collaborate with recipients...in setting goals and priorities throughout the intervention process including full disclosure of the nature, risk, and potential outcomes of any interventions" (AOTA, 2005, p. 640). This principle also is contained within the *Core Values and Attitudes of Occupational Therapy Practice*, that we be "faithful to facts and reality" (AOTA, 1993, p. 1086). Further, this document states that, despite basic inviolable values,

> [The] degree to which certain values will take priority at a given time is influenced by the specifics of a situation and the environment in which it occurs. The practitioner… is required to engage in thoughtful deliberation to determine where the priority lies in a given situation. (p. 1086)

In sorting through any ethical dilemma presented in practice, the good of the recipient of services must always serve as the focal point from which intervention decisions are made, regardless of ongoing changes in the external environment. Payment regulations may present ethical dilemmas for occupational therapy practitioners. As AOTA members, an important component of our professional role is knowledge about payment guidelines for our services and strategies to assist clients in obtaining beneficial services. The ongoing knowledge base needed to maintain competence in the payment for services area includes financial information from federal and state laws, regulations, and guidelines that cover Medicare and Medicaid payment, as well as private payer sources in both fee-for-service model and managed care models. The occupational therapy role of educator and advocate also must be acknowledged. The concepts of informed decision making by both occupational therapy practitioner and client must be part of the service delivery process.

CONCLUSION

Guidelines and regulations for payment change. However, the need for current competency in this area does not change. The *Occupational Therapy Code of Ethics (2005)*, *Guidelines to the Occupational Therapy Code of Ethics*, *Core Values and Attitudes of Occupational Therapy Practice*, and other cited documents in this advisory opinion support the knowledge base to provide cost-effective services in an ethical manner. The EC believes that, as members of AOTA, it is incumbent on occupational therapists and occupational therapy assistants to be familiar with these documents and use them in clinical practice.

REFERENCES

American Occupational Therapy Association. (1993). Core values and attitudes of occupational therapy practice. *American Journal of Occupational Therapy, 47*, 1085–1086.

American Occupational Therapy Association. (2005). Occupational therapy code of ethics (2005). *American Journal of Occupational Therapy, 59*, 639–642.

American Occupational Therapy Association. (2006). Guidelines to the occupational therapy code of ethics. *American Journal of Occupational Therapy, 60*, 652-658.

Kyler, P. (1996). Ethics in managed care. *OT Week, 10*, 9.

Povar, G. J., Blumen, H., Daniel, J., Daub, S., Evans, L., Holm, R. P., et al. (2004). Ethics in practice: Managed care and the changing health care environment. *Annals of Internal Medicine, 141*, 131–136.

Slater, D. Y., & Kyler, P. L. (1999, June). Management strategies for ethical practice dilemmas. *Administration and Management Special Interest Section Quarterly*, pp. 1–2.

Author

Deborah Y. Slater, MS, OTR/L, FAOTA
Chairperson, Standards and Ethics Commission, 2000–2001
Originally written July 17, 2000

Deborah Yarett Slater, MS, OT/L, FAOTA
AOTA Staff Liaison to the Ethics Commission
Revised December 2005, February, 2008

CHAPTER 10

Patient Abandonment

SUMMARY

The duty to treat, patient abandonment, and occupational therapy are examined in this advisory opinion. Occupational therapy practitioners have a variety of resources available to enable their adherence to high ethical standards. The advisory opinion encourages practitioners to abide with rather than abandon the recipient of services.

ABANDONMENT IN THE HEALTH CARE SETTING

In the *New Expanded Webster's Dictionary*, *abandonment* is defined as "a total desertion" (Patterson, 1991, p. 5). *Taber's Cyclopedic Medical Dictionary* clarifies what *abandonment* means in the health care setting: "The abandoning, without adequate warning, of a patient needing further medical care by the person responsible for that care" (Thomas, 1993, p. 1).

One should note that, according to this second definition, a health care professional can indeed "abandon" a patient as long as some notice has been given. Tangential to withdrawing from a case in which treatment has already begun is the refusal to initiate treatment, which many patients also take as an act of abandonment. This "right" (as it sometimes called) of health care professionals to withdraw from the treatment of a patient, or to refuse to initiate treatment, is supported by the *American Medical Association's [AMA's] Principles of Medical*

Ethics, Principle VI: "A physician shall, in the provision of appropriate patient care, except in emergencies, be free to choose whom to serve, with who to associate, and the environment in which to provide medical services" (AMA, 1994, p. 101). Similarly, the *Comprehensive Accreditation Manual for Hospitals* (JCAHO, 1998) calls for the development of policies and procedures within health care facilities governing "how staff may request to be excused from participating in an aspect of patient care on grounds of conflicting cultural values, ethics, or religious beliefs...." (p. HR-21).

Belief in this "right" of health care professionals to refuse to treat can be found throughout the health care system in this country, because it flows out of the strong value Americans place on freedom of choice. As Albert R. Jonsen (1995) explains,

> There has long been, in the United States, a reluctance to force one person to provide services to another against his or her will.... the right to refuse to care for a particular patient, either by not accepting that person as a patient or by discharging oneself from responsibility in a recognized way, is deeply embedded in the ethos of American medicine. (p. 100)

The issue of patient abandonment versus health care professional's rights is one of several problems that contribute to the growing tension between patients and medical personnel. Finding and maintaining a balance between patient needs and the personal rights of those involved with health care delivery on this issue of abandonment would go far toward easing such tensions as we move into the next millennium.

CLARIFYING PATIENT ABANDONMENT

We must recognize that there are legitimate reasons across all fields of health care to cease providing treatment to a patient. Some of these are clear-cut. First, when treatment needs exceed the ability and expertise of a health care professional, the patient is best served by having care transferred to a more qualified practitioner. Since the goal of health care is the well-being of the patient, withdrawing from a case when one's skill can no longer be of benefit is justified, even though claims of abandonment may be raised by the patient. However, the manner in which one presents the need for a transfer of care and the degree to which the patient is made aware of this need and involved in the choice of a new practitioner are important factors in lessening the patient's perception of abandonment.

Second, it is commonly agreed that a health care practitioner may withdraw from the care of a patient who acts inappropriately within the health care setting. The most common situation discussed is when a patient becomes violent or acts in ways that endanger the practitioner, other patients, or staff. However, this would also include inappropriate sexual advances from a patient (e.g., or possibly from a patient's guardian, spouse, parent). In such cases, a practitioner may, if necessary, withdraw from the treatment of the patient without abandoning the patient, as the health care relationship has already been severed and the bond of trust damaged.

A third area, but one that involves more difficulty, arises from issues regarding the cultural and religious values of health care practitioners.

As noted in the *Comprehensive Accreditation Manual for Hospitals*—Refreshed Core (JCAHO, 1998), in the delivery of health care there should be respect for a health care practitioner's, "cultural values, ethics, and religious beliefs and the impact these may have on patient care" (p. HR-21). The *Manual* emphasizes that to respect all staff members, a health care institution (or practice) should establish policies for how staff members can make requests to discontinue care for ethical, religious, and cultural reasons, as well as policies for ensuring that patient care will not be negatively affected. It is further noted that addressing such issues in advance, even at the time of hiring or contracting, will be the most helpful for maintaining an appropriate level of patient care.

What makes these issues difficult is the subjective nature of "personal values." Who is to say what represents a cultural value? What if one's culture is in the minority—do minority values still have weight? Religious values also might be difficult to determine, because not all members of the same religion hold the same values. Should those making the decisions recognize only mainstream values of the staff member's religion? And of course, ethical values flow from the individual's own conscience. How should a manager or a supervisor regard a staff member's ethical claims? Should all expressed values carry the same weight, simply because someone claims they are important? The *Manual* goes on to note that if an appropriate (*in the judgment of the manager or supervisor*) request has been made, accommodations should be made where possible and cites the following "Examples of Implementation" to support Standard HR.6:

- There will be an understanding that if events prevent the accommodation at a specific point because of an emergency situation, the employee will be expected to perform assigned duties so he or she does not negatively affect the delivery of care or services.

- If an employee does not agree to render appropriate care or services in an emergency situation because of personal beliefs, the employee will be placed on a leave of absence from his or her current position and the incident will be reviewed. (JCAHO, 1998, p. HR-21)

Such cases surely will be difficult for all involved, especially if they have not been addressed prior to the emergent situation. The issue here is further complicated by the fact that, even though health care is becoming more diverse, when we work with each other we are not always aware of each other's diverse beliefs, nor are we always open and understanding about such differences. Supervisors and employers will need to become more aware of their staff's values, while staff will need to continue to keep patient care at the focus of their work during times of personal conflict.

Beyond the above reasons for discontinuing patient care, disagreement begins to arise. What about refusing to treat a noncompliant patient? What if that patient is *extremely* noncompliant versus occasionally noncompliant? In another vein, what about the patient who does not pay her or his bills? Is refusing to treat such a patient justifiable? What if the patient is unable to pay the bills? Would this make a difference? Or, one might consider an especially demanding patient. If a patient takes time away from the care of others and continually calls the practitioner beyond normal care hours, is withdrawal from the care of such a patient acceptable? Yet another problematic case might involve a patient whose appearance or manners disgusted a practitioner. If a practitioner is so put off by a patient that it impedes her or his ability to be an effective therapist, would withdrawing from the case be an act of abandonment or patient benefit? Finally, perhaps the most addressed cases involve persons with AIDS. Does the fear of contagion validate withdrawal from treating such a patient? Across the literature, there is little agreement as to what constitutes abandonment in such situations. Legal cases have not added much clarity (Southwick, 1998, pp. 37–41).

THE DUTY TO TREAT

Although there is disagreement about the issue of abandonment and the duty of health care professionals to treat patients, even in the face of personal inconvenience or risk, some helpful insights can be gained from the thoughts of Edmund D. Pellegrino. In his article "Altruism, Self-Interest, and Medical Ethics," Pellegrino (1991) addresses the particular case of physicians and the treatment of persons with AIDS. To begin, the author questions the notion that "medicine is an occupation like any other, and the physician has the same 'rights' as the businessman or the craftsman" (p. 114). As a counter to this notion, Pellegrino draws out three things specific to the nature of medicine that he argues establish a duty of physicians to treat the sick, even in the face of personal risk.

Pellegrino first points out the uniqueness of the medical relationship, in that it involves a vulnerable and dependent person who is at risk of exploitation who must trust another to be restored to health. As he explains, "physicians invite that trust when offering to put knowledge at the service of the sick. A medical need in itself constitutes a moral claim on those equipped to help." Next, the author points out that, in short, medical education is a privilege. Societies make special allowances for people to study medicine for the good of the society, thereby establishing a covenant with future health care professionals. Based on this, Pellegrino concludes, "the physician's knowledge, therefore, is not individually owned and ought not be used primarily for personal gain, prestige, or power. Rather, the profession holds this knowledge in trust for the good of the sick." Finally, Pellegrino points to the oath that physicians take before practicing medicine: "That oath—whichever one is taken—is a public promise that the new physician understands the gravity of this calling and promises to be competent and to use that competence in the interests of the sick." Although the debate continues, several have asserted that Pellegrino has made a strong case for the duty to treat (see, e.g., Arras, 1991, pp. 115–121; Jonsen, 1995, pp. 97–106). And although Pellegrino's comments are directed toward physicians, his reasoning cuts across all fields of medical practice.

THE DUTY TO TREAT, PATIENT ABANDONMENT, AND OCCUPATIONAL THERAPY

The three points presented by Pellegrino above have direct bearing on the profession of occupational therapy. Occupational therapists recognize the vulnerability of the people who seek their services and are aware of the trust that is required in the healing relationship. This is exhibited first in the *Core Values and Attitudes of Occupational Therapy Practice* (AOTA, 1993). Even though the recipient of treatment depends upon the occupational therapist, the core value of *equality* "requires that all individuals be perceived as having the same fundamental human rights and opportunities" (p. 1085). The core value of *dignity* "emphasizes the importance of valuing the inherent worth and uniqueness of each person. This value is demonstrated by an attitude of empathy and respect for self and others" (p. 1086). The need for respecting the vulnerability of patients and building trust is also expressed in the *Occupational Therapy Code of Ethics (2000)*. Principle 1 states "Occupational therapy personnel shall demonstrate a concern for the well-being of the recipients of their services" (AOTA, 2000). Principle 2 adds that "Occupational therapy personnel shall take all reasonable precautions to avoid imposing or inflicting harm upon the recipient of services or to his/her property." Item A under Principle 2 also explicitly states that "Occupational therapy personnel shall maintain relationships that do not exploit the recipient of services sexually, physically, emotionally, financially, socially, or in any other manner." Principle 3 further demonstrates the concern of occupational therapists for building trust between practitioners and the persons in

their care: "Occupational therapy personnel shall respect the recipient and/or their surrogate(s) as well as the recipient's rights." Under this principle, the importance of collaborating with, gaining informed consent from, and respecting the confidentiality of recipients is recognized.

As to the second point raised by Pellegrino, occupational therapists do indeed recognize the importance of their training and education. This is emphasized in Principle 4 of the *Occupational Therapy Code of Ethics (2000)*: "Occupational therapy personnel shall achieve and continually maintain high standards of competence" (AOTA, 2000). The impact of this principle goes beyond just receiving specialized training. Occupational therapists seek to maintain "competence by participating in professional development and educational activities." This fourth principle also directs occupational therapists to "protect service recipients" in the discharge of their knowledge and skill "by ensuring that duties assumed by or assigned to other occupational therapy personnel match credentials, qualifications, experience, and the scope of practice." Through these actions, occupational therapists can truly demonstrate that they do not acquire their knowledge for "personal gain, prestige, or power. Rather, the profession holds this knowledge in trust for the good of the sick" (Pellegrino, 1991, p. 114).

Finally, occupational therapists also make a public pledge to promote the well-being of others through the *Occupational Therapy Code of Ethics (2000)*. The Preamble to the Code states "The American Occupational Therapy Association and its members are committed to furthering the ability of individuals, groups, and systems to function within their total environment" (AOTA, 2000). Principle 1 of the Code further supports this pledge for the "well-being of the recipients" of occupational therapy. Finally, the dedication of occupational therapists to the well-being of those they treat is echoed in the core value of *altruism*: "the unselfish concern for the welfare of others. This concept is reflected in actions and attitudes of *commitment, caring, dedication, responsiveness,* and *understanding*" (AOTA, 1993, p. 1085, italics added).

This understanding of the duty of health care professionals to treat patients as drawn from the perspective of occupational therapy can provide some guidance for the initial concern of patient abandonment. There is, indeed, a strong claim here to treat all patients to the fullest of one's ability as an occupational therapist. The two limiting factors to this are when a more competent therapist is needed and when the patient's actions make further treatment imprudent. But aside from such cases, both the *Occupational Therapy Code of Ethics (2000)* and the *Core Values and Attitudes of Occupational Therapy Practice* challenge occupational therapists to act from a higher level of responsibility than the general norms of society. Thus, even though it may be standard practice to refuse to serve customers and clients at one's discretion in business, occupational therapists have a higher standard to follow. Prudential decisions will need to be made about initiating or ceasing treatment when such actions are valid and necessary. However, to avoid the genuine abandonment of patients, occupational therapists must act according to both the letter and the spirit of the *Occupational Therapy Code of Ethics (2000)* and the *Core Values and Attitudes of Occupational Therapy Practice.*

Penny Kyler (1995) sums up these points well when she writes,

> As ethical health care practitioners, we are guided by the fundamental belief in the worth of our clients. This belief is based on our social responsibility, as stated in the AOTA *Code of Ethics* and in the *Standards of Practice.* An ethical practitioner treats clients and delivers services not simply because of a contractual agreement, but because of a social responsibility to do so. (p. 176)

CONCLUSION: ABIDE, NOT ABANDON

As Ruth Purtilo (1993) notes, the actual *physical* abandonment of patients by health care professionals is no longer as prevalent as it had once been. However, she adds that "psychological abandonment often replaces what used to be experienced as the more obvious bodily abandonment of the patient" (p. 156). Psychological abandonment still involves treating a patient but in such a manner "that the patient becomes a total non-person to the health professional." One of the dangers here is that physical abandonment is rather obvious and can be empirically validated. Psychological abandonment is far more subtle and may even occur without the practitioner's conscious knowledge, for example, as a type of defense mechanism in a difficult case. Nonetheless, even this form of abandonment must be guarded against.

But how? Purtilo (1993) offers a simple but thought-provoking suggestion. She explains that the "opposite of abandonment is to stay with or abide with the patient." Learning to *abide* with those in need, those who are difficult, those whose actions appear immoral to us, those whom we fear because of their specific health problems will certainly not be easy. However, as Purtilo notes, health care professionals "can overcome their tendency to flee (physically or psychologically) only when the attitude of compassion is combined with an understanding of how much harm is induced by abandonment" (p. 157). Learning to abide with the recipients of occupational therapy may be one of the most important ways to safeguard against patient abandonment.

REFERENCES

American Medical Association. (1994). American Medical Association's principles of medical ethics. In G. R. Beabout & D. J. Wennemann (Eds.), *Applied professional ethics* (p. 101). New York: University Press of America.

American Occupational Therapy Association. (1993). Core values and attitudes of occupational therapy practice. *American Journal of Occupational Therapy*, 47, 1085–1086.

American Occupational Therapy Association. (2000). Occupational therapy code of ethics (2000). *American Journal of Occupational Therapy*, 54, 614–616. (*Note:* This document was updated. American Occupational Therapy Association. (2005). *American Journal of Occupational Therapy, 59*, 639–642.)

Arras, J. D. (1991). AIDS and the duty to treat. In T. A. Mappes & J. S. Zembaty (Eds.), *Biomedical ethics* (3rd ed., pp. 115–121). St. Louis, MO: McGraw-Hill.

Beabout, G. R., & Wennemann, D. J. (1994). *Applied professional ethics*. New York: University Press of America.

Joint Commission on Accreditation of Healthcare Organizations. (1998). *Comprehensive accreditation manual for hospitals*. Washington, DC: Author.

Jonsen, A. R. (1995). The duty to treat patients with AIDS and HIV infection. In J. D. Arras & B. Steinbock (Eds.), *Ethical issues in modern medicine* (4th ed., pp. 97–106). Mountain View, CA: Mayfield.

Jonsen, A. R., Siegler, M., & Winslade, W. J. (1998). *Clinical ethics* (4th ed.). St. Louis, MO: McGraw-Hill.

Kyler, P. (1995). Ethical commentary (Chapter 10, "Contracts and Referrals to Private Practice"). In D. M. Bailey & S. L. Schwartzberg (Eds.), *Ethical and legal dilemmas in occupational therapy* (pp. 174–176). Philadelphia: F. A. Davis.

Pellegrino, E. D. (1991). Altruism, self-interest, and medical ethics. In T. A. Mappes & J. S. Zembaty (Eds.), *Biomedical ethics* (3rd ed., pp. 113–114). St. Louis, MO: McGraw-Hill.

Purtilo, R. (1993). *Ethical dimensions in the health professions* (2nd ed.). Philadelphia: W. B. Saunders.

Southwick, A. F. (1988). *The law of hospital and health care administration* (2nd ed.). Ann Arbor, MI: Health Administration Press.

Author

John F. Morris, PhD
Member-at-Large, Standards and Ethics Commission (1998–2001, 2001–2004)

Last Updated June 2000, February, 2008

CHAPTER 11

Plagiarism

WHAT IS PLAGIARISM?

The *Oxford Desk Dictionary and Thesaurus* defines *plagiarize* as taking and using "the thoughts, writings, inventions, etc., of another" as one's own, or "passing off thoughts, etc., (of another) as one's own" (Abate, 1997). Among its word alternatives to plagiarism, the thesaurus lists *piracy, theft, stealing, appropriation,* and *thievery.*

These definitions remind readers that plagiarism's scope extends beyond the failure to reference a published quote. Plagiarism involves the taking of another's ideas, thoughts, and concepts from any source. The sources can include printed or formally published works, electronic media, presentations or workshops, video or audiotaped materials, and information obtained from the World Wide Web.

Plagiarism can occur in several contexts. Individuals can take someone else's complete work and represent an identical work as their own (University of Victoria, 2003). One can omit references to borrowed phrases or sentences incorporated into his or her work. Authors can paraphrase statements from other sources and fail to cite the source. And ?nally, writers can represent another's ideas or concepts as their own without including a reference to the creator or source.

Plagiarism can take several forms. One can actively or intentionally use the words, ideas, or concepts of another without citing the author as the source (Drummond, 1998). Unintentional plagiarism occurs as well. Sometimes after dedicating

long hours to research on a specific topic, one may find it difficult to discern his or her own ideas from the ideas of the many readings one has undertaken. Unintentional confusion of another's ideas with one's own still constitutes plagiarism. One also may engage in passive plagiarism when one cuts and pastes "the ideas and words of others from various sources" and arranges them into a new order to form a "new" work (Drummond, 1998). One should understand that a "pastiche of ideas and words of other people" fails to rise to the level of an original work (Drummond, 1998). One also may commit unintentional plagiarism when one "fails to *adequately* cite" another's ideas or concepts because of ignorance of how or when to use citations (Kalikoff, 1995).

HOW DOES THE OCCUPATIONAL THERAPY PROFESSION VIEW PLAGIARISM?

As a profession, occupational therapy embraces a set of basic beliefs as put forth in the *Core Values and Attitudes of Occupational Therapy Practice* (AOTA, 1993) and the *Occupational Therapy Code of Ethics* (AOTA, 2000). According to the *Core Values and Attitudes document,*

> Truth requires that we be faithful to facts and reality. Truthfulness or veracity is demonstrated by being accountable, honest, forthright, accurate, and authentic in our attitudes and actions. There is an obligation to be truthful with ourselves,

those who receive services, colleagues, and society. (AOTA, 1993)

AOTA's *Occupational Therapy Code of Ethics* expands on the concept of truth in Principles 6 and 7 (AOTA, 2000). Principle 6C states that "occupational therapy personnel shall refrain from using or participating in the use of any form of communication that contains false, fraudulent, deceptive, or unfair statements or claims" (AOTA, 2000). Principle 7 states that "occupational therapy personnel shall treat colleagues and other professionals with fairness, discretion, and integrity (*fidelity*)" (AOTA, 2000, italics added). Subsection B of Principle 7 elaborates further on truth: "Occupational therapy practitioners shall accurately represent the qualifications, views, contributions, and findings of colleagues" (AOTA, 2000). The Code also reminds us that we need to comply with laws and policies relevant to plagiarism such as federal copyright laws. Principle 5A explicitly states that "occupational therapy personnel shall familiarize themselves with and seek to understand and abide by applicable Association policies; local, state, and federal laws; and institutional rules" (AOTA, 2000). The *Guidelines to the Occupational Therapy Code of Ethics* further clarify the prohibition against plagiarism (AOTA, 1998). Section 2, which addresses communication, states that "communication is important in all aspects of occupational therapy. Individuals must be conscientious and truthful in all facets of written, verbal, and electronic communication." Subsection 2.8 further explains that "occupational therapy personnel must give credit and recognition when using the work of others."

EXAMPLES OF PLAGIARISM IN OCCUPATIONAL THERAPY

- A local charity asks an occupational therapy practitioner to write an article for a local charity newsletter explaining how occupational therapy can help the charity's constituents.

The occupational therapy practitioner reads all of the major occupational therapy literature on the subject and surfs the Internet. She paraphrases the materials as she goes, collecting several pages of notes. At the end of her search, she puts her notes together in a coherent manner and submits her article. If the occupational therapy practitioner omits references to the ideas she paraphrased from the work of others, she commits plagiarism. (*intentional plagiarism*)

- Before writing a paper, a graduate student reads another student's paper. Two days later, she sits down and writes her own paper. Upon review of the paper, many ideas sound strikingly similar to the other student's paper. Although the student never intended to copy her fellow student's ideas, her conduct falls under the umbrella of plagiarism. (*confusion of one's own ideas with another's ideas*)

- An occupational therapy practitioner accepts a position to open a new, community-based occupational therapy program. As she develops her evaluation forms and policies and procedures, she reviews a collection of material she gathered from previous employers and others. She cuts and pastes pieces from the various sources to form her "new" forms and policies and procedures. She includes no references in her documents. Because the practitioner took materials written by others and failed to give them credit, this constitutes plagiarism. (*cutting and pasting ideas of others*)

- An occupational therapy practitioner attends a workshop. Upon her return, her employer requests that she present the material to the other occupational therapy practitioners. The occupational therapy practitioner copies and distributes to her colleagues the handout given out at the workshop. She reproduces the slide handout onto overheads and presents the material to the staff. Although everyone knows this material comes from a workshop presented by a world-renowned occupational therapy practitioner, none of the materials or slides contain a reference. If the occupational therapy practitioner uses the materials without referencing their source, she plagiarizes the materials. This also may violate copyright laws. (*unintentional plagiarism due to ignorance*)

HOW CAN OCCUPATIONAL THERAPY PRACTITIONERS AND STUDENTS AVOID PLAGIARISM?

Occupational therapists, occupational therapy assistants, and occupational therapy students may take several steps to avoid committing plagiarism. One must always put direct quotes in quotation marks and include the appropriately cited source (Writing Resource Center, 2003). If authors borrow significant words from the work of another, they must quote those words and give credit to the author who coined them. When paraphrasing statements or borrowing concepts or ideas from another's work, one must include a reference to the source following the adopted information. One should consider introducing the quote or paraphrased language by including the author's name in an introductory statement, such as "According to Mary Reilly..." (Writing Resource Center, 2003).

As members of AOTA, we respect a standard of professionalism. Professionalism requires occupational therapists, occupational therapy assistants, and students of occupational therapy at all levels to treat the works of others as an extension of respect for the author. When in doubt, one should cite the source of words, thoughts, and ideas that may have originated from others. Writers must never represent someone else's words, thoughts, or ideas as their own. Plagiarism is not acceptable in any form.

REFERENCES

Abate, F. R. (1997). *Oxford desk dictionary and thesaurus*. New York: Berkley Books.

American Occupational Therapy Association. (1993). Core values and attitudes of occupational therapy practice. *American Journal of Occupational Therapy, 47*, 1085–1086.

American Occupational Therapy Association. (1998). Guidelines to the occupational therapy code of ethics. *American Journal of Occupational Therapy, 52*, 881–884. (*Note:* This document was updated in 2006. American Occupational Therapy Association. (2006). *American Journal of Occupational Therapy, 60*, 652–658.)

American Occupational Therapy Association. (2000). Occupational therapy code of ethics. *American Journal of Occupational Therapy, 54*, 614–616. (*Note:* This document was updated in 2005. American Occupational Therapy Association. (2005). *American Journal of Occupational Therapy, 59*, 639–642.)

Drummond, L. (1998, August 25). *Research and argumentation course: Plagiarism*. Austin, TX: St. Edward's University. Retrieved June 10, 2004, from http://www.stedwards.edu/hum/drummond/23pol.html

Kalikoff, B. (1995). *Plagiarism*. Tacoma: University of Washington, Tacoma Writing Center. Retrieved June 10, 2004, from http://www. tacoma. washington.edu/ctlt/learning/resources/plagiarism.pdf

University of Victoria. (2003). *Plagiarism and cheating*. Victoria, BC: Author. Retrieved June 10, 2004, from http://web.uvic.ca/calendar2003/GI/AcRe/PaCh.html

Writing Resource Center. (2003). *Avoiding plagiarism*. Bemidji, MN: Bemidji State University. Retrieved June 10, 2004, from http://cal.bemidji. msus.edu/WRC/Handouts/avoidPlag.html

Author

Barbara L. Kornblau, JD, OT/L, FAOTA, AAPM, ABDA, CCM, CDMS
Commission on Standards and Ethics, Chairperson (1998–2001)

Last Updated January 26, 2005, February, 2008

State Licensure, Professionalism, and the AOTA Occupational Therapy Code of Ethics

WHEN DOES YOUR STATE LICENSE EXPIRE?

If you are unable to answer this question, please read on to heighten your awareness regarding the importance of state licensure renewal. Although not all states and territories of the United States require licensure per se, they all require some form of regulation for those wishing to provide occupational therapy services. Depending on your location, except in a state with trademark law, all occupational therapists in the United States, District of Columbia, and Puerto Rico are required to be licensed, state certified, registered, or to hold a temporary license/permit in order to provide services to clients. The same is true for occupational therapy assistants, except in states with trademark law or those that do not regulate occupational therapy assistants. As such, all occupational therapy practitioners are required to adhere to state occupational therapy statutes and regulations. States' statutes and regulations governing occupational therapy practice vary in how titles and initials are used.

Occupational therapists and occupational therapy assistants need to be aware of the specific provisions in their states so that they and their practice are in compliance with the law. It is unlawful for an unlicensed occupational therapist or occupational therapy assistant to represent oneself as an occupational therapy practitioner unless he or she is licensed by the state. State licensees who practice occupational therapy without renewing their license may be subject to criminal prosecution depending on the regulations of the state, district, or province.

AOTA's *Occupational Therapy Code of Ethics (2000)* (Code; AOTA, 2000) identifies standards that support regulatory bodies and licensing of occupational therapy practitioners. Licensure laws and the AOTA Code are requisite to protect recipients of services, the practitioner, and the profession. According to the AOTA Code as published in AOTA's *Reference Guide to the Occupational Therapy Code of Ethics,* "any action in violation of the spirit and purpose of this Code shall be considered unethical" (AOTA, 2003, p. 10). In other words, when practicing without a license, regardless of the reason, the offender is not only violating his or her licensing regulatory board laws but is also breaching the AOTA Code. Unfortunately, it is not uncommon for many occupational therapy practitioners to have such hectic personal and professional lives that they may neglect to take the time to check when their state license requires renewal.

In today's busy world, a variety of life situations can arise that may interfere with obtaining or renewing your license to practice occupational therapy. Relocating without leaving a forwarding address for your licensure board or moving to a new state may disrupt your typical pattern for licensure renewal. Having a baby, having a serious personal illness, or coping with the illness of a family member or some other major life event may be distracting and leave practitioners forgetful about licensure renewal. New practitioners may lack knowledge about how to obtain a license. Practitioners who change employment or work in a variety of states may not be aware of each state's licensure requirements. Traveling and international practitioners face the challenge of keeping up with state licensing processes, which are contingent on their relocation, which can change several times within a year.

These examples may sound familiar to you, and there can be understandable reasons for failing to apply or renew one's license. However, regardless of the situation, each practitioner is ultimately responsible for ensuring that her or his license is current before practicing as an occupational therapist or occupational therapy assistant. AOTA's State Affairs Group maintains detailed information about state occupational therapy laws on the Association's Web site (www.aota.org), including a directory of state occupational therapy regulatory authorities.

Practitioners should contact individual state boards or agencies for specific questions about state regulatory requirements. Licensure is not only a legal measure to protect consumers, it also serves as a safeguard for the profession, the practitioner, and the community at large, thus preventing nonqualified individuals from practicing occupational therapy. As a protective measure for recipients of service, licensure requirement is a process that affords patients safety in that it prevents individuals who are not trained occupational therapists from assuming such a role and providing spurious intervention under false pretense. An employer, a client, the client's family members, an occupational therapy practitioner, a colleague of another discipline, licensing organizations, or a related professional organization may report practitioners who provide occupational therapy services without a license. Practitioners reported to be providing occupational therapy

services without a license may undergo a review and or penalty from several professional oversight organizations such as the licensing state, district, or province; the AOTA; and the National Board for Certification in Occupational Therapy (NBCOT). Unlicensed practitioners who are members of AOTA may be reported to the Association's Commission on Standards and Ethics (SEC [now Ethics Commission or EC]) through a formal complaint process by one of the aforementioned groups or individuals.

Depending on the nature of the violation as ascertained from thorough and objective information from relevant sources (e.g., the state regulatory board, NBCOT, the complainant, and/or the respondent), the EC determines the principles of the Code that have been violated. State and national regulatory boards and professional organizations such as NBCOT *(Certificant Code of Conduct)* may adopt AOTA's Code or similar ethical language. Following are examples of principles of the Code that reflect the violation of practicing without a license or with an expired or lapsed license:

- **Principle 4.** "Occupational therapy personnel shall achieve and continually maintain high standards of competence. *(duties)*
  A. Occupational therapy practitioners shall hold the appropriate national and state credentials for the services they provide" (AOTA, 2000, p. 615).
  All occupational therapy practitioners are ethically bound to adhere to and follow the credential requirements of their state, territory, or district, in particular, maintaining the required credentials in a timely manner as required.

- **Principle 5.** "Occupational therapy personnel shall comply with laws and Association policies guiding the profession of occupational therapy. *(justice)*
  A. Occupational therapy personnel shall familiarize themselves with and seek to understand and abide by applicable Association policies; local, state, and federal

laws, and institutional rules" (AOTA, 2000, p. 615).

In the case of licensure, and its legal ramifications, the understanding here is that occupational therapy practitioners are ethically responsible for securing, reading, and understanding licensure rules and requirements for their state, territory, or district.

B. "Occupational therapy practitioners shall remain abreast of revisions in those laws and Association policies that apply to the profession of occupational therapy and shall inform employers, employees, and colleagues of those changes" (AOTA, 2000, p. 615).

Occupational therapy practitioners are responsible for maintaining up-to-date knowledge about changes and additions to their state licensure requirements.

C. "Occupational therapy practitioners shall require those they supervise in occupational therapy–related activities to adhere to the *Occupational Therapy Code of Ethics (2000)*" (AOTA, 2000, p. 615).

Occupational therapy practitioners who function in a leadership capacity are responsible for ensuring that occupational therapy professionals under their supervision have met all state requirements for licensure in the timely manner required by law.

D. "Occupational therapy practitioners shall take reasonable steps to ensure employers are aware of occupational therapy's ethical obligations, as set forth in this *Occupational Therapy Code of Ethics (2000)* and of the implications of those obligations for occupational therapy practice, education, and research" (AOTA, 2000, p. 615).

All occupational therapy practitioners are responsible for communicating to their employer, supervisor, director, etc., up-to-date information regarding their licensure status.

- **Principle 6.** "Occupational therapy personnel shall provide accurate information about occupational therapy services. *(veracity)*

A. Occupational therapy personnel shall accurately represent their credentials, qualifications, education, experience, training, and competence. This is of particular importance for those to whom occupational therapy personnel provide their services or with whom occupational therapy practitioners have a professional relationship" (AOTA, 2000, p. 615).

Any individual declaring themselves an occupational therapy practitioner and providing services to clients in that regard are required by the laws of their state, territory, or district and AOTA to be credentialed according to the board regulations in their geographical area. This assures recipients of occupational therapy services that they are receiving care from individuals who are qualified to do so.

There are three core values inherent in the *Core Values and Attitudes of Occupational Therapy Practice* (AOTA, 1993) that are part of the ethics standards that reflect the commitment and responsibility of occupational therapy practitioners to maintain up-to-date practice credentials.

- **Justice**—The concept of justice is most relevant, as it requires the practitioner to adhere to laws and standards that are established by governing bodies. "The occupational therapy practitioner must understand and abide by the local, state, and federal laws governing professional practice" (AOTA, 1993, p. 1086).
  It is the responsibility of the occupational therapist and occupational therapy assistant to ensure that they are informed about regulatory requirements in their state, territory, or district to provide services they identify as occupational therapy.

- "**Truth** requires that we be faithful to facts and reality. Truthfulness or veracity is demonstrated by being accountable, honest, forthright, accurate, and authentic in our attitudes and actions" (AOTA, 1993, p. 1086).

Occupational therapists and occupational therapy assistants should be accountable by acquiring their initial license and renewal thereafter as required by their regulatory board. Occupational therapists and occupational therapy assistants are responsible for providing information to employers regarding their licensure status.

- "**Prudence** is the ability to govern and discipline oneself through the use of reason. To be prudent is to value judiciousness, discretion, vigilance, moderation, care, and circumspection in the management of one's affairs… and respond on the basis of intelligent reflection and rational thought" (AOTA, 1993, p. 1086). *Although regulatory boards may provide renewal information to practitioners, it is the sole responsibility of the professional to be self-disciplined in securing and maintaining the credentials required by their state, territory, or district.*

When a credentialing violation has occurred, the SEC applies the *Enforcement Procedures for the Occupational Therapy Code of Ethics,* (AOTA, 2004) as a disciplinary and protective measure based on the range of circumstances. AOTA fully supports the legal and practice intent of credentialing out of concern for consumer and practitioner protection and, as such, will enforce the AOTA's ethics in an effort to maintain the integrity of the profession. Examples of disciplinary actions that may be applied to cases involving the practice of occupational therapy without the appropriate credentials are

- **Reprimand**—"a formal expression of disapproval of conduct communicated privately by a letter from the Chairperson of the SEC that is nondisclosable and non-communicative to other bodies (e.g., state regulatory boards, National Board for Certification in Occupational Therapy…)" (AOTA, 2004, p. 655).
- **Censure**—"a formal expression of disapproval that is public" (AOTA, 2004, p. 656).

- "**Probation of membership subject to terms**—failure to meet terms will subject a member to any of the disciplinary actions or sanctions" (AOTA, 2004, p. 656).
- **Suspension**—"removal of membership for a specified period of time" (AOTA, 2004, p. 656).
- **Revocation**—the most critical of the enforcement procedures, which is "permanent denial of membership" in AOTA (AOTA, 2004, p. 656).

CASE SCENARIO

You are an occupational therapy practitioner with 15 years of experience. You have been married for slightly over 2 years and have a 4-month-old baby. Your husband received a job transfer, and you have recently moved to a new state. Two months after relocating to your new state, you join the state occupational therapy association. Through the state association, you learn of a job opening; you apply and are hired. Although the state requires licensure, they provide you with a grace period of 3 months to get the process completed. You have worked in three other states, so you need to supply past licensure information from those states, as well as information about having successfully completed the National Certification Exam for occupational therapy practitioners. You develop a case of influenza and are very ill for at least 2 weeks. During this time, you are worried about your family and your new employment. Eventually you recover and return to work with a great deal to catch up on, both at work and home. Along the way, you forget about the licensure requirements. It is now 15 months later and you receive a notice from the state board stating that you are facing disciplinary action as a result of practicing without a license. Your initial response is that you actually completed the licensure process. You search for the information but are unable to locate any paperwork to verify that you actually completed the licensure process.

DISCUSSION

Even though your circumstances were challenging, the overriding issue is that you violated the law and practiced without a license for a significant period of time. Because of the collaborative professional relationship between organizations, state licensing boards routinely communicate information regarding lapsed licenses to the AOTA EC. Referencing the aforementioned principles from the *Reference Guide to the Occupational Therapy Code of Ethics* (2003), the likelihood of disciplinary action from a variety of sources is probable. Regardless of your personal circumstances, the final determination will be influenced by the sum of information collected from all parties involved, including your supervisors from your place of employment.

CONCLUSION

In many states, achieving regulatory status required extensive lobbying and legislative efforts. The collaborative effort between AOTA and state associations has been instrumental in assisting states to achieve this professional status. This widespread, successful effort legally ensures the quality of occupational therapy service for consumers and prevents illegal behavior on the part of individuals without professional training and certification in occupational therapy who call themselves occupational therapists, thus aiding in the preservation of the integrity of the profession. Occupational therapy practitioners are legally bound by state requirements and are ethically responsible for compliance with them. An increased awareness and knowledge regarding the importance of state license renewal will protect us from unnecessary legal problems, work interruption, and professional and personal embarrassment.

REFERENCES

American Occupational Therapy Association. (1993). Core values and attitudes of occupational therapy practice. *American Journal of Occupational Therapy, 47,* 1085–1086.

American Occupational Therapy Association. (2000). Occupational therapy code of ethics (2000). *American Journal Occupational Therapy, 54,* 614–616. (*Note:* This document was updated in 2005. American Occupational Therapy Association. (2005). *American Journal of Occupational Therapy, 59,* 639–642.)

American Occupational Therapy Association. (2003). *Reference guide to the occupational therapy code of ethics.* Bethesda, MD: AOTA Press.

American Occupational Therapy Association. (2004). Enforcement procedures for occupational therapy code of ethics. *American Journal of Occupational Therapy, 58,* 1085–1086. (*Note:* This document was updated in 2007. American Occupational Therapy Association. (2007). *American Journal of Occupational Therapy, 61,* 679–685.)

Arnold, M. J., Hill, D., & Shephard, J. (2001). Everyday ethics: State licensure, the law and ethics. *OT Practice, 6*(11).

Slater, D. Y. (Ed.) (2006). *Reference guide to the occupational therapy code of ethics.* Bethesda, MD: AOTA Press.

Authors

Melba J. Arnold, MS, OTR/L
Member, Standards and Ethics Commission, 1999–2005; Assistant Professor, St. Louis University, St. Louis, MO

Diane Hill, COTA/L, AP, ROH
Member, Standards and Ethics Commission, 1999–2005; Senior Practitioner, Longwood at Oakmont, Verona, PA

Reviewed/updated February 2008

Ethical Considerations When Occupational Therapists Engage in Business Transactions With Clients

INTRODUCTION

Selling products to recipients of occupational therapy services requires an awareness of the various regulatory and ethical issues that guide how occupational therapists and occupational therapy assistants may engage in this business. Selling equipment and supplies to clients has become a common business activity for many occupational therapy practitioners (i.e., occupational therapists and occupational therapy assistants).

However, careful consideration must be made to uphold an objective, professional, and therapeutic relationship with clients who require both goods and services. This relationship may become confusing and unclear when practitioners hold outside interests beyond the therapeutic interaction. Having a financial interest in a business venture such as product sales related to occupational therapy while providing occupational therapy services to the client may be perceived as a *conflict of interest,* which exists when there is a "conflict between the private interests and the official or professional responsibilities of a person in a position of trust" (*Merriam-Webster's Dictionary of Law,* 1996). When conflict of interest occurs in business matters such as these, a practitioner's professional integrity may be questioned if care has not been given as to how the equipment, supplies, or other items were sold to clients. Moreover, if financial benefits exceed acceptable reimbursement rates, this could be indicative of impaired or altered professional judgment by the practitioner.

THE ISSUES

A variety of products may be sold by occupational therapists directly to their clients, such as adaptive, durable medical, and exercise equipment, as well as books. Less common and sometimes questionable items, such as pain-relieving magnets and aromatherapy supplies, also may be sold to clients. Serious ethical questions can arise when selling products to clients while providing professional services. Thoughtful reflection on the responses to the following types of questions can be helpful in determining the appropriateness of this behavior.

- What types of products are being sold?
- If the item is related to a client's therapeutic goals, should the product be sold to the client by the therapist providing the services?
- Should the therapist hold ownership in the company from which the product is being sold?

The answers to these questions help clarify if financial interest in completing this transaction is influencing the therapeutic recommendation. These questions are not easily answered and are further complicated by the increased emphasis toward less-traditional occupational therapy practice settings. This emphasis has led to greater opportunities for occupational therapy practitioners to sell both goods and services to recipients of their services.

In situations in which an occupational therapy practitioner also assumes the role of product vendor, clients will need to be assured that the practitioner has adhered to compliance regulations. For example, as a vendor, a practitioner may be required to provide the client with documentation of written warranty information; policies for complaints, questions, returns, and repairs; nondiscrimination policies, a consumer bill of rights, and the Health Insurance Portability and Accountability Act of 1996 (HIPAA, P.L. 104–191) compliance regulations. Practitioners need to be aware of all of the Federal Trade Commission and or state consumer protection agencies' rules and regulations for product safety and liability.

Another potential area for concern is the potential for harm. What happens if a client is injured from the product a practitioner sold to him or her? Practitioners could be subjecting themselves to sanctions or exposure to professional liability issues from federal regulatory agencies such as the Center for Medicare and Medicaid Services (CMS; see http://www.cms.hhs.gov/default.asp). The product may require specific standards of infection control such as those regulated by agencies such as the Joint Commission for the Accreditation of Hospitals Organization (JCAHO, 2004–2005). Practitioners also may be required to meet prevailing industry standards as a product vendor, which may require additional state licensure. For example, durable medical equipment vendors must meet CMS standards if they want to bill CMS for the equipment. Items must be medically necessary and prescribed by a physician. The vendor must demonstrate adherence to a variety of rules and regulations ranging from product safety, storage of equipment, patient's bill of rights (i.e., right to refuse equipment), complaint process, and return policy.

The *Standards of Practice for Occupational Therapy* (AOTA, 2005b) supports practicing according to association and institutional policies and other relevant documents. When selling products, practitioners may be in a position to use their referral base as a source for potential customers. In such cases, it would be critical to use this source objectively, considering the existing trust that clients have for practitioners. Occupational therapy practitioners have an ethical obligation to inform clients (i.e., disclose) of outside business relationships that may give the appearance of conflict of interest and to assure service recipients that therapeutic decisions are devoid of coercion. Whether financial interest in the business transaction is for direct or indirect monetary gain, practitioners' disclosures must be completely transparent.

The AOTA *Occupational Therapy Code of Ethics (2005)* (AOTA, 2005a; e.g., Principles 2A and B, 6B and C) requires that practitioners disclose financial conflicts of interests that may involve clients. Because of the broad spectrum of this topic, several principles from the AOTA Code (AOTA, 2005a) as well as values from the *Core Values and Attitudes of Occupational Therapy* statement (AOTA, 1993) are applicable to the issue of selling goods and services to clients (see Table 13.1).

Primary among the core values are *justice* and *altruism.* "Justice places value on the upholding of such moral and legal principles as fairness, equity, truthfulness, and objectivity. This means . . . we maintain a goal directed and objective relationship with all those served" (AOTA, 1993, p. 1086). It is important for practitioners to reflect on their therapeutic practice and business interests to ensure that the two are clearly separate and that clients have full disclosure and information on both.

Occupational therapy practitioners have a "duty" and an obligation to provide occupational therapy services in an altruistic manner to clients. Altruism is one of seven core concepts that guide the values, actions, and attitudes of occupational therapy practitioners (AOTA, 1993). Occupational therapy interventions should be goal directed, avoiding any perceived potential to exploit recipients of service for financial gain. Participating in activities outside of this focus may damage the therapeutic relationship according to Principle 2A of the Code (AOTA, 2005a). According to

JCAHO (2004–2005), *exploitation* is defined as "taking an unjust advantage of another individual for one's own advantage or benefit" (p. GL7). Health care providers have an obligation to protect clients from real or perceived abuse, neglect, or exploitation from anyone. Individuals who operate a private occupational therapy practice and sell therapeutic supplies and equipment to clients must ensure that the items are necessary for the client's return to function; that the amount charged for products is fair and reasonable according to industry standards and practices; and that disclosures meet all of the legal, federal, and professional requirements.

CASE SCENARIO AND DISCUSSION

An occupational therapist who works in a private practice setting also is part owner of a durable medical equipment company. She recommends to a client the need to purchase certain items to enhance functional performance in home safety and provides the client with the name of her company as a resource for this equipment. She does not tell the client of her financial holdings in this company, nor does she provide a list of other vendors who also can supply the same equipment.

The client follows the occupational therapist's instructions and purchases the equipment. Later, when the client receives the invoice for the equipment, he notices that the therapist is listed as an owner of the company. The client calls and expresses anger in the occupational therapist failing to inform him of her financial holdings in the company.

Disclosure of the occupational therapist's role in this company may have prevented the client from feeling exploited. It is possible that

TABLE 13.1. Principles From the *Occupational Therapy Code of Ethics (2005)* Applicable to Selling Goods and Services to Clients

2. Occupational therapy personnel shall take measures to ensure a recipient's safety and avoid imposing or inflicting harm. *(Nonmaleficence)*	Occupational Therapy Personnel Shall:
	2A. Maintain therapeutic relationships that shall not exploit the recipient of services sexually, physically, emotionally, psychologically, financially, socially, or in any other manner.
	2B. Avoid relationships or activities that conflict or interfere with therapeutic professional judgment and objectivity.
3. Occupational therapy personnel shall respect recipients to assure their rights. *(Autonomy, Confidentiality)*	
6. Occupational therapy personnel shall provide accurate information when representing the profession. *(Veracity)*	Occupational Therapy Personnel Shall:
	6B. Disclose any professional, personal, financial, business, or volunteer affiliations that may pose a conflict of interest to those with whom they may establish a professional, contractual, or other working relationship.
	6C. Refrain from using or participating in the use of any form of communication that contains false, fraudulent, deceptive, or unfair statements or claims.

the situation could have been avoided by offering a list of other potential vendors from which the client could make the purchase. Doing so could avoid the perception of impropriety and enable the client to make an informed decision, which is supported by Principles 2B and 3 of the Code (AOTA, 2005a).

According to Principle 6B, occupational therapy personnel shall "disclose any professional, personal, financial, business, or volunteer affiliations that may pose a conflict of interest to those with whom they may establish a professional, contractual, or other working relationship" (AOTA, 2005a, p. 5). "Disclosure would at least be unlikely to have as corrosive an effect on that trust as would clients learning of the same undisclosed and apparently hidden conflict" (Brock, 1990, p. 35). What would happen if this client were referred to the therapist in the future? Would the objective therapeutic relationship be compromised? Would the client respect the therapist's role as his health care provider *(fidelity)*? The trust so critical to a therapeutic relationship may be breached and ultimately reflect negatively on the profession of occupational therapy and those that provide services (Principle 6D).

GUIDELINES TO THE OCCUPATIONAL THERAPY CODE OF ETHICS

The *Guidelines to the Occupational Therapy Code of Ethics* (AOTA, 2006) are overarching statements of morally correct action intended to help practitioners attain a high level of professional behavior. The guidelines can be applied to complex situations in which further clarification of perplexing problems would be helpful. Guideline 6, Conflict of Interest, states that "avoidance of real or perceived conflict of interest is imperative to maintaining the integrity of interactions" (AOTA, 2006). Guideline 6.2 states that "occupational therapy personnel shall not take advantage of or exploit anyone to further their own personal interests" (AOTA, 2006). Truthfulness *(verac-*

ity) is demonstrated by being accountable, honest, forthright, accurate, and authentic in our attitudes and actions.

Engaging in business ventures in a competitive health care environment obligates occupational therapy practitioners to become educated in all of the rules and regulations that govern these endeavors. Practitioners must become educated on the ethics of prudent practice as well as appropriate business behaviors such as disclosure when dual roles of practitioner and entrepreneur are assumed. For example, maintaining objectivity can become clouded if a practitioner prescribes a wheelchair for a client and also sells this equipment to the client. Are the practitioner's intentions to provide the proper basic wheelchair, or is he motivated by profit to provide the most expensive wheelchair covered by the client's insurance?

Medicare regulations stipulate that practitioners should not engage in "self-dealing." According to Goldman (2004, italics added), "*self-dealing* occurs when a decision maker is motivated in part for personal gain and not entirely on what is good for the company" (client). Financial rewards can be quite tempting but may be a breach of the honesty and trust that are a professional responsibility toward those whom occupational therapy practitioners serve.

Further, "[occupational therapists] . . . have a fiduciary responsibility to safeguard the well-being of beneficiaries, and health professionals may not engage in self-dealing" (Baker, Caplan, Emanuel, & Latham, 1999, p. 182). When potential conflicts arise, fiduciaries are required to make a full disclosure of the conflict. According to Edge and Groves (1999),

> A *fiduciary relationship* is a special relationship of loyalty and responsibility that is formed between the client and practitioner. The client has the right to believe that the practitioner will maintain a higher level of accountability in regard to health care than that expected from most other relationships. (p. 296, italics added)

A critical point made by Sulmasy (1993) about physicians and the selling of goods and services, is that

> The client is an exceptionally vulnerable person in the hands of the physician. The client entrusts his body, his dignity, and his secrets to you. The physical effects of being ill compound this vulnerability, affecting to varying degrees the client's decision-making, communicative, and motor capacities in ways that always limit, even minimally, the autonomous agency of the individual who is sick. (p. 32)

According to Principle 2 of the Code, "OT personnel shall take reasonable precautions to avoid imposing or inflicting harm upon the recipient of services or to his or her property" (*nonmaleficence;* AOTA, 2005a, p. 640). So conceivably, Sulmasy's point of view is appropriate to occupational therapy practitioners as well.

CONCLUSION

This advisory opinion is not intended to exclude occupational therapists from entrepreneurial ventures; instead, it is intended to educate them on the numerous issues related to product sales and potential ramifications if conducted in a manner contrary to industry standards. Business, professional, and legal issues should be considered when conducting business for profit with clients.

Occupational therapy practitioners' behavior is representative of the therapeutic relationships they seek to achieve as well as a demonstration and reflection of the profession of occupational therapy. Practitioners have an obligation to cause no harm, real or perceived, toward clients and to retain public trust. Participation in behaviors that may cast a shadow or negatively reflect the professional standards that practitioners seek to uphold should be avoided. "Professionalism extols attributes such as being knowledgeable and skillful; altruistic; respectful; honest; compassionate;

committed to excellence and on-going professional development; and showing a responsiveness to the needs of clients and society that supersedes self-interest" (Jecker, 2004, pp. 47–48). It is, therefore, always important for occupational therapy practitioners to ask "to what end do these interactions contribute to the therapeutic goals?"

"Our professional training provides us with the skills and obligation to maintain objectivity and transparency in all interactions. We must adhere to our professional boundaries and remain committed to maintain appropriate limits . . . with clients or their families" (Purtilo & Haddad, 2002, p. 213).

REFERENCES

American Occupational Therapy Association. (1993). Core values statement and attitudes of occupational therapy practice. *American Journal of Occupational Therapy, 47,* 1085–1086.

American Occupational Therapy Association. (2005a). Occupational therapy code of ethics (2005). *American Journal of Occupational Therapy, 59,* 639–642.

American Occupational Therapy Association. (2005b). Standards of practice for occupational therapy. *American Journal of Occupational Therapy, 59,* 663–665.

American Occupational Therapy Association. (2006). Guidelines to the occupational therapy code of ethics. *American Journal of Occupational Therapy, 60, 652–658.*

Baker, R., Caplan, A., Emanuel, L., & Latham, S. (1999). *The American medical ethics revolution.* Baltimore, MD: Johns Hopkins University Press.

Brock, D. (1990). Medicine and business: An unhealthy mix? *Business and Professional Ethics Journal, 9,* 21–37.

Edge, R., & Groves, J. R. (1999). *Ethics of health care: A guide for clinical practice* (2nd ed.). New York: Delmar.

Goldman, S. (2004). Three pillars of ethics lead to strong sound business. *Silicon Valley/San Jose Business Journal.* Available online at http://www.

bizjournals.com/sanjose/stories/2004/04/26/editorial3.html?page=1

Health Insurance Portability and Accountability Act of 1996, P.L. 104–191, retrieved October 20, 2005, from http://www.cms.hhs.gov/hipaa/

Jecker, N. (2004). The theory and practice of professionalism. *American Journal of Bioethics, 4*(2), 47–48.

Joint Commission on Accreditation of Health Care Organizations. (2004–2005).Glossary: Exploitation. In *Comprehensive accreditation manual for home care* (p. GL7). Washington, DC: Author.

Merriam-Webster's Dictionary of Law. (1996). Conflict of interest. Retrieved August 24, 2005, from http://dictionary.reference.com/search?q=conflict%20of%20interest

Purtilo, R., & Haddad, A. (2002). *Health professional and client interaction.* Philadelphia: W. B. Saunders.

Sulmasy, D. (1993). What's so special about medicine? *Theoretical Medicine, 14,* 377–380.

Author

Darryl Austin, MS, OT/L
Practice Representative to the Ethics Commission, 2001–2008

CHAPTER 14

Cultural Competency and Ethical Practice

VIGNETTE 1

Joan, a pediatric therapist, is asked to make a home visit to a Vietnamese child who was recently burned. On examination of the child, she notes red, round, coin-sized marks over the child's back. The mother is never asked about the marks. After leaving the home Joan wonders if the mother is using a traditional healing treatment. "How can I give this child ethical and quality care while allowing the mother to continue with this harmful practice?"

INTRODUCTION

People face problems, dilemmas, and issues with ethical significance that necessitate action or nonaction every day. Doing the right thing in practice is always a challenge. In an increasingly pluralistic society, health care providers are finding themselves confronting choices that may depend more on moral and ethical values than on medical knowledge. Joan's dilemma is not a question of what intervention method should be used but whether quality ethical care can be provided. Culturally competent practitioners realize that behaviors are shaped and defined differently by every culture. Rather than being distressed by another culture's health practice, a culturally competent practitioner welcomes collaboration and cooperation in making sound ethical decisions.

This advisory opinion will outline and discuss those provisions within the most recent version of *Occupational Therapy Code of Ethics*

(2005) (AOTA, 2005) that address culturally competent services. Vignettes are presented to demonstrate the range of ethical concerns that cultural encounters can generate. This advisory paper was developed to provide guidance to the AOTA membership so that they can provide ethically and culturally appropriate services to all populations while recognizing their own cultural or linguistic background or life experience and that of their clients, colleagues, or students.

CULTURAL COMPETENCE

Cultural competency is a journey rather than an end. It refers to the process of actively developing and practicing appropriate, relevant, and sensitive strategies and skills in interacting with culturally different persons (AOTA, 1995). It is a set of congruent behaviors, attitudes, and policies that come together in a system, agency, or among professionals and enables that system, agency, or those professionals to work effectively in cross-cultural situations (Cross, Bazron, Dennis, & Isaacs, 1989). *Cultural competence* entails

understanding the importance of social and cultural influences on patients' health beliefs and behaviors; considering how these factors interact at multiple levels of the health care delivery system; and finally, devising interventions that take these issues into account to assure quality health care delivery to diverse patient populations.

(Betacourt, Green, Carrillo, & Ananeh-Firempong, 2003, p. 297)

Clinically, cultural competence means having the self-awareness, knowledge, skills, and framework to make sound, ethical, and culturally appropriate decisions. It is the integration and transformation of knowledge about individuals and groups of people into specific standards, policies, practices, and attitudes used in appropriate cultural settings to increase the quality of services, thereby producing better outcomes (Davis & Donald, 1997). In Vignette 2 below, the therapist does not take into account the socioeconomic level, living environment, or culture of Mrs. Jones before training her to use a variety of adaptive equipment. A culturally competent practitioner is not afraid to ask the client culturally pertinent questions upfront.

Competence in practice means learning new patterns of behaviors and effectively applying them in appropriate settings. Examples (Wells & Black, 2000) include the following:

1. Involve the extended family in the intervention process.
2. Address elderly persons more formally (by their last name and title) than younger clients.
3. Acknowledge and work with traditional or faith healers.
4. Be cautious about touching.
5. Make small talk at the beginning of a session, which will be considered good manners and will keep you from appearing too rushed.
6. Conduct the session in the preferred language of the client or arrange for a professional interpreter.
7. Add culturally related questions during the evaluation process.

Cultural competence is key to effective therapeutic interactions and outcomes. It implies a heightened consciousness of how clients experience their uniqueness and deal with their differences and similarities within a larger social context. It enhances the occupational therapy provider's knowledge of the relationship between sociocultural factors and health beliefs and behaviors. It equips providers with the tools and skills to manage these factors appropriately, with quality occupational therapy delivery as the gold standard. Cultural competence is an evolving and developing process that depends on self-exploration, knowledge, and skills.

VIGNETTE 2

Mrs. Jones is in her mid-60s and of Hispanic ethnicity. She is dependent for her existence on food stamps and Supplemental Security Income benefits. Somewhat hard of hearing, she has a slight tremor in her voice and arthritis in her hands. The three-bedroom house in which she lives is in poor condition. The house is unkempt. For meals she relies on her neighbors and junk food.

Mrs. Jones is admitted to the rehabilitation unit after experiencing a mild stroke that leaves her impaired on the right side. Her treatment sessions consist of transfer training, learning one-handed cooking, and dressing with adaptive equipment. A variety of equipment and devices are recommended and ordered for her. At the discharged planning session, the occupational therapist states that "Mrs. Jones has refused all the equipment even though she is able to use them safely and properly."

ETHICAL CONFLICTS

There are several Western bioethical principles and concepts that may be in opposition to certain cultural values and beliefs. These can be the source of some ethical conflicts and dilemmas. There are many therapist–client interactions in which culture affects health, but they are not perceived as culturally or ethically related. Western bioethics places the "self" at the center of all decisionmaking *(autonomy)*. However, there are many cultures that place the family, community, or society above the rights of the individual. The disclosing *(truthtelling)* of a diagnosis of serious illness or disability to the client is not universally accepted.

Many believe that the family, not the client, should make important health care decisions. Some people believe that health is maintained and restored through positive language. When disclosing risks of a treatment or approach, health care providers speak in a negative way *(informed consent)*. Questions of race, ethnicity, and cultural beliefs have become part of the equation when resources are finite or scarce *(justice)*. Some cultures believe that it is the duty of the family to care for its sick member *(self-independence)*. When the therapist promotes independence in self-care or activities of daily living, the role of the family may be negated (Wells, 2005).

Ethical dilemmas can be further complicated by the unequal distribution of power in the relationship between the client and therapist. Clients and families faced with medical decisions are often subject to being over- or underinfluenced by the health care system and providers *(power and dominance)*. The therapist–client relationship is one in which the therapist has the ultimate responsibility for developing conclusions and proposing treatment. These issues can lead to dilemmas in which the practitioner must either accede to the family's wishes or withdraw care. Respect for autonomy grants clients, who have been properly informed in a manner appropriate to the client's beliefs and understanding, the right to refuse a proposed treatment (Wells & Black, 2000).

THE ISSUE

In view of the changing demographics in the United States, occupational therapists and occupational therapy assistants will have the opportunity to work with a growing number and types of diverse clients. They will encounter individuals with different values and belief systems about health, well-being, illness, disabilities, and activities of daily living. Evaluation and intervention plans will be developed for consumers, who may not speak their language; differ on socioeconomic and educational levels,

ethnicity and race, religion; and have diverse beliefs about and reactions to illness. Clients and families, as well as practitioners, bring many different cultures to the therapeutic setting. The interaction of clients and practitioners embodies a form of multiculturalism in which several cultures—the health care profession, institution, family, community, traditional culture, and so forth—are all merged (Genao, Bussey-Jones, Brady, Branch, & Corbie-Smith, 2003). Therefore, every therapeutic interaction is a cross-cultural interaction. It is this overlap and interaction of cultures and dialects that can create ethical conflicts and dilemmas in providing occupational therapy services.

Without cultural competence, one can easily imagine the possible adverse consequences that can result when distrust, miscommunication, and misunderstanding interfere with the therapeutic relationship. The outcome can range from frustration, confusion, or shame to anger by the client, family, and practitioner. Cultural incompetence can result in compromised quality of care, noncompliance by the client, inability to recognize differences, fear of the new or unknown, denial, and inability to look in-depth at the individual needs of the client and their family (Wells & Black, 2000). On the other hand, cultural competence can produce a positive outcome, a feeling of professional satisfaction from knowing that you helped a client at a time of need.

Individual cultural beliefs affect how occupational therapy practitioners approach, speak to, and measure outcomes with clients. Within a personal context, we tend to make assumptions and judgments about individuals based upon their particular culture, ethnicity, race, religion, sexual orientation, language, disability, or life experiences, and this can lead to improper intervention. In the clinical environment, the responsibility for making sound ethical decisions rests with the individual practitioner. Ethical situations can arise when the behavior of the practitioner is in conflict with the behavior of the client or family. When two values present themselves and we choose one rather than another, we are saying, based on our cultural context and beliefs, that one is more valuable than another (Iwana, 2003). Problems arise when the participants have a different interpretation of illness and treatment and use language or decision-making frameworks differently. As individuals and professionals, we take a particular action based on our own sense of right and wrong, values, knowledge, and skills.

APPLICATION OF THE CODE

Professional codes of ethics provide a moral framework for and define the ideal standard of practice. They and associated documents provide guidelines and standards for resolving ethical conflicts, dilemmas, and issues. The relevant ethical principles of the *Occupational Therapy Code of Ethics (2005)* valid for culturally competent occupational therapists, occupational therapy assistants, and students are contained under the following:

- **Principle 1.** *Occupational therapy personnel shall demonstrate a concern for the safety and well-being of the recipients of their services. (beneficence)*
  Occupational therapy personnel shall:
  A. Provide services in a fair and equitable manner. They shall recognize and appreciate the cultural components of economics, geography, race, ethnicity, religious and political factors, marital status, age, sexual orientation, gender identity, and disability of all recipients of their services.

This principle speaks directly to the prohibition of discrimination in the delivery of professional services. This principle holds the welfare of those we serve as paramount. Occupational therapists and occupational therapy assistants must consider all relevant contexts that influence the performance, skill, and patterns that determine the behaviors of their client. According to the *Occupational Therapy Practice Framework* (AOTA,

2002), "the cultural context, which exists outside of the person but is internalized by the person, also sets expectations, beliefs, and customs that can affect how and when services may be delivered" (p. 614). The entire process of service delivery begins with a collaborative relationship with the client and family; therefore, incompetence in cross-culture interaction, knowledge, and skill can lead to unethical decision-making.

- **Principle 4.** *Occupational therapy personnel shall achieve and continually maintain high standards of competence. (duty)*

This principle reminds practitioners of the importance of and duty to lifelong learning to develop the knowledge and skills required to provide culturally appropriate service. It also speaks to requiring occupational therapy practitioners to strive to deliver culturally competent services to an increasingly broad range of clients. It holds practitioners accountable for continuing their professional development and seeking knowledge throughout their careers, which is required to provide culturally competent care. Principle 4.F prohibits delegation of tasks that are beyond the competence of the designee and requires that the certified individual provide adequate supervision. This is especially important when linguistic differences exist and bilingual assistants, aides, and interpreters are used.

- **Principle 7.** *Occupational therapy personnel shall treat colleagues and other professionals with respect, fairness, discretion, and integrity. (fidelity)*

This principle provides guidance on interactions with individuals, colleagues, and students from diverse backgrounds. It bars discrimination against these individuals on the basis of race, ethnicity, gender, age, religion, sexual orientation, gender identity, national origin, or disability. Culturally diverse students and practitioners bring a special skill and knowledge to the profession. They are entitled to professional equity and should not be exploited or debased because of their differences. They should not be held to different expectations, roles, or behaviors. Discrimination in any professional interaction and against any individual with whom we interact ultimately debases the profession and harms all those within the practice.

The *Guidelines to the Code of Ethics* (AOTA, 1998) specifically state that

> Occupational therapy personnel shall develop an understanding and appreciation for different cultures in order to be able to provide culturally competent service. Culturally competent practitioners are aware of how service delivery can be affected by economics, ethnic, racial, geographic, gender, religious and political factors, as well as marital status, sexual orientation, and disability [4.4], [and]. . . . In areas where the ability to communicate with the client is limited (aphasia, different language, literacy), occupational therapy personnel shall take appropriate steps to ensure comprehension and meaningful communication [4.5].

Under the *Core Values and Attitudes of Occupational Therapy Practice* (AOTA, 1993), the concepts that are related to cultural competence are equality, justice, dignity, and truth.

DISCUSSION

The *Occupational Therapy Code of Ethics (2005)* recognizes that culture may influence how individuals cope with problems and interact with each other. The way in which occupational therapy services are planned and implemented needs to be culturally sensitive to be culturally effective. Cultural competence builds on the profession's ethical concepts of *beneficence, nonmaleficence, autonomy, justice, veracity, fidelity,* and *duty,* adding *inclusion, tolerance,* and *respect* for diversity in all its forms.

The direct service provider, educator, supervisor, researcher, and professional leader must be mindful of the impact of cultural diversity in interactions with clients, families, students, and colleagues. Some materials and approaches may be inappropriate and even offensive to some individuals. Clients and families may choose complementary and alternative medicine or traditional or faith healing practices as opposed to mainstream therapeutic approaches. Colleagues and students will approach issues and events from their own cultural perspective. Cultural competence requires occupational therapy practitioners to enter into the therapeutic relationship with awareness about their own culture and cultural biases, knowledge about other cultures, and skills in cross-communication and intervention (Wells & Black, 2000).

Practitioners need a nonjudgmental attitude toward unfamiliar beliefs and health practices. They should be prepared to be open and flexible in the selection, administration, and interpretation of intervention approaches. They must be willing to negotiate and compromise when conflicts arise. And when cultural or linguistic differences may negatively influence outcomes, practitioners must be ready to refer to or collaborate with others who have the needed knowledge, skill, and experience. Cultural competence requires occupational therapy practitioners to detect and prevent exclusion or exploitation of diverse clients. This includes monitoring cultural competence among agencies, policies and procedures, and delivery systems.

VIGNETTE 3

You are attending a lecture about a disabling condition and its effect on specific populations. A multitude of groups and populations are presented and discussed. The only time that gay men and lesbians are mentioned is in connection with the total number of deaths resulting from the condition. When asked by an attendee about the effects of this condition on the gay and lesbian population, the speaker ignores the individual and goes on to another question.

Caution must be taken not to attribute stereotypical characteristics to individuals. Rather, an attempt should be made to gain better understanding of the culture of clients, colleagues, and students. Practitioners should devise a plan to continually acquire the training and education necessary to be culturally competent. The *Occupational Therapy Code of Ethics (2005)* clearly shows that occupational therapists and occupational therapy assistants have an ethical responsibility to be culturally competent practitioners.

Conclusion

To effectively reach diverse populations, the field of occupational therapy must have culturally competent professionals. Cultural competence is a basic reminder to all practitioners of their responsibility in protecting the rights of clients and their families and to act as their advocates. Recognizing the link among trust, cultural competence, and the therapeutic relationship is critical to providing ethical care. Being culturally competent can help occupational therapy practitioners develop intervention approaches, health delivery systems, and health policies that fully recognize and include the effects of culture on the ethics of health decisions. It can aid practitioners in integrating fair and equitable services of all people and the holistic, contextual, and need-centered nature of such services. It can assist practitioners in achieving their goals of providing sound ethical decision-making, practice, and care to all persons.

Ethical considerations dictate that cultural competence should be considered in activities such as hiring practices, teaching, evaluation, and supervision of staff and students. There is an equally important need for all occupational therapists and occupational therapy assistants to continually improve their level of cultural competence and to establish a mechanism for the evaluation of competence-based practice. Guided by the AOTA *Occupational Therapy Code of Ethics (2005)*, occupational therapists and occupational therapy assistants should take the leadership role not only in disseminating knowledge about diverse client groups but also in actively advocating for fair, equitable, and

culturally appropriate treatment of all clients served. This role should extend within and outside the profession. It is through the principles of the *Occupational Therapy Code of Ethics (2005)* that therapists have a framework to guide their decisions when cultural conflicts arise.

References

American Occupational Therapy Association. (1993). Core values statement and attitudes of occupational therapy practice. *American Journal of Occupational Therapy, 47,* 1085–1086.

American Occupational Therapy Association, Multicultural Task Force. (1995). *Definition and terms.* Bethesda, MD: Author.

American Occupational Therapy Association. (1998). Guidelines to the occupational therapy code of ethics. *American Journal of Occupational Therapy, 52,* 881–884. (*Note:* This document was updated in 2006. American Occupational Therapy Association. (2006). *American Journal of Occupational Therapy, 60,* 652–658.)

American Occupational Therapy Association. (2002). Occupational therapy practice framework: Domain and process. *American Journal of Occupational Therapy, 56,* 609–639.

American Occupational Therapy Association. (2005). Occupational therapy code of ethics. *American Journal of Occupational Therapy, 59,* 639–642.

Betacourt, J. R., Green, A. R., Carrillo, J. E., & Ananeh-Firempong, O. (2003). Defining cultural competence: A practical framework for addressing racial/ethnic disparities in health and health care. *Public Health Report, 118,* 293–302.

Cross, T. L., Bazron, B. J., Dennis, K. W., & Isaacs, M. R. (1989). *Towards a culturally competent system of care, volume 1.* Washington, DC: Georgetown University Child Development Center, CASSP Technical Assistant Center.

Davis, P., & Donald, B. (1997). *Multicultural counseling competencies: Assessment, evaluation, education and training, and supervision.* Thousand Oaks, CA: Sage.

Genao, I., Bussey-Jones, J., Brady, D., Branch, W. T., & Corbie-Smith, G. (2003). Building the case for cultural competence. *American Journal of the Medical Sciences, 326,* 136–140.

Iwana, M. (2003). Toward culturally relevant epistemologies in occupational therapy. *American Journal of Occupational Therapy, 57,* 582–588.

Wells, S. A. (2005). An ethic of diversity. In R. B. Purtilo, G. M. Jensen, & C. B. Royeen (Eds.), *Educating for moral action: A sourcebook in health and rehabilitation ethics* (pp. 31–41). Philadelphia: F. A. Davis.

Wells, S. A., & Black, R. (2000). *Cultural competency for health professionals.* Bethesda, MD: American Occupational Therapy Association.

Author

Shirley A. Wells, MPH, OTR, FAOTA
Chairperson, Standards and Ethics Commission, 2001–2004

Last Updated August 9, 2005

CHAPTER 15

Ethical Considerations for Professional Education of Students With Disabilities

INTRODUCTION

Assisting individuals with disabilities and valuing diversity are core tenets of the profession of occupational therapy. According to the American Occupational Therapy Association (AOTA; 2004b),

> The occupational therapy profession affirms the right of every individual to access and full participation within society. … We maintain that society has an obligation to provide the reasonable accommodations necessary to allow individuals access to social, educational, recreational, and vocational opportunities. (p. 668)

Most often the individual with a disability is a client, but sometimes the individual is a student in an occupational therapy educational program. Regardless of whether the student has a disability, educational programs must balance the needs of their students with their obligations to the future clients that programs' graduates will serve. Occupational therapy classroom and fieldwork educators must treat students fairly and act in accordance with the AOTA "Ethics Standards" and federal and state laws. The AOTA Ethics Standards are comprised of the AOTA *Occupational Therapy Code of Ethics* (AOTA, 2005a), *Core Values and Attitudes of Occupational Therapy Practice* (AOTA, 1993), and the *Guidelines to the Occupational Therapy Code of Ethics* (AOTA, 2006).

This advisory opinion discusses ethical issues that may arise during the classroom and fieldwork portions of the educational process of occupational therapy students who have disabilities. First, a brief background of key legislation is provided, including the Americans with Disabilities Act (ADA) of 1990, Section 504 of the Rehabilitation Act of 1973, and the Family Education Rights and Privacy Act (FERPA, 1974). Next, the AOTA Ethics Standards will be applied to two case studies that describe situations that may arise in the classroom and in fieldwork education. Last, the opinion will summarize key issues. When the term *educational program* is used, it applies to both the academic and fieldwork portion of the educational program unless otherwise stated.

BACKGROUND

The ADA (1990) extended civil rights to individuals with disabilities. Similarly, the Rehabilitation Act of 1973, specifically Section 504, defines exactly how services must be provided to people with disabilities who request assistance. These legislative mandates pertain to all aspects of American life, from housing and education, to employment, recreation, and religion. In any situation in which an otherwise qualified person might be prevented from achieving their potential due to a disability, ADA and the Rehabilitation Act demand assurances that opportunities be available for all.

The ADA and Section 504 are antidiscrimination acts, not entitlement acts. As such they are outcome neutral, and the responsibility for initiating accommodation rests with the student. The ADA and Section 504 require that individuals, such as those entering higher education, receive the opportunity to participate in educational and vocational endeavors for which they are otherwise qualified. An equal opportunity to participate does not mean that there will be equal outcomes. Just as their peers without disabilities, some students with disabilities will fail coursework and fieldwork. The ADA focuses on whether students with disabilities in higher education have equal access to an education. It is not intended to optimize academic success. "The intent of the law, again, was to level the playing field, not to tilt it" (Gordon & Keiser, 1998, p. 5).

Because the ADA's intention is to protect against discrimination based on a disability, a student can receive such protection only if he or she has substantial impairments that affect major life activities and he or she is found to be disabled relative to the general population (Gordon & Keiser, 1998). Some conditions warrant intervention but may not rise to the level of impairment as defined by the ADA. Furthermore,

[D]ocumentation of a specific disability does not translate directly into specific accommodations. Reasonable accommodations are individually determined and should be based on the functional impact of the condition and its likely interaction with the environment (course assignments, program requirements, physical design, etc.). As such, accommodation recommendations may vary from individual to individual with the "same" disability diagnosis and from environment to environment for the same individual. (Association on Higher Education and Disability, 2004)

There are specific requirements for diagnosis and documentation to qualify for protection under the ADA as an individual with a disability. The diagnosis must be made and documented by a qualified professional, such as a physician, neuropsychologist, or educational psychologist, among others. "The general expectation is that people conducting evaluations have terminal degrees in their profession and are fully trained in differential diagnosis" (Gordon & Keiser, 1998, p. 13). Additional information on best practices in documentation of a disability in higher education may be found at the Association on Higher Education and Disability's Web site at http://www.ahead.org/resources/bestpracticeselements.htm. The report based on the evaluator's findings must also be sufficient to allow for careful administrative review.

The coordination of the documentation and services for students with disabilities is usually managed through an administrative office at the college or university. This office is frequently called the Office of Disability Accommodations (ODA). The ODA determines if the student qualifies for accommodations and what accommodations are allowable by disability law and regulations.

The above process assumes that the student is aware of his or her disability and self-identifies. If a student chooses not to self-identify, he or she is within individual rights to pursue post-secondary education. However, such a student is not protected by the law. Simply stated, unless a student self-identifies as being eligible for protections under the ADA and Section 504, no associated privileges are afforded.

Because occupational therapy practitioners in their professional role assist people with impairments to be successful, it is sometimes difficult for a faculty member to refrain from making special arrangements for a student who appears to have a disability but who has not self-identified or who has not completed the process to qualify for accommodations. However, educators must consider fundamental fairness to all students, including those who may struggle for a variety of other reasons but who do not qualify for accommodations.

It is not unusual for a disability to be discovered after a student enters professional school or as late as Level II fieldwork. Sometimes students with learning or emotional disabilities have succeeded up to the point of professional school through extremely hard work and dedication. However, the demands of professional school and fieldwork can push such a student past her or his ability to compensate.

If the student is otherwise qualified, the educational program must determine if the student can perform the essential job function of being an occupational therapy student with or without reasonable accommodations. For a more complete discussion of essential job functions and reasonable accommodations in academic and practice settings, see Gupta, Gelpi, and Sain (2005). A variety of documents exist that contribute to understanding the essential job functions of an occupational therapist or occupational therapy assistant (AOTA, 2004a, 2004c, 2005b; U.S. Department of Labor, 2003, 2004).

In the field of health education, essential job functions are generally referred to as technical standards. Many occupational therapy programs include the technical standards as part of the admissions process (e.g., Medical College of Georgia, Samuel Merritt College, Stony Brook University, University of Kansas, University of Tennessee).

The last federal law relevant to this advisory opinion is the Family Education Rights and Privacy Act (FERPA) of 1974, which protects the privacy of all students' educational records. Generally, "institutions must have written permission from the student in order to release any information from a student's educational record" (Van Dusen, 2004, p. 4). This protection of privacy applies to all students regardless of disability.

Protection of confidential information is part of FERPA, the ADA, and Section 504. The Association on Higher Education and Disability (1996) states that "Disability-related information should be treated as medical information and handled under the same strict rules of confidentiality as is other medical information" (p. 1). The student alone determines whether to share information, what information to share, and selects which faculty member(s) may receive information.

> In the U.S., the Department of Justice has indicated that a faculty member generally does not need to know what the disability is, only that it has been appropriately verified by the individual (or office) assigned this responsibility on behalf of the institution. (p. 1)

APPLICATION TO PRACTICE: CASE STUDIES

Analysis of two case studies will be used to apply ethical reasoning to students with disabilities.

Case 1

Ashley is an occupational therapy student with a learning disability. Ashley is your advisee and in the first semester in the occupational therapy program. She makes an appointment with you and tells you about her learning disability and the difficulties she has had, shows you a psychological report describing her disability, and asks to be given extra time to complete exams and assignments. You advise her to go to the university's ODA. Ashley does not want to go to the ODA because she thinks that the university would label her as a student with a disability. You inform Ashley of the risks of not seeking accommodations and encourage her to reconsider. She leaves your office undecided. You do not hear from Ashley again until after midterm exams when she discovers she has a failing grade in two classes. She admits that she did not go to the ODA and thought she could make it on her own. Ashley says that one of her instructors gave her more time, and she can't understand why the other occupational therapy instructors did not. Ashley finally agrees to go to the ODA, but she also wants to be able to retake her midterm exams in the two courses she is failing. She wants more time for exams and to turn in assignments. The ODA determines that Ashley does qualify as a student with learning disabilities and that her accommodations can include time and a half for exams, but she must turn in assignments on the dates they are due in the syllabi. She is also not allowed to retake the two midterm exams.

Discussion Case 1

Your behavior as Ashley's advisor demonstrates understanding, caring, and responsiveness (*altruism*) to Ashley's situation. By requiring Ashley to go to the ODA, you followed procedures (*procedural justice*), which requires that you are familiar with and comply with institutional rules and federal laws, in this case the ADA and Section 504. The instructor who gave Ashley more time on the exam before accommodations were in place demonstrated altruism but violated Principle 5A of the Code (*procedural justice*) because university procedures stipulate that accommodations should not be given until the ODA determines that the student is entitled to them and what the accommodations should be. Otherwise other students who may have had extenuating circumstances affecting their performance did not have an equal opportunity for extra time.

Principle 4 of the Code, *duty*, applies to all faculty involved in this case. Specifically, 4D reads "Occupational therapy personnel shall be competent in all topics in which they provide instruction to consumers, peers, and/or students" (AOTA, 2005a, p. 640). While academic and fieldwork educators may typically think of competence in terms of educating students without disabilities, knowledge of laws related to educating students with disabilities is also required.

Case 2

Tanisha is preparing for her first Level II fieldwork experience. She has a diagnosis of anxiety disorder for which she has received accommodations during the academic portion of her education. As the academic fieldwork coordinator, you encourage Tanisha to contact the ODA to determine what accommodations she would qualify for during clinical education. Tanisha states that she does not want to reveal to the fieldwork site that she has a disability because she plans to apply for jobs in this city after graduation. She says she feels more confident now and wants to prove to herself that she can perform without assistance. After you explain the risks and benefits of disclosure, Tanisha decides not to disclose or ask for accommodations from her clinical site. You contact Tanisha after Week 2 to review her progress. Tanisha says things are okay. At Week 4, Jeremy, Tanisha's clinical educator, calls you to say that he is concerned about Tanisha's difficulty with time management and turning in documentation on time. He says that Tanisha's level of knowledge appears solid but that she sometimes "shuts down" in stressful situations. Jeremy asks if Tanisha has some learning or emotional issues that he should know about. He wants your advice on how to help Tanisha be more successful.

Discussion Case 2

As the academic fieldwork coordinator you must consider the ethical principles of *autonomy* and *confidentiality*. Principle 3D is especially applicable to this case:

> Occupational therapy personnel shall protect all privileged confidential forms of written, verbal, and electronic communication gained from educational, practice, research, and investigational activities unless otherwise mandated by local, state, or federal regulations. (AOTA, 2005a, p. 640)

In a similar fashion, *fidelity* requires that "occupational therapy personnel shall preserve, respect, and safeguard confidential information about colleagues and staff, unless otherwise mandated by national, state, or local laws"

(AOTA, 2005a, p. 641). *Veracity* also applies to this case: "Occupational therapy personnel shall accept responsibility for their professional actions that reduce the public's trust in occupational therapy services and those that perform those services" (AOTA, 2005a, p. 641). The latter principle creates tension between your duty to your student and your duty to consumers of occupational therapy services. However, you realize that you have a greater obligation to avoid breaching confidentiality with Tanisha *as you do not have evidence at this point that Tanisha's behavior is putting clients at risk.* If you had information to indicate that clients were at risk, you would have a greater obligation to protect the clients, and you must focus on Tanisha's lack of competence in the area of client safety.

You must also consider *procedural justice*, which requires that you are familiar and comply with institutional rules and federal laws, which in this case are the ADA, Section 504, and FERPA. Finally, you consider *ensuring the common good*, which states that "occupational therapy personnel in educational settings are responsible for promoting ethical conduct by students, faculty, and fieldwork colleagues" (AOTA, 2006, p. 654). It is important that you model ethical conduct for Jeremy and Tanisha.

A more thorough discussion of ethical dilemmas involving confidentiality of students with disabilities during fieldwork education can be found in an article by Brown and Griffiths (2000). AOTA's Web site also provides useful information on this topic under the section titled "Occupational Therapy Fieldwork Information for Practitioners Most Frequently Asked Questions." The following question and answer are relevant to this advisory opinion:

Does the academic program have to tell the fieldwork setting that the student has a disability? The academic program is not required to, nor should it, inform the fieldwork site of a student's disability without the student's permission. It is the student's decision whether or not to disclose a disability. The academic fieldwork coordinator will counsel students on the pros and cons of sharing this type of information prior to beginning fieldwork. If a student decides not to disclose this information, the academic fieldwork coordinator is legally not allowed to share that information with the fieldwork setting.

A fieldwork setting cannot refuse to place a student with a disability unless that student is unable to perform the essential job functions with or without reasonable accommodations. To refuse placement solely on the student's disability is discriminatory and illegal. (AOTA, 2000)

After considering the above Ethics Standards and other documents, you decide you cannot directly answer Jeremy's question about a disability, but you could brainstorm with Jeremy about strategies that might help Tanisha be more successful. You could encourage Jeremy to document Tanisha's difficulties and to give her frequent and specific feedback. If these suggestions don't correct the problems, a learning contract or site visit could be considered. You could contact Tanisha to assist her with making an informed decision by providing her with the potential risks of nondisclosure. However, as an autonomous person with freedom to exercise choice and self-direction, Tanisha must make the final decision. Autonomous persons can and do take risks. Tanisha may be risking failure of her first Level II fieldwork, but taking the risk is her choice.

Wells and Hanebrink (2000) noted that

The decision to disclose or not to disclose as well as when and how to disclose is solely the right of the student. The fieldwork site can be held accountable only from the point in which they are informed or receive a request for accommodation. (p. 9)

Education programs should provide clinical sites with information about educating students with disabilities and the requirements of the ADA and Section 504 in regard to education and encourage sites to call the academic fieldwork coordinator when questions arise. AOTA's *Self-Assessment Tool for Fieldwork Educator Competency* (AOTA, n.d.) is a potential resource for educating fieldwork educators in general. Under Administration Competencies, Item 7 is pertinent to this discussion: "[T]he fieldwork educator defines essential functions and roles of a fieldwork student, in compliance with legal and accreditation standards (e.g., ADA, Family Education Rights and Privacy Act, fieldwork agreement, reimbursement mechanism, state regulations, etc.)" (p. 7).

DISCUSSION AND SUMMARY

Occupational therapy faculty and fieldwork educators must remain mindful of their obligations to both their occupational therapy students and to the clients those students will someday serve. Patient safety is always paramount. However, there will be students who can become competent occupational therapists despite their disabilities, if given reasonable accommodations. Although the student has rights and responsibilities, so do the academic and clinical sites. "The institution is always responsible for students who are participating in its programs whether on or off campus. The question is whether the institution has primary or secondary responsibility. The institution has the ultimate responsibility for the provision of reasonable accommodations. The intern site generally assumes the duty for providing accommodation on site; the institution, however, must monitor what happens in that environment to ensure that its students are not discriminated against and are provided necessary accommodations" (Scott, Wells, & Hanebrink, 1997, p. 44).

"Students with disabilities have a right under ADA (Title II) to be seen first as capable people with marketable skills and only secondarily as people who happen to have disabilities" (Scott et al., 1997, p. 46). According to

the Northeast Technical Assistance Center (n.d.), faculty should not

make assumptions about a student's ability to work in a particular field. Most often, concerns that students may not be able to "cut it" are based on fears and assumptions, not facts. Remember too, that employers are also required to comply with the ADA.

REFERENCES

American Occupational Therapy Association. (1993). Core values and attitudes of occupational therapy practice. *American Journal of Occupational Therapy, 47*, 1085–1086.

American Occupational Therapy Association. (2000). *Most frequently asked fieldwork questions.* Retrieved January 14, 2008, from http://www.aota.org/Educate/EdRes/Fieldwork/NewPrograms/38242.aspx

American Occupational Therapy Association (2004a). Guidelines for supervision, roles, and responsibilities during the delivery of occupational therapy services. *American Journal of Occupational Therapy, 58*, 663–667.

American Occupational Therapy Association (2004b). Occupational therapy's commitment to nondiscrimination and inclusion. *American Journal of Occupational Therapy, 58*, 668.

American Occupational Therapy Association (2004c). Scope of practice. *American Journal of Occupational Therapy, 58*, 673–677.

American Occupational Therapy Association. (2005a). Occupational therapy code of ethics (2005). *American Journal of Occupational Therapy, 59*, 639–642

American Occupational Therapy Association (2005b). Standards of practice of occupational therapy. *American Journal of Occupational Therapy, 59*, 663–665.

American Occupational Therapy Association. (2006). Guidelines to the Occupational Therapy Code of Ethics. *American Journal of Occupational Therapy, 60*, 652–658.

American Occupational Therapy Association (n.d.). *Self-assessment tool for fieldwork educator competency.* Retrieved November 24, 2007, from

http://www.aota.org/Educate/EdRes/Fieldwork/
Supervisor/Forms/38251.aspx

Americans with Disabilities Act of 1990, Pub. L.
No. 101-336.

Association on Higher Education and Disability.
(1996). *Confidentiality and disability issues in higher
education* [Brochure]. Huntersville, NC: Author.

Association on Higher Education and Disability.
(2004). *AHEAD best practices: Disability documentation in higher education.* Retrieved December 11,
2007, from http://www.ahead.org/resources/best-
practicesprinciples.htm.

Brown, K., & Griffiths, Y. (2000). Confidentiality
dilemmas in clinical education. *Journal of Allied
Health, 29*, 13–17.

Family Education Rights and Privacy Act, 0 USC §
1232(g) (1974).

Gordon, M., & Keiser, S. (1998). *Accommodations in
higher education under the Americans with Disabilities Act (ADA): A no-nonsense guide for clinicians,
educators, administrators, and lawyers.* DeWitt, NY:
GSI Publications.

Gupta, J., Gelpi, T., & Sain, S. (2005, August).
Reasonable accommodations and essential job
functions in academic and practice settings. *OT
Practice*, pp. CE1–CE7.

Medical College of Georgia. (n.d.). *Technical standards for occupational therapy.* Retrieved November 24, 2007, from http://www.mcg.edu/sah/ot/
TechnicalStandards.html

Northeast Technical Assistance Center. (n.d.).
Nondiscrimination in higher education. Retrieved
January 21, 2007, from http://www.netac.rit.edu/
publication/tipsheet/ADA.html

Rehabilitation Act of 1973, Section 504, P.L.
93–112, 29 USC § 701 et seq.

Samuel Merritt College. (n.d.). *Occupational therapy
technical standards.* Retrieved July 2, 2007, from
http://www.samuelmerritt.edu/occupational_ther
apy/technical_standards

Scott, S. S., Wells, S., & Hanebrink, S. (1997). *Educating college students with disabilities: What academic and fieldwork educators need to know.* Bethesda,
MD: American Occupational Therapy Association.

Stony Brook University. (n.d.). *Technical standards
for admission and continuation in the occupational
therapy program.* Retrieved June 7, 2007, from
http://www.hsc.stonybrook.edu/shtm/ot/tech-
standards.cfm

University of Kansas. (n.d.). *Occupational therapy education department policy, technical standards, and
essential functions for occupational therapy students.*
Retrieved November 24, 2007, from http://
alliedhealth.kumc.edu/programs/ot/docu-
ments/PDF/techstds_preadm.pdf

University of Tennessee. (n.d.). *Occupational therapy technical standards.* Retrieved July 3, 2007,
from http://www.utmem.edu/allied/ot_techni-
calstandards.html

U.S. Department of Labor, National O*NET Consortium. (2003). *Summary report for occupational
therapists.* Retrieved January 14, 2008, from
http://online.onetcenter.org/link/summary/ 29-
1122.00

U.S. Department of Labor, National O*NET Consortium. (2004). *Summary report for occupational
therapy assistants.* Retrieved January 14, 2008, from
http://online.onetcenter.org/link/summary/31-
2011.00

Van Dusen, W. R. (2004). FERPA: Basic guidelines for faculty and staff: A simple step-by-step
approach for compliance. Retrieved January 21,
2007, from *NACADA Clearinghouse of Academic
Advising Resources,* http://www.nacada.ksu.edu/
Resources/FERPA-Overview.htm

Wells, S. A. & Hanebrink, S. (2000). Students with
disabilities and fieldwork. In *Meeting the fieldwork challenge* (Self-Paced Clinical Course).
Bethesda, MD: American Occupational Therapy
Association.

Authors

Linda Gabriel, PhD, OTR/L
*Education Representative, Ethics Commission
2003–2006, 2006–2009*

Betsy DeBrakeleer, COTA/L, ROH
*OTA Representative , Ethics Commission
2005–2008*

Lorie J. McQuade, M.Ed. C.R.C.,
*Public Member, Ethics Commission
2004–2007*

CHAPTER 16

Balancing Patient Rights and Practitioner Values

INTRODUCTION

Clinical reasoning in occupational therapy involves art, science, and ethics, according to Joan Rogers (1983). The relationship between rights and duties is one of the ethical issues that may arise in clinical practice. The art and science of care delivered by occupational therapy personnel relates directly to the correlation between rights and duties. The rights of a person who presents for intervention should be met with a trained practitioner's duty to provide care that benefits that individual.

The following question is raised: "Do circumstances exist whereby occupational therapy personnel can ethically refrain from providing services?" Although there is an overarching professional duty to provide benefit to clients, there may be unsafe situations in which the practitioner may ethically refrain from providing service. On the other hand, the practitioner may feel unsafe due to a significant difference of personal values that impedes therapeutic interaction. Some argue that there are situations in which the practitioner's moral duty or personal values will outweigh the patient's right to receive services. However, in a diverse society, ideas of right and wrong vary as much as the individuals themselves.

It is increasingly difficult to identify what constitutes an ethical right of conscience in healthcare and the limits of decisions based on conscience (Stein, 2006). Although some may agree with the provider's right to refrain from

care in scenarios in which the practitioner has a personal moral conflict with a patient, moral consensus as to the provider's rights versus responsibilities has not been reached. Therefore, the practitioner must be prudent and diligent in differentiating between a conflict of values and a truly unsafe environment to obtain a balance with the rights of the patient.

Many occupational therapy personnel have experienced working with difficult patients who are uncooperative, appear to lack motivation, or are in some way repugnant. This may be manifested by harsh and inappropriate language spoken during the therapy session or complete unresponsiveness. A homebound patient unable to perform daily hygiene activities or who does not have anyone responsible for overseeing such basic needs as nutrition and cleansing may become offensive to the practitioner. In these situations it is important for occupational therapy personnel to separate their personal feelings of aversion from the treatment protocol and deliver the prescribed care. Occupational therapy practitioners must acknowledge the dignity of patients regardless of their unpleasant nature or condition. Within the boundaries of the provider–patient relationship, the continuation of care is essential to upholding the ethical guidelines of patient autonomy and beneficence. In other words, patients have choices about personal behaviors and are entitled to receive the benefit of services and care. However, if environmental conditions exist that truly jeopardize the practitioner's safety, he or she has the right to refrain from providing services in that context.

CASE SCENARIOS
Scenario 1. Conflict of Values

Keisha, a home care therapist, meets her new patient, Rafaella, who recently had a hip replacement as a result of long-standing rheumatoid arthritis. Rafaella is currently estranged from her husband, who has been abusive in the past. On the second visit, the therapist notices a large bruise on her neck, which she attempted to cover up with a scarf. The therapist inquires as to how she got bruised, and she says she fell out of bed but seems withdrawn and does not make eye contact while speaking. The therapist is concerned about the situation and suspects abuse. As Keisha continues to treat Rafaella, they establish a therapeutic relationship whereby Rafaella discloses that her husband continues to stop by when he is intoxicated and can become quite physically abusive. Keisha encourages Rafaella to file a police report and get a restraining order. Rafaella adamantly refuses this advice, stating that she still loves her husband and would not want to get him in trouble. The occupational therapist questions her ability to continue treating Rafaella because she does not feel that she can support Rafaella's choice to remain in an abusive relationship.

Scenario 2. Unsafe Environment

During the scenario above, while Keisha is treating Rafaella, her estranged husband arrives with alcohol on his breath, is verbally abusive, and is swaggering around. Keisha notices a gun in his waistband. The husband confronts Keisha and orders her to leave, yelling that he will shoot if she returns. Keisha feels that she cannot continue to treat Rafaella in her home because she fears for her own safety. Keisha also fears for Rafaella but feels that she has done all she can to encourage Rafaella to seek assistance from the police.

DISCUSSION

Although both of these scenarios portray a situation in which the provider, Keisha, questions her duty to continue treating Rafaella, her professional ethics may require her to act differently based on the circumstances at hand. The moral dilemma facing Keisha stems from conflicts between the client's and the professional's autonomy as well as beneficence. Respect for an individual's autonomy, or the right to make their own decisions (self-determination), has historically been a pervasive concept in the field of ethics. Respect for the client's autonomy requires the practitioner to acknowledge the individual as a moral agent as well as recognize the client's "right to hold views, to make choices, and to take actions based on personal values and beliefs" (Beauchamp & Childress, 2001, p. 63).

The overriding question is, How far does this right extend? Does respect for client autonomy require the practitioner to place himself or herself in a situation that places him or her in danger? Although patient autonomy plays a significant role in the ethical delineation of services, according to Fleming (2005), "a successful and ethically grounded [provider]–patient relationship presumes respect for autonomy, bolstered by good communication and shared decision-making that requires careful balancing of the values and beliefs of both participants" (p. 263). Neither scenario supports abandonment of the patient; instead, both scenarios call for communication and decision-making as described by Fleming.

Following this line of thinking, in Scenario 1 Keisha needs to work with Rafaella to facilitate a safe environment. However, if Rafaella does not ultimately agree to Keisha's involvement in changing her environment, according to Principle 3 of the *Occupational Therapy Code of Ethics (2005)*, occupational therapy personnel are required to assure the rights of service recipients (American Occupational Therapy Association [AOTA], 2005). Moral objections to a person's life or lifestyle would not warrant discontinuation of services. Therefore, Keisha must respect Rafaella's autonomy and does not have an ethical right to refrain from providing services based on her moral objections regarding Rafaella's decision. However, note that if there is a law that requires a health care practitioner to report abuse (e.g., children, elderly people), then the occupational therapy practitioner must do so regardless of the autonomy principle.

Scenario 2 also calls for shared decision making between the client and the provider. However, Keisha can ethically remove herself from the immediate situation, which violates her own rights as a provider. Keisha is not ethically required to subject herself to danger to serve her clients. However, Keisha does have an extended responsibility to acknowledge the provider–patient relationship and thus work with Rafaella to find a safe place in which to continue therapy services. This extended responsibility of the provider is supported through Principle 1, Beneficence, of the *Occupational Therapy Code of Ethics* (AOTA, 2005), which requires occupational therapy personnel to "demonstrate a concern for the safety and well-being of the recipients of their services" (p. 639). In addition, Principle 1C requires the practitioner to "make every effort to advocate for recipients to obtain needed services through available means" (p. 639). Again, through shared-decision making and communication, Keisha should partner with Rafaella to ensure access to services in the safest environment available.

SUMMARY AND CONCLUSION

The actions on the part of a practitioner must benefit the health of the patient in addition to acknowledging the autonomy of the patient as established by his or her rights to be informed, to privacy, and to confidentiality. The recipient of occupational therapy services has duties and the provider has rights that affect the therapeutic relationship. For example, the recipient has the duty to arrive on time for therapy, follow through with intervention plans, and pay

for services rendered. Occupational therapy personnel have the right to work in safe environments and in clinical settings that support the ethical nature of their role with clients.

Given these parameters, when questions arise regarding rights versus responsibilities of the provider, one must thoughtfully determine which justifiable course of action to take. Practitioners must be grounded by not only a moral conscience to do what is right but also by the courage to proceed and ensure the best interests of the patient. This may require occupational therapy personnel to apply a framework of ethical decision-making. Such action highlights the specific details of the case, assessment of the patient's condition, and determination of realistic alternatives for intervention, if needed. Therapeutic interventions should be interrupted only after all potential avenues to continue care have been exhausted. Acknowledging these moral obligations within the provider–patient relationship clearly delineates the role of occupational therapy personnel.

REFERENCES

American Occupational Therapy Association. (2005). Occupational therapy code of ethics (2005). *American Journal Occupational Therapy, 59,* 639–642.

Beauchamp, T. L., & Childress, J. F. (2001). *Principles of biomedical ethics* (5th ed.). New York: Oxford University Press.

Fleming, D. A. (2005). Futility: Revisiting a concept of shared moral judgment. *HEC Forum, 17,* 260–275.

Rogers, J. C. (1983). Eleanor Clarke Slagle Lecture—Clinical reasoning: The ethics, science, and art. *American Journal of Occupational Therapy, 37,* 601–616.

Slater, D. Y. (Ed.). (2006). *Reference guide to the Occupational Therapy Code of Ethics.* Bethesda, MD: AOTA Press.

Stein, R. (2006, July 16). A medical crisis of conscience: Faith drives some to refuse patients medication or care. *Washington Post,* p. A01.

Authors

Lea C.Brandt, OTD, OTR/L,
*Member at Large, Ethics Commission,
2005–2008*

Donna F. Homenko, PhD, RDH,
*Public Member, Ethics Commission,
2005–2009*

REFERENCE GUIDE TO THE OCCUPATIONAL THERAPY ETHICS STANDARDS

CHAPTER 17

Ethics in Governance

INTRODUCTION

Ethics in governance is about the qualities of leadership and the values expressed by the leaders themselves. Leaders set the tone and character of the organization of which they are stewards. Values are a core set of beliefs that guide actions. Ethics are derived from and based on a particular code of values (Campbell, 2003). Occupational therapy leaders are guided by the core values of the profession (American Occupational Therapy Association [AOTA], 1993).

THE ISSUES

Leaders in volunteer organizations, such as a professional association, are frequently faced with expectations by members to increase performance of the organization but also are faced with limited resources and options. There are pressures to maintain or expand existing programs, membership benefits, and ideals while at the same time to change, be innovative, be creative, and be different (Merrill Associates, 2002). Leadership training to deal effectively with membership expectations often is learned in the course of performing the leadership role. The result may be ethical dilemmas and tough choices for the volunteer or elected leaders that challenge the profession's core values and beliefs. Dilemmas may evolve from conflicts of interest, conflict of commitment (e.g., accepting addi-

tional roles that have a negative impact on the ability to meet current responsibilities), or misunderstanding one's fiduciary responsibility.

The values in leadership are similar to the values in practice: *trustworthiness, respect, responsibility, fairness, caring,* and *citizenship* (Seel, 1996). The six values are based in part on the six pillars of character developed by the Josephson Institute for Ethics (2007). *Trustworthiness* includes "integrity, honesty, reliability, and loyalty" (Josephson Institute for Ethics, 2007, para. 7). *Respect* includes dignity, tolerance, acceptance, nonviolence, and courtesy. *Responsibility* includes duty, accountability, pursuit of excellence, and self-control. *Fairness* includes justice, impartiality, and openness. *Caring* includes concern for others and altruism. *Citizenship* includes doing your share and respecting authority. These six values are consistent with the core values of the American Occupational Therapy Association (AOTA, 1993): *altruism, equality, freedom, justice, dignity, truth,* and *prudence.*

DISCUSSION

These leadership values also are expressed and covered in the *Occupational Therapy Code of Ethics (2005)* (AOTA, 2005). *Trustworthiness* is part of *veracity* (Principle 6) and is supported by *fidelity* (Principle 7). *Respect* is supported by *fidelity* (Principle 7) and *autonomy/confidentiality* (Principle 3). *Responsibility* relates to *duty* (Principle 4). **Fairness** is of *procedural justice* (Principle 5). **Caring** is part of *beneficence* (Principle 1) and *nonmaleficence* (Principle 2). **Citizenship** involves all seven principles. In addition, *Guidelines to the Occupational Therapy Code of Ethics* 1.1 (leadership roles and honesty), 6.5 (conflict of interest), and 10.3 (resolving ethical issues in professional organizations) (AOTA, 2006) also are relevant.

Leaders need to constantly monitor their behavior to avoid the perception of seeking secondary gains from their position. For example, one situation in which the ethical conduct of leaders can be challenged is when they are called on to speak to members at local or state meetings and to represent AOTA at other organizational events. The content of their presentations and the conduct during their representations reflects directly on the reputation of the association. Therefore, a volunteer who is in an AOTA leadership role must avoid projecting personal opinions or promoting his or her employer or policies that would benefit his or her employer. Following the principles of ethical conduct and good leadership provides a sound guidance toward ensuring that AOTA will continue to be well respected and maintain its good reputation with both its members and outside groups.

Some examples of the ethical values in application may include the following statements adapted from the American Heart Association (AHA, 2006) and Josephson Institute (2007):

- Be honest and truthful in personal conduct related to association business, including the "handling of actual or apparent conflicts of interest between personal and professional relationships" (AHA, 2006, para.11) *(trustworthiness)*.
- Be loyal to the association and committed to maintaining its good reputation *(trustworthiness)*.
- Treat members of the association, fellow volunteers, and employees, with good man-

ners and with tolerance for differences *(respect)*.
- Resolve disagreements without resorting to anger and insults *(respect)*.
- "Comply with all applicable government laws, rules, and regulations" (AHA, 2006, para. 11) *(responsibility)*.
- "Protect and ensure the proper use of" (AHA, 2006, para. 11) association assets *(responsibility)*.
- Be open-minded and listen to what others (e.g., members, fellow volunteers, employees) have to say *(fairness)*.
- Do not take advantage of others or blame others carelessly *(fairness)*.
- Provide association members "with information that is accurate...objective, relevant, timely, and understandable" (AHA, 2006, para. 11) *(caring)*.
- "Proactively promote ethical behavior" (AHA, 2006, para. 11) among association members, fellow volunteers, and employees *(caring)*.
- Complete assigned tasks on time and perform to the best of personal ability *(citizenship)*.
- Stay informed on topics of interest and concern to the association and its members *(citizenship)*.
- Cooperate with others to accomplish the goals and objectives of the association and its members *(citizenship)*.
- Be accountable for personal behavior and actions at all times *(citizenship)*.

SUMMARY

Ethical behavior in governance is based on the same principles as the expected ethical conduct of all AOTA members. However, volunteer and elected leaders have accepted, by virtue of their position, additional responsibilities within the association. These responsibilities include behaviors that require a higher level of ethical conduct than members without such responsibilities. The welfare and well-being of AOTA must remain the number one concern of all leaders involved in Association governance. Adherence to the AOTA *Occupational Therapy Code of Ethics* and the values on which the Code is based provides a sound approach to ensuring that AOTA will remain a vital force and voice in expressing the goals and objectives of the profession.

REFERENCES AND RESOURCES

American Heart Association. (2006). *Ethics policy*. Retrieved February 1, 2007, from http://www.americanheart.org/presenter.jhtml?identifier=3023721

American Occupational Therapy Association. (1993). Core values and attitudes of occupational therapy practice. *American Journal of Occupational Therapy, 47*, 1085–1086.

American Occupational Therapy Association. (2005). Occupational therapy code of ethics (2005). *American Journal of Occupational Therapy, 59*, 639–642.

American Occupational Therapy Association. (2006). Guidelines to the occupational therapy code of ethics. *American Journal of Occupational Therapy, 60*, 652–658.

Campbell, K. H. (2003, Fall/Winter). Ethics today: Personal, practical, and relevant. *The Connection*. Retrieved September 13, 2006, from www.casanet.org/

Josephson Institute for Ethics. (2007). *The six pillars of character*. Retrieved May 14, 2007, from http://www.josephsoninstitute.org/MED/MED-2sixpillars.htm

Merrill Associates. (2002). *Topic of the month: April 2002*. Retrieved September 13, 2006, from www.merrillassociates.net

Seel, K. (1996). The new AVA statement of professional ethics in volunteer administration. *Journal of Volunteer Administration, 14*(2), 33–38.

Author

Kathlyn L. Reed, PhD, OTR, FAOTA, MLIS

Deborah Yarett Slater, MS, OT/L, FAOTA
Liaison to the Ethics Commission
Liaison to the Special Interest Sections

CHAPTER 18

Organizational Ethics

The current health care system has changed in recent years from a model where health care relationships were defined primarily by the provider and patient to a more complex model where the organization in which the health care professional practices has a direct impact on the care provided to patients. The role of the organization in the delivery of care has introduced business, financial, and management pressures into the health care environment, often leading to ethical conflict between delivery, access, and reimbursement for service. As stated by the American Society for Bioethics and Humanities, "Ethical issues in organizational behavior have become more evident in recent years with the emergence of a more explicit market approach to medicine" (p. 24).[1] The market approach has resulted in the need for integrating organizational ethics into the health care environment. This integration has led to speculation regarding how business ethics and clinical ethics will coexist within the infrastructure of the health care institution. However, organizational ethics is more than clinical ethics and business ethics combined. Organizations must take into account values and moral positions that are defined both internally and externally,[2] including the professionals and the codes that shape their behavior and guide practice.

Strategies for shaping an ethical organization must include health care values and codes of ethics. Health care professionals have always been held to a high ethical standard; therefore, organizations that provide health care services also must be held to this standard. Ethics in organizations are often complicated by business pressures. Health care organizations have become more complex and more involved in managing care, especially in times of limited resources. There are ethical tensions resulting from pressures to do more with less. Health care organizations are expected to improve quality and expand access while reducing cost.[3] However, these pressures do not excuse organizations from their primary purpose of caring for people. In addition, if a health care professional works for an organization, ethical or otherwise, he or she cannot hide behind the policies or administration of the institution; his or her professional code and values must continue to guide practice. Ethical action requires the organization and the health care provider to demonstrate "integrity in the face of patients' exploitable vulnerability, [and] loyalty even to the point of personal sacrifice" (p. 155).[4]

THE ISSUES

Occupational therapists are not immune to these market-based pressures. Most clinicians are familiar with the pressure to do more with less, whether manifested in lack of resources or increased productivity standards. Constraints in time and money will continue to exist in health care; therefore, occupational therapy practitioners must understand how to handle these problems ethically while addressing the needs of the patients and the communities they serve. Practitioners may work within an organization, but they also belong to a profession with core values based on concepts of altruism, equality, freedom, justice, dignity, truth, and prudence.

Health care providers are finding themselves enmeshed in relationships that extend beyond the provider and patient. These providers "interact on matters of accountability over many different domains and mechanisms [creating] what we might call a complex reciprocating matrix of accountability" (p. 231).[5] The organization in which a health care professional practices often acts as a domain that influences his or her behavior. If the practitioner is an employee of the organization, then a level of accountability to that organization's culture, standards, and viability is subsumed. Although the focus of accountability is often limited to the dynamic of the provider–patient relationship, service delivery is influenced by relationships external to this dyad. The occupational therapy practitioner may be placed in situations where it is difficult to protect and maintain the provider–patient relationship. In some circumstances, occupational therapy practitioners will be pressured to provide services that conflict with their personal or professional code of ethics, in order to support decisions made by individual physicians or made within the organization.

> Ethics focuses on choices in at least three domains: [1] choices about what we ought to do or not do, that is, the actions we might undertake; [2] choices about the kind of persons we ought to be or not be, that is, the kind of character we ought to have or develop; [3] and, more abstractly, choices about the conditions of doing and being, which are perhaps best illustrated in the context by the organizational cultures, structures, or policies that influence but do not determine what we do and who we are as persons. (p. 346)[6]

It is this influence of the organization that often leaves practitioners in the difficult position of attempting to respect the patient's rights while also attempting to support the organization's policies, procedures, and financial viability. Organizations are dominant moral actors in today's health arena, not only influencing policies within the hospital but also creating role expectations for health care providers that influence how they perform professionally within the organization.[7]

In years past, relationships in health care were arguably less complicated. Practitioners' ethical obligations were primarily limited to the patient and acting within that patient's best interest.[8] Practitioners' roles and accountabilities were outlined by oaths and professional codes of ethics. These codes are designed to address conflict specific to the patient–provider relationship but are lacking when used to address more complex ethical dilemmas that extend beyond the bedside and encompass organizational ethics issues. With growing changes in health care, and with the shift in focus from health care providers to corporate institutions, "greater attention must be paid to the moral content or moral character of the actions of health care organizations" (p. 69).[9] In particular, one must be aware of the impact an organization's moral character has on its practitioners. Although organizations must consider the relationships between "institutions and patients, patient populations, professionals, and other institutions" (p. 133),[10] the organization cannot undermine the integrity of the provider–patient relationship.

> [Organizations must take into] account interaction among individuals, health care workers, institutions, integrated delivery systems, and the entire health care environ-

ment. Any account of organizational ethics that focuses only on one level of the environment, such as the team or the institution, without examining and accounting for interaction among the levels of the environment, is inadequate. (p. 8)[11]

This goal of organizations to meet individual as well as comprehensive societal needs may at times seem to conflict with the provider's responsibility to the patient. When this conflict occurs, the provider is often presented with a dilemma to support either the organization's goals or the patient's rights. An ethical dilemma will be encountered when a morally correct course of action requires the therapist to support both the organization and the patient, but the supporting actions are mutually exclusive, meaning that the therapist cannot do both.[12]

Although the organization is responsible for responding to all of these levels of the environment, the occupational therapist working within the organization cannot be accountable to all of these groups without risking an erosion of the provider–patient relationship. This dynamic appears to be a conflict between organizational ethics and those of the practitioner. A health care organization must be accountable to multiple parties and the community, but this extended accountability should not detract from the provider's relationship with the patient. The organization, therefore, cannot ethically require a practitioner to engage in decision making or actions that will undermine the provider–patient relationship. "Any social, organizational, administrative, and financial arrangement with practice settings that contribute to distancing [providers] from their patients will result in tendencies to dehumanize them and will ultimately diminish the [provider's] competence to heal" (p. 81).[13] Therefore, although organizational and clinical ethics may seem to conflict initially, the care of the individual patient is the common tenet in

both areas of ethics, and ultimately the destruction of the provider–patient relationship detracts from delivery of care and patients' outcomes.[14] Unfortunately, not all health care organizations recognize the role the institution plays in sustaining the provider–patient relationship, and inevitably the provider encounters situations in which he or she must choose to act as directed by organizational administration or on behalf of the patient.

The conflict that arises from the health care professional's complex matrix of accountability often erodes trust between patients and providers.[15] Yet "the need for trust and the reliance on trust are especially important in health care because of the patient's acute vulnerability to suffering, lost opportunity, and lack of power" (p. 26).[7] Within the provider–patient relationship, the occupational therapy practitioner has more power, and how he or she wishes to use that power can quickly enhance or degrade the trust of a patient. One potential abuse of that power presents itself in the form of paternalism. Practitioners who independently define the patient's best interest and provide care based on their assumptions of best interest—without the consent, or worse, against the will of the patient—are acting in a paternalistic manner. Health care in the United States has shifted away from a paternalistic manner that affords the professional the power to make decisions in the health care environment and has moved toward a focus on patient autonomy.[16]

CASE SCENARIO AND DISCUSSION

An occupational therapist has received a referral to see a patient on the cardiac floor of a community hospital. When the therapist enters the room to complete her evaluation, the patient refuses occupational therapy services. The occupational therapist continues to see the patient over the course of the next week. On all occasions, the patient refuses to participate in therapy. During each visit the therapist explains to the patient and her family the importance of occupational therapy services, why her physician has referred her for treatment, and the risks of minimal activity after cardiac surgery. In addition, the occupational therapist speaks with the nursing staff to determine whether the patient has been seen by a psychiatrist to rule out depression or any other emotional state that may be affecting participation. The nurse refers the occupational therapist to a report compiled by the psychiatrist, indicating that the patient is slightly depressed but has full decision-making capacity and is therefore able to make health-care-related decisions. The occupational therapist decides to contact the physician to tell her she will be discharging the patient from services, due to the patient's informed refusal of treatment. During this discussion, the physician states that the therapist will need to continue treatment and that she should "not allow the patient to refuse services" and then abruptly hangs up the phone.

When the occupational therapist arrives to work the next day, she has another written physician referral on her desk stating "evaluate and treat for occupational therapy services; do not allow the patient to refuse." This new order places the occupational therapist in a difficult position, and she does not know how to proceed. She wants to respect the patient's autonomy, and yet she feels a responsibility to maintain a positive working relationship with the physician. Her confusion is complicated by her obligation to the health care organization for which she is working, fearing that aggravating the physician may result in a decrease in referrals for patients who may benefit from occupational therapy services and subsequent decreased revenue for the department.

Occupational therapists often work under the direction of a physician and within a health care organization. Organizations drive care because they have a vested interest in services provided and in ensuring continued physician referrals that support the financial solvency of the institution. This situation is especially true in communities where the physicians are not employed by the facility itself but also have privileges at competing hospitals within the same town. Of the three relationships—patient, physician, and organization—the patient relationship is often seen as the one to whom the occupational therapy practitioner is most responsible. In contrast, there are sometimes serious questions about what accountability occupational therapy practitioners have to the organizations that employ them. Do employees have a fiduciary responsibility to support the organizations that employ them as well as other health care professionals within the organization, even if that relationship conflicts with their patient relationship?

Occupational therapy practitioners may perceive that the organization would support a team environment, which favors the physician, because there may be a negative financial fallout if physician relationships are strained. However, it is in the organization's best interest to support provider–patient relationships that build trust, because these relationships make for better medical care.[7] Ethical health care organizations should not require a practitioner to compromise standards in the delivery of care. Organizations that place providers in situations that jeopardize the patient–provider relationship are also jeopardizing the organization's relationship with the customer. In the case scenario above, if the occupational therapist were to violate the trust of the patient by forcing her to participate in therapy against her will, the therapist would inadvertently make the institution less trustworthy in her eyes. Because of this need to support individual provider–patient relationships, most organizations have policies and resources in place that can support the provider in making ethical choices.

In the case scenario, the occupational therapist should utilize her supervisor to help her in communicating with the physician. If a supervisor is not available, there is generally a medical director or administrator who can facilitate communication with the physician. Often, organizational managers can communicate with physicians in a way that minimizes power imbalances. In addition, a supervisor or administrator should be familiar with and able to locate patients' rights policies that objectively identify patient and provider roles and can help the employee in identification of other organizational resources. The hospital ethics committee or consultation services may help resolve conflict between health care providers within the confines of the organization. In addition, organizational structures, such as incident reporting systems or safety hotlines, can be used to influence the behavior of providers in order to protect patient rights while keeping the reporting source anonymous so as to avoid strained relationships among team members. The occupational therapist walks a difficult line in balancing these team relationships with his or her responsibilities to the patient.

Helping patients to exercise their autonomy effectively in today's health care environment has become more and more complicated. However, Principle 3 of the *Occupational Therapy Code of Ethics (2005)* requires occupational therapy personnel to respect their patients and assure that their rights are being upheld.[17] Due to the complex matrix of accountability faced when practicing in health care organizations, practitioners often find themselves not only in a relationship with the patient but also in collegial relationships with other health care providers and the institution. Although the provider–patient relationship is typically the theoretical focus of conflict resolution, other relationships also must be maintained by the provider to ensure safe, effective, and ethical delivery of health care services. This concept of fidelity is also present in the Code under Principle 7: "Occupational therapy personnel shall treat colleagues and other professionals with re-

spect, fairness, discretion, and integrity" (p. 641).[17] However, an occupational therapist need not compromise a relationship with a patient in order to maintain other relationships. In fact, respecting the patient's right to refuse—thus maintaining the integrity of the provider–patient relationship—is ethically mandated in order to ensure ethical practices that support the moral structure of the health care environment.

In the case scenario above, the occupational therapist does have options for justifying a course of action. The therapist should pursue opportunities for communication with the physician; however, if the physician continues to rebuff the therapist's attempts at dialogue, the therapist should pursue another avenue for communication, involving the administration. Depending on the organization's understanding of its role in fostering relationships between providers and patients, the therapist may or may not encounter a supportive advocate for resolution of the ethical dilemma. If this option does not resolve the conflict, the therapist may ultimately decide to transfer care of the patient to another therapist; refuse to treat the patient, which may result in termination of employment; or continue treating the patient. Continuing to treat a patient who is refusing services and has decision-making capacity would not be ethically justifiable. This option could lead to many adverse outcomes, including a decline in trust between patient and provider; the potential harm—both psychological and physical—imposed on the patient; the lack of benefit incurred when treating a patient against his or her will (*Note:* This is also a legal issue because it can be construed as assault and battery); and, ultimately, a decline in trust between health care providers, organizations, and the individuals served.

Although the previously mentioned options are viable, it is important to actively advocate for the patient, but in a respectful manner that is least damaging to relationships between the physician and therapist. Although patient trust is essential, one must also work to maintain trust between colleagues and team members.

CONCLUSION

Research demonstrates over and over again that patients most highly value having a strong relationship with their health care provider.[8] The humanistic characteristics of the occupational therapy profession, in which emphasis is placed on the patient's view of meaningful life, morally require respect for the patient's wishes, even when these wishes seem to conflict with clinical reasoning and his or her own benefit. It is not that autonomy-based obligations trump beneficence-based obligations; however, when there is no compelling beneficence-based obligation to consider, as demonstrated in the case study, a health care provider has no morally based option but to adhere to the patient's informed choice.[18] Although other health care professionals are often apprehensive about sharing decision-making powers with the patient,[19] occupational therapists rely on patient input to help identify the direction intervention should take. The American Occupational Therapy Association acknowledges that "ethical decision making is a process that includes awareness regarding how the outcome will impact occupational therapy clients in all spheres" (p. 5) and encourages the implementation of core occupational therapy tenets that require the active participation of the client.[20] Occupational therapy is a traditionally holistic profession with humanistic roots implying a "theoretical and practical commitment to treating patients in a caring, respectful, and holistic manner that appreciates their dignity, individual needs, and meaningful life circumstances" (p. 11).[21]

The occupational therapy practitioner has an ethical responsibility to maintain the integrity of the provider–patient relationship in the face of organizational pressures. Whether this relationship is maintained through respect for autonomy or advocating for patient rights and needs with regard to care, occupational therapists must be aware of their responsibilities to the well-being of the patient. Within the AOTA *Occupational Therapy Code of Ethics* (2005), the first principle calls on practitioners to act with beneficence. Although therapists cannot disregard or neglect their relationships within an organization, they must remember that undermining the patient's trust promotes neither the integrity of the organization nor the integrity of the patient–provider relationship.

REFERENCES

1. American Society for Bioethics and Humanities. (1998). *Core competencies for health care ethics consultation: The report of the American Society for Bioethics and Humanities.* Glenview, IL: Author.
2. Spencer, E. M., & Mills, A. E. (1999). Ethics in health care organizations. *HEC Forum, 11*(4), 323–332.
3. Veterans Health Administration, National Center for Ethics. (2002, February). *Developing an integrated ethics program.* Presentation for Veterans Health Administration on Ethics Training, Detroit, MI.
4. Emanuel, L. (2000). Ethics and the structures of healthcare. *Cambridge Quarterly of Healthcare Ethics, 9*, 151–168.
5. Emanuel, E. J., & Emanuel, L. L. (1996). What is accountability in health care? *Annals of Internal Medicine, 124*, 229–239.
6. Heller, J. C. (1999). Framing healthcare compliance in ethical terms: A taxonomy of moral choices. *HEC Forum, 11*, 345–357.
7. Goold, S. (2001). Trust and the ethics of health care institutions. *Hastings Center Report, 31*(6), 26–33.
8. Gervais, K. G. (1998). Changing society, changing medicine, changing bioethics. In R. DeVries & J. Subedi (Eds.), *Bioethics and society: Constructing the ethical enterprise* (pp. 216–232). Upper Saddle River, NJ: Prentice Hall.
9. Goold, S., Kamil, L., Cohan, N., & Sefansky, S. (2000). Outline of a process for organiza-

tional ethics consultation. *HEC Forum, 12,* 69–77.

10. Khushf, G. (1998). The scope of organizational ethics. *HEC Forum, 10,* 127–135.

11. Boyle, P. J., DuBose, E. R., Ellingson, S. J., Guinn, D. E., & McCurdy, D. B. (2001). *Organizational ethics in health care: Principles, cases, and practical solutions.* San Francisco: Jossey-Bass.

12. Purtilo, R. (2005). *Ethical dimensions in the health professions* (4th ed.). Philadelphia: Elsevier/Saunders.

13. Scott, R., Aiken, L., Mechanic, D., & Moravcsik, J. (1995). Organizational aspects of caring. *Milbank Quarterly, 73*(1), 77–95.

14. Mills, A. E., Spencer, E. M., Rorty, M. V., & Werhane, P. H. (2000). *Organization ethics in health care.* New York: Oxford University Press.

15. Haskell, C. M. (2000, September/October). Healthcare ethics and integrity. *Veterans Health Systems Journal,* pp. 53–60.

16. Quill, T. E., & Brody, H. (1996). Physician recommendations and patient autonomy. *Annals of Internal Medicine, 125,* 763–769.

17. American Occupational Therapy Association. (2005). Occupational therapy code of ethics (2005). *American Journal of Occupational Therapy, 59,* 639–642.

18. Chervenak, F. A., & McCullough, L. B. (1991). Justified limits on refusing intervention. *Hastings Center Report, 21*(2), 7–12.

19. Henderson, S. (2003). Power imbalance between nurses and patients: A potential inhibitor of partnership in care. *Journal of Clinical Nursing, 12,* 501–508.

20. Slater, D. Y. (Ed.). (2006). *Reference guide to the occupational therapy code of ethics.* Bethesda, MD: AOTA Press.

21. Lohman, H., & Brown, K. (1997). Ethical issues related to managed care: An in-depth discussion of an occupational therapy case study. *Occupational Therapy in Healthcare, 10,* 1–12.

Author

Lea Cheyney Brandt, OTD, OTR/L, is manager of occupational therapy and speech pathology at Boone Hospital Center in Columbia, MO.

She is also the member at large on AOTA's Ethics Commission, 2002–2008, 2008–2011.

EDUCATIONAL TOOLS

CHAPTER 19

Introductory Statement

The Ethics Commission (EC) has two roles: (1) enforcement and (2) education. This section of the *Reference Guide to the Occupational Therapy Ethics Standards* provides tools for members to understand and apply ethics in their professional and volunteer work. Professional ethics applies to all *licensed (or otherwise regulated) occupational therapists* and *occupational therapy assistants* inclusive of those who work in practice, education, or research as well as to students and individuals who work in other paid or volunteer positions related to occupational therapy.

The chapters in this section provide foundational information about the role of ethics in our profession and additional resources to assist with practical application of the *Ethics Standards* in a variety of situations. One overarching theme, both explicitly and implicitly, is the importance of conduct, which positively reflects the behavior and values of the occupational therapy profession. This is critically important not only among colleagues within a work setting but also in relationships and collaborative activities with outside organizations and the public.

New content in this edition of the *Guide* includes the article "Occupational Therapy Values and Beliefs: The Formative Years: 1904–1929," which serves as an underpinning for the ethics documents of the Association. In addition, a new article on "The Ethics of Productivity" delineates current challenges in this important clinical topic and strategies to address them from an ethical and practical perspective. This and other articles discuss the personal obligations practitioners have to maintain ethical standards in the face of increasing pressure to maximize productivity and reimbursement, often at the expense of appropriate clinical judgment and the client's best interests. An article by John Morris that outlines a process and framework for analysis and decision-making around ethical issues is included for use when confronted with potential ethical dilemmas. The difference between *illegal and unethical*, a frequent source of confusion, is addressed directly in a brief article and more extensively in the context of working within a legal scope of practice in the *OT Practice* article on "Legal and Ethical Practice: A Professional Responsibility" Additional content in this section focuses on areas in which member queries have shown greater need for ethical awareness and assistance with resolving issues.

CHAPTER 20

The Function of Professional Ethics

A profession organizes its ethics code based on the activities of its members. Generally, professionals are expected to uphold a higher degree of ethical behavior than the general public. In turn, the public grants rights or privileges to professionals beyond those normally granted to all citizens. This arrangement is designed to protect the public and the recipients of professional services.

The American Occupational Therapy Association (AOTA) has adopted eight ethical concepts, which have been organized into seven statements. These statements are the *Occupational Therapy Code of Ethics (2005;* AOTA, 2005b). Four of the concepts are considered moral principles: *beneficence, autonomy, nonmaleficence,* and *procedural justice* (Principles 1, 2, 3, and 5). Four concepts are viewed as rules that service providers must follow: *confidentiality, duty, veracity,* and *fidelity* (Principles 3, 4, 6, and 7). These concepts are further illustrated in the following summary of the seven ethical statements in the Code:

- *Beneficence* concerns the well-being of the recipients of services, which occupational therapists and occupational therapy assistants are expected to provide for and maintain as a moral principle (Principle 1).
- *Professional competence* is a duty that all occupational therapy personnel must maintain to fulfill the moral principles of nonmaleficence (Principles 2 and 4).

- *Autonomy* and *confidentiality* are rights of recipients that occupational therapy professionals are expected to respect (Principle 3).
- *Procedural justice* involves complying with all laws, rules, and regulations applicable to occupational therapy services and abiding by association policies guiding the profession (Principle 5).
- *Veracity* requires that occupational therapy personnel provide accurate information about occupational therapy services to recipients of services, including family members and reimbursement entities (Principle 6).
- *Fidelity* and *veracity* are expressed through fairness, discretion, and integrity expected of occupational therapy personnel toward students, colleagues, peers, and other professionals (Principle 7).

Professionals usually develop their concepts of moral ideals and accepted rules of ethical behavior by preparing a written code of ethics through a professional association or organization. Three types of ethical codes can be adopted: aspirational, educational, or regulatory. *Aspirational codes* encourage competent and moral behavior but do not provide guidelines for ethical conduct or sanctions for failure to follow the intent of the code. *Educational codes* state what constitutes ethical behavior and may provide case examples as illustrations but still do not provide sanctions for failure to follow the code. *Regulatory codes,* on the other hand, spell out the expected behavior, state guidelines of expected conduct, and give specific descriptions of sanctions for failures to follow the code.

AOTA's Ethics Commission (EC) has described the *Occupational Therapy Code of Ethics* as aspirational. The Code is complemented by the *Enforcement Procedures to the Occupational Therapy Code of Ethics* (AOTA, 2007), which offers members and the public the regulatory component to support the Code. The *Enforcement Procedures* help ensure compliance with the ethics standards established in the Code, the *Core Values* (AOTA, 1993), and the *Guidelines to the Code of Ethics* (AOTA, 2006).

The process used by the EC is advantageous in that collective thinking is used to develop and update the Code, and peers are encouraged to monitor the behavior of their colleagues. The disadvantage is that the Code can be applied only to members of the professional association. Occupational therapists and occupational therapy assistants who are not AOTA members are not subject to the Code or to the behaviors that the Code embraces. However, the public's access to the Code and its *Enforcement Procedures* may result in their expectation that the ethical standards approved by the professional association are adhered to by all members of the profession. Many of the state regulatory boards (SRBs) over time have adopted the Code in whole or part; subsequently, many of the ethical concepts articulated by AOTA have been incorporated to varying degrees throughout occupational therapy.

Although the AOTA *Enforcement Procedures* are regulatory, primary reliance on regulatory action to enforce the Code does not meet the intent and spirit of the Code. Ethical behavior is a learned process that is best enforced through daily practice. Thus, voluntary compliance is both encouraged and endorsed. That is, members are encouraged to educate themselves and help other members conform to the behavior stated in the Code before any sanctions are considered or applied. This approach of attracting and supporting desired behavior is in contrast

with standards that require certain behavior and have specific sanctions for noncompliance, even for a first offense.

Finally, ethics are a dynamic process. As society changes, so do the ideas about ethical behavior. AOTA has recognized the changing concepts of ethics by adopting a (minimum) 5-year review cycle to consider revisions of the Code. The process begins with members of the EC conducting an internal review of the Code and then drafting the revisions for review by the AOTA membership. Once the review process is complete, the revised *Occupational Therapy Code of Ethics* is sent to the Representative Assembly for action. The final copy is published in the *American Journal of Occupational Therapy* as part of the Association's official documents. The Code also is posted on AOTA's Web site (www.aota.org).

In the past, a variety of complaints have been received by the chairperson of the EC concerning alleged violations of the *Occupational Therapy Code of Ethics*. An analysis of these complaints suggests that members may not understand clearly the criteria on which professional ethics can be applied. The problems can be organized into 10 major areas:

1. The *Occupational Therapy Code of Ethics (2005)* "applies to persons who are or were members of the AOTA at the time of the conduct in question. Later non-renewal or relinquishment of membership does not affect AOTA jurisdiction. The Code that is applicable to any complaint shall be the Code in force at the time the alleged act or omission occurred, unless the date of the alleged act or omission cannot be precisely determined. In that case, the conduct shall be judged by the Code in force on the date of the complaint" (AOTA, 2007, p. 679). If the alleged violator was not a member at the time of the incident, other language related to professional conduct may apply, such as that stated in a state licensure law.

2. The Code includes those behaviors that occupational therapists and occupational ther-

apy assistants have agreed are important. Other professions and professionals may have different ideas about ethical and unethical behavior. To determine the ethics that apply to another professional, occupational therapists must read the code of ethics adopted by that professional's organization or licensure law. Most, if not all, professional codes of ethics are publicly available on that professional organization's Web site. If an occupational therapist feels that a member of another profession has violated an ethics principle, he or she must review that profession's code of ethics for instructions or procedures to follow in reporting alleged violations.

3. When AOTA members or the public suspect that an occupational therapist or occupational therapy assistant has violated a regulation governing occupational therapy practice, an established code of conduct, or the *Occupational Therapy Code of Ethics (2005)*, the alleged violations should be reported to the appropriate body. It is permissible to report alleged violations to more than one agency, organization, or association (e.g., SRB and AOTA, the National Certification Board for Occupational Therapy [NBCOT] and AOTA). Occupational therapy professionals can refer to "Overview of the Ethical Jurisdictions of AOTA, NBCOT, and SRBs" (see Chapter 8 in this book) for additional information. Note that alleged breaches of ethical conduct by AOTA members (occupational therapists, occupational therapy assistants, occupational therapy students) should be reported to the EC.

4. The Code of Ethics is a set of desired behaviors. A code does not take the place of disciplinary procedures that may be applied for failure to perform according to one's position description or employee policy manual. Managers should take action to ensure that an occupational therapy practitioner performs duties stated in the position description or apply the remedy as stated in the manual of the employing organization. In-

stitutional rules and guidelines articulated in student handbooks should be considered for those in academia (e.g., students, faculty).

5. The AOTA code is an aspirational guide to appropriate behavior but cannot substitute for a position description or contract. Occupational therapists need to know what their position description or contract states. Questions about job duties should be addressed to the manager in charge of occupational therapy. If the manager is unable or unwilling to address the problem or questions, the occupational therapist should follow the procedures outlined in the employee policy manual for addressing grievances. Advice of a lawyer specializing in business and contracts may be useful. Examples of problems related to job duties are productivity requirements, alleged inappropriate referrals, lack of equipment or supplies, disagreements about the use of various therapy media or modalities, disputes about the number of therapy sessions to be provided, and termination procedures to end therapy. In some cases, fraud also may be involved (see No. 7 below).

6. If an AOTA member is convicted of an offense or violation of federal, state, or local laws and regulations, the EC will review the charges. The member will be afforded due process. Only after careful review of the details of the charge will the EC determine if disciplinary action is indicated and the nature and extent of such action.

7. The EC and AOTA officials cannot resolve disputes about billing procedures, record keeping, and documentation. False billing for services not rendered, double billing, or overcharging are examples of fraud. Deviations from accepted record keeping and documentation procedures done for financial gain also are examples of fraud. All states have mechanisms to oversee and review reported cases of suspected fraud through the state attorney general or similar state official

or office. In addition, questionable business practices can be reported to the Better Business Bureau. Accrediting agencies for health and educational organizations may be notified, as fraud convictions can adversely affect accreditation. Insurance companies are usually quick to respond to reported cases of alleged fraud, because fraud usually increases the cost of doing business, may increase premiums, or will divert funds that could be used to provide additional services. If federal funds are involved, fraud is a misappropriation of tax money, which is a federal offense. If an AOTA member is cited or convicted of fraudulent behavior, the EC and the Association may subject that member to disciplinary action.

8. The EC or AOTA officials cannot resolve complaints about unsafe working conditions, such as electrical equipment improperly maintained, exposure to hazardous chemicals or waste, unsanitary conditions, improper storage of dangerous substances, structural weaknesses, or other alleged safety violations. Local building inspectors or fire departments often are charged with making local inspections. The federal Occupational Safety and Health Administration maintains offices in all states. If a member is convicted of or fined for violations related to health and safety, that person may be subjected to disciplinary action by the EC and the Association.

9. The EC and AOTA officials cannot intervene on behalf of a student who alleges unfair grading procedures, lack of opportunity to take specific courses or assignment to fieldwork placement, or problems with other educational activity. Such complaints must be handled through college or university grievance procedures or civil courts. In some cases, notification of educational accrediting agencies may be in order. However, if an educational institution determines that an AOTA member has engaged in unfair or discriminatory practices against a student or colleague, that

member may be subjected to disciplinary action by the EC and the Association.

10. The ultimate sanction that AOTA can apply to a member is permanent revocation of membership. AOTA cannot remove an occupational therapist's right to practice occupational therapy. Removal of occupational therapy certification is the responsibility of NBCOT. Only a court of law or governmental agency (state or federal) with legal authority (e.g., state licensure board) can take away or suspend a person's ability to practice occupational therapy. AOTA may, however, be called to testify about actions that it has taken against the member. If the member loses certification as an occupational therapy practitioner or is convicted of a crime by a legal authority related to services provided by that person in the capacity of an occupational therapist or occupational therapy assistant, disciplinary action will be initiated by the EC and the Association.

SUMMARY

A professional code of ethics contains statements of desired behaviors that members are encouraged to follow. Peers should support the efforts of members to adopt the desired behavior. When a code of ethics is thought to have been violated, enforcement of ethics should begin as an educational process between the individuals directly involved. If the resolution cannot occur on the "local" level, a complaint should be filed with the most appropriate agency or body, depending on the level of infraction and desired outcome (refer to Chapter 7 in this guide). The AOTA Ethics Office also can provide guidance with this decision. If violations of the *Occupational Therapy Code of Ethics* are alleged that may involve an AOTA member, these allegations should be reported to the EC, even if complaints have been filed with other regulatory authorities. The ultimate sanction that the AOTA can supply is revocation of membership or a permanent denial of membership, which should be applied only on sound evidence of failure or unwillingness to comply with appropriate conduct.

REFERENCES

American Occupational Therapy Association. (1993). Core values and attitudes of occupational therapy practice. *American Journal of Occupational Therapy, 47,* 1085–1086.

American Occupational Therapy Association. (2005). Occupational therapy code of ethics (2005). *American Journal of Occupational Therapy, 59,* 639–642.

American Occupational Therapy Association. (2006). Guidelines to the occupational therapy code of ethics. *American Journal of Occupational Therapy, 60,* 652–658.

American Occupational Therapy Association. (2007). Enforcement procedures for the occupational therapy code of ethics. *American Journal of Occupational Therapy, 61,* 679–685.

Author

Kathlyn L. Reed, PhD, OTR, FAOTA, MLIS, AHIP
At the request of the Standards and Ethics Commission, January 1997

Janie B. Scott, MA, OT/L, FAOTA
Revised December 2005

Deborah Yarett Slater, MS, OT/L, FAOTA
Revised February 2008

CHAPTER 21

Scope of the AOTA Ethics Commission

The Ethics Commission (EC) is a body of the Representative Assembly (RA) of the American Occupational Therapy Association (AOTA). The purpose of the EC is to serve the Association members and public through the identification, development, review, interpretation, and education of the occupational therapy "Ethics Standards" and to provide the process whereby the Ethics Standards of the Association are enforced (AOTA Bylaws, Section 7—Bodies of the Assembly; AOTA, 2007a). It serves to promote and maintain professional conduct in all occupational therapy roles, and support the delivery of high-quality services, and contributions to society's health and well-being.

The AOTA *Occupational Therapy Code of Ethics* (2005), (AOTA, 2005) is a public statement of the values and principles that guide the behavior of members of the profession and to which they should aspire. The *Occupational Therapy Code of Ethics (2005)*, along with the *Core Values and Attitudes* (AOTA, 1993) and the *Guidelines to the Code of Ethics* (AOTA, 2006), collectively are known as the "Ethics Standards." The EC is responsible for the development and oversight of the Ethics Standards, which apply to occupational therapy personnel at all levels. They apply to professional roles such as those of practitioner, educator, fieldwork educator or coordinator, clinical supervisor, manager, administrator, consultant, faculty, program director, researcher/scholar, private practice owner, entrepreneur, student, and other professional roles such as elected and appointed volunteer roles within AOTA. To ensure adherence by members of the AOTA, procedures have been developed for the investigation and adjudication of alleged violations. The *Enforcement Procedures for the Occupational Therapy Code of Ethics* (AOTA, 2007b) define the scope of disciplinary action for the Code. These procedures are intended to enable AOTA to implement its responsibilities in a fair and equitable manner to best serve its members and society.

ROLE OF THE EC

The EC has two roles: education and enforcement. The EC's jurisdiction for enforcement is limited to individuals who are members of the Association, including occupational therapists, occupational therapy assistants, associates, and students.

FUNCTIONS OF THE EC

The functions of the EC include the following:

- Shall develop and revise principles of the AOTA *Occupational Therapy Code of Ethics* and submit such revisions to the RA for approval
- Shall provide a process whereby existing and proposed documents can be reviewed and monitored from an ethical perspective for consistency with the Ethics Standards
- Shall inform and educate Association members and consumers regarding the Ethics Standards
- Shall establish and maintain procedures for considering and reviewing allegations of non-conformance with Association standards and ethics
- Shall serve as a resource for any Association body requiring interpretation of the Ethics Standards

- Shall issue Advisory Opinions on the interpretation and application of the AOTA Ethics Standards) as well as ethical trends
- Shall provide members and the Association bodies with descriptions of the roles of regulatory or associated agencies or bodies (e.g., National Board for Certification in Occupational Therapy [NBCOT], state regulatory boards [SRBS]) that oversee the delivery of occupational therapy services and educational programs (AOTA 2007c).

MEMBERS OF THE EC

The EC chairperson, elected by the AOTA membership, serves 1 year in the role of chairperson-elect and 3 years as chairperson. The chairperson appoints AOTA member volunteers and public members to serve on the EC. The Commission is made up of a representative from occupational therapy assistants, education, practice, a member at large, and two public members (a total of 7 members, including the chairperson). The chairperson and appointed volunteers serve 3-year terms. The chairperson serves one term, but EC members have the possibility of serving a maximum of two consecutive terms.

AOTA's National Office staff liaison and legal counsel support the work of the EC. Specifically, the liaison provides administrative and procedural support, while the legal counsel provides legal expertise as needed.

OVERVIEW OF THE EC

- One of the primary roles of the EC is ethics education. Accordingly, the EC periodically issues Advisory Opinions; provides an "Everyday Ethics" Workshop at the AOTA Annual Conference & Expo; and develops and provides other educational materials in response to member needs, inquiries, and ethical trends.

- The EC reviews and investigates ethics complaints filed against AOTA members. Disciplinary actions that may be recommended by the EC include reprimand, censure, probation, suspension, and revocation. For spe-

cific information about the disciplinary process used by the EC, see the *Enforcement Procedures for the Occupational Therapy Code of Ethics* in this *Reference Guide*.

- The EC meets face-to-face at least once a year at the Association's headquarters with additional meetings by conference call. Members of the AOTA may attend these meetings; however, executive sessions (i.e., for case discussions) are closed to the public.

- Meeting minutes, with the exception of those for executive sessions, are distributed to the AOTA Board of Directors and RA leadership.

- Along with AOTA EC, other agencies that have oversight over the occupational therapy profession include SRBs and NBCOT. Each has a defined jurisdiction and areas of specific concern. More information on the ethical jurisdictions of AOTA, NBCOT, and SRBs is available in this *Reference Guide*.

REFERENCES

American Occupational Therapy Association. (1993). Core values and attitudes of occupational therapy practice. *American Journal of Occupational Therapy, 47*, 1085–1086.

American Occupational Therapy Association. (2005). Occupational therapy code of ethics. *American Journal of Occupational Therapy, 59*, 639–642.

American Occupational Therapy Association. (2006). Guidelines to the occupational therapy code of ethics. *American Journal of Occupational Therapy, 60*, 652–658.

American Occupational Therapy Association. (2007a). The official bylaws of the American Occupational Therapy Association, Inc. *American Journal of Occupational Therapy, 61*, 640–651.

American Occupational Therapy Association. (2007b). Enforcement procedures for the occupational therapy code of ethics. *American Journal of Occupational Therapy, 61*, 679–685.

American Occupational Therapy Association. (2007c). *Ethics Commission standard operating procedures.* [Available from AOTA, 4720 Montgomery Lane, Bethesda, MD 20814]

CHAPTER 22

Occupational Therapy Values and Beliefs: The Formative Years: 1904–1929

The social values of a professional group are its basic and fundamental beliefs, the unquestioned premises upon which its very existence rests. Foremost among these values is the essential worth of the service which the professional group extends to the community" (p. 36).[1] "One of the major differences between the professions and other occupations is that the professions are assumed to be concerned with the fulfillment of certain intrinsic values…" (p. 307).[2]

Occupational therapy values and beliefs were shaped by the times and events of the 19th and early 20th centuries, during which the profession was created. The Progressive Era (1890–1914) was at its height of influence as occupational therapy was being formally organized. The United States was being transformed by political, social, and economic reform.[3] There was a "revolution in manners and morals" (p. xvi)[4] that "was part of a broader shift from a Protestant ethos of salvation through self-denial to a therapeutic ideal of self-fulfillment in this world through exuberant health and intense experience" (p. xiv).[4]

As Elizabeth Greene Upham said in 1918,

> Occupational therapy is neither a new movement nor one which has suddenly come into prominence through a spectacular publicity campaign. It is, rather, a movement which has gradually developed by justifying itself over a long period of years. It was initiated by the doctors in insane hospitals who first dared the experiment of putting their patients to work; and by those other doctors who were groping after something which might give to their neurasthenic patients a healthy interest and a new grip on life. The healing value of occupation is so well established that occupational therapy is no longer confined to the insane or neurasthenic but has been found equally beneficent in tuberculosis, in long orthopedic treatments, and in extensive convalescences in a general hospital. (pp. 48–49)[5]

As the profession approaches its 100th year of formal organization, a review of the values and beliefs that formed the basic premises is in order.

IN THE BEGINNING

The development of occupational therapy as a profession is unique. According to Maxwell and Maxwell, "The development appeared to reflect not so much the emergence of a new technology or scientific advance, such as the development of the occupational role of X-ray technician following the invention of X-rays by Roentgen, but rather the organizing of existing knowledge into a new occupational role…. Since the knowledge base was not specific, occupational therapists faced from the beginning the problem of identity" (p. 339).[6] In other words, the development of occupational therapy did not fit the existing pattern recognized in sociology for a new profession—that is, as a consequence of a new technology or an advance in scientific knowledge. Instead, occupational therapy was created by selecting among knowledge already established from a variety of sources, including educators, artists, craftsmen and craftswomen, religious and spiritual leaders, engineers, nurses, physicians, social services workers, women's social groups, civic leaders and reformers, attendants, aides, and the patients or clients themselves. Such a variety of sources provided many values and beliefs, and even the early leaders were aware of the need to organize them into a set of principles. The first set of principles proposed to the professional organization was published in 1919 in the January issue of the *Maryland Psychiatric Quarterly*[7] and in a book by William R. Dunton, Jr., MD.[8] They were reprinted in 1923,[9] 1925,[10] and 1940[11] (see Figure 22.1). The last two printings appeared in *Occupational Therapy and Rehabilitation,* the organization's official journal before the *American Journal of Occupational Therapy.* The principles were written by Eleanor Clarke Slagle, William L. Russell, and Norman L. Burnette (from Canada). Dunton had already published a shorter set of principles in 1918[12] (see Figure 22.2). After the early efforts, the idea of documenting the values and beliefs of occupational therapy was not revisited for many years.

WHY LOOK BACK?

The current project grew from a concern expressed by members of the Representative Assembly Coordinating Committee (RACC) in 2003 that the historical and philosophical roots of occupational therapy were not known to all current members of the profession. Responding to this concern, the 2003 Representative Assembly (RA) adopted a motion to form an ad hoc committee to identify those roots. The committee consists of myself as the chair, along with Suzanne Peloquin, PhD, OTR, FAOTA, and Christine Peters, MA, OTR.

The project began by identifying a time frame, 1904 to 1929, that represents a significant period of formation for the profession, based on an analysis of historical patterns in occupational therapy. We identified several subject areas that emerged during that time and that had an influence on the development or application of occupational therapy. The subject areas relate to social, educational, and philosophical movements; to the national government; to the application of therapeutic techniques; and to important contributions by particular individuals. By 1930 only Slagle, Kidner, and Dunton remained active; the other founders and early leaders had died or were inactive. In addition, no new textbooks were published from 1928 until the 1940s.

To assemble information from the subject areas, we created an outline for data collection that included a description of the subject area; dates when the subject began and ended; names and places associated with the subject; the purpose(s) of the subject; where, when, and how the subject interacted with occupational therapy; names and places associated with occupational therapy interaction; and the beliefs and values relevant to occupational therapy based on its involvement with the subject area. As might be expected, some outlines were more complete than others because of the availability of more source material. Cross-references to other subjects were listed because many were interrelated. All references identified from the occupational therapy literature about each subject were listed. However, a separate literature search on each subject area was not done, such as searching several data sources for all articles and books on the Arts and Crafts movement or all articles published about humanism.

Of the 42 subject areas identified, developmental psychology, play as a skill for children, and progressive education did not produce useful literature or references. The remaining 39 subject areas are listed in Figure 22.3.

Reference sources included textbooks on the treatment of war injuries (during World War I), vocational reeducation and training, and occupational therapy literature published from 1904 to

FIGURE 22.1. Basic Principles of Occupational Therapy, 1919

To the members of the National Society for the Promotion of Occupational Therapy: Your Committee on Principles has agreed upon the following as representing the basic principles of occupational therapy:
  1. Occupational therapy is a method of treating the sick or injured by means of instruction and employment of productive occupation.
  2. The objects sought are to arouse interest, courage, and confidence; to exercise mind and body in healthy activity; to overcome functional disability; and to re-establish capacity for industrial and social usefulness.
  3. In applying occupational therapy, system and precision are as important as in other forms of treatment.
  4. The treatment should be administered under constant medical advice and supervision, and correlated with the other treatment of the patient.
  5. The treatment should, in each case, be specifically directed to the individual's needs.
  6. Though some patients do best alone, employment in groups is usually advisable because it provides exercise in social adaptation and the stimulating influence of example and comment.
  7. The occupation selected should be within the range of the patient's estimated interests and capability.
  8. As the patient's strength and capability increase, the type and extent of occupation should be regulated and graded accordingly.
  9. The only reliable measure of the value of the treatment is the effect on the patient.
  10. Inferior workmanship, or employment in an occupation which would be trivial for the healthy, may be attended with the greatest benefit to the sick or injured. Standards worthy of entirely normal persons must be maintained for proper mental stimulation.
  11. The production of well-made, useful, and attractive articles, or the accomplishment of a useful task, requires healthy exercise of mind and body, gives the greatest satisfaction, and thus produces the most beneficial effects.
  12. Novelty, variety, individuality, and utility of the products enhance the value of an occupation as a treatment measure.
  13. Quality, quantity, and salability of the products may prove beneficial by satisfying and stimulating the patient but should never be permitted to obscure the main purpose.
  14. Good craftsmanship, and ability to instruct, are essential qualifications in the occupational therapist; understanding, sincere interest in the patient, and an optimistic, cheerful outlook and manner are equally essential.
  15. Patients under treatment by means of occupational therapy should also engage in recreational or play activities. It is advisable that gymnastics and calisthenics, which may be given for habit training, should be regarded as work. Social dancing and all recreational and play activities should be under the definite head of recreations.

Committee members: Eleanor Clarke Slagle, Dr. William. L. Russell, and Mr. Norman L. Burnette (Canada)

Source: [Dunton, W. R.] (1919). N.S.P.O.T. *Maryland Psychiatric Quarterly, 13*(3), 68–73. Reprinted in Dunton, W. R. (1919). Appendix. In *Reconstruction therapy* (p. 229). Philadelphia: Saunders.

1929. Journal articles came from four primary sources: *Maryland Psychiatric Quarterly* (1914–1923), *Archives of Occupational Therapy* (1922–1924), *Occupational Therapy and Rehabilitation* (1925–1929), and *Modern Hospital* (1917–1929). Other relevant journals related mostly to psychiatry, mental hygiene, tuberculosis, orthopedics, surgery, and social welfare. Historical review articles were also identified to examine the values, beliefs, and ideas of the time. Approximately 40 books and 400 articles were scanned and screened for content. We used the Internet to identify some resources that were not readily available in the occupational therapy literature, such as major names and places associated with the manual training movement.

FIGURE 22.2. Principles Written by Dr. William R. Dunton, Jr., 1918

1. That work should be carried on with cure as the main object.
2. The work must be interesting.
3. The patient should be carefully studied.
4. The one form of occupation should not be carried to the point of fatigue.
5. That it should have some useful end.
6. That it preferably should lead to an increase in the patient's knowledge.
7. That it should be carried on with others.
8. That all possible encouragement should be given the worker.
9. The work resulting in a poor or useless product is better than idleness.

Source: Dunton, W. R. (1919). Appendix. In *Reconstruction therapy* (p. 229). Philadelphia: Saunders. Original source: Dunton, W. R. (1918). The principles of occupational therapy. *Public Health Nurse, 18*, 316–321. Committee members: Eleanor Clarke Slagle, Dr. William. L. Russell, and Mr. Norman L. Burnette (Canada)

From these data we extracted values and beliefs, then organized them by principle (see Figure 22.4). McKenzie may have best summarized the uniqueness of occupational therapy as a therapeutic agent when he wrote that "treatment by occupation differs from all other forms…in that the remedy is given in increasing doses with its patient's improvement" (p. 105).[13] Hall, a past president of AOTA, reminded all practitioners that, although the values and beliefs of a profession change little over the years, "the technic [sic] of the art, its practical application, is due for many changes, improvements, and readjustments" (p. 73).[14] All occupational therapists and occupational therapy assistants should know and retain the inherent values and beliefs of the profession, even as societal and technological changes affect the technique.

NEXT STAGE

The members of the Ad Hoc Committee on Historical Foundations are continuing to review professional values and beliefs during additional time periods. The second stage of our research covers the years from 1930 to 1949. Early data show that, although we expect the original values and beliefs to remain intact, the profession continued its practice of drawing on knowledge from other fields. As this new knowledge was incorporated into practice, additional values and beliefs may have been added to the existing ones. Also, as changes occur in the politics, society, and economics of practice, some values and beliefs may be competing with others for the attention of occupational therapy practitioners. We look forward to sharing the report when it is completed.

REFERENCES

1. Greenwood, E. (1966). The elements of professionalization. In H. M. Vollmer & D. L. Mills (Eds.), *Professionalization* (pp. 9–19). Englewood Cliffs, NJ: Prentice Hall.
2. Lipset, S. M., & Schwartz, M. A. (1966). The politics of professionals. In H. M. Vollmer & D. L. Mills (Eds.), *Professionalization* (pp. 299–321). Englewood Cliffs, NJ: Prentice Hall.
3. Gould, L. L. (2001). *America in the Progressive Era: 1890–1914.* Harlow, UK: Pearson Education.
4. Lear, T. J. (1981). *No place of grace: Antimodernism and the transformation of American culture, 1880–1920.* New York: Pantheon.
5. Upham, E. G. (1918). *Training of teachers for occupational therapy for the rehabilitation of disabled soldiers and sailors.* Washington, DC: Federal Board of Vocations Education.
6. Maxwell, J. D., & Maxwell, M. P. (1984). Inner fraternity and outer sorority: Social structure and the professionalization of occupational therapy. In A. Wipper (Ed.), *The sociology of work: Papers in honour of Oswald Hall* (pp. 330–358). Ottawa, Ontario, Canada: Carleton University Press.

FIGURE 22.3. Subject Areas (in alphabetical order)

Arts and Crafts movement	Interest or interests	Progressive era
Curative workshops	Manual training	Public health and welfare
Education of occupational therapists	Mechanism or mechanistic philosophy	Purposive psychology
Emmanuel movement	Mechano-therapy	Reconstruction aides
Federal Board of Vocational Education	Medical education	Re-education of the disabled
Feminism	Mental hygiene	Settlement houses
Functional re-education	Meyer and psychobiology	The simple life
Habit training	Moral treatment	Surgeon General's Office (including divisions and departments)
Holism and gestalt psychology	Motion study (Gilbreths)	Therapeutic occupation
Humanism	Motivation	Treatment of tuberculosis
Humanitarianism	Neuropsychiatry	Vocational re-education and training
Idleness	Occupational therapy	Work and the work ethic
Industrial re-education	Orthopedics	
	Pragmatism	

7. [Dunton, W. R.] (1919). N.S.P.O.T. *Maryland Psychiatry Quarterly, 13*(3), 68–73.

8. Dunton, W. R. (1919). Appendix. In *Reconstruction therapy* (pp. 227–229). Philadelphia: W. B. Saunders.

9. American Occupational Therapy Association. (1923). *Bulletin No. 4.* Baltimore: Sheppard Hospital Press.

10. American Occupational Therapy Association. (1925). An outline of lectures on occupational therapy to medical students and physicians. *Occupational Therapy and Rehabilitation, 4,* 280–281.

11. American Occupational Therapy Association. (1940). Principles of occupational therapy. *Occupational Therapy and Rehabilitation, 19,* 19–20.

12. Dunton, W. R. (1918). The principles of occupational therapy. *Public Health Nurse, 18,* 316–321.

13. McKenzie, R. T. (1919). *Reclaiming the maimed.* New York: Macmillan.

14. Hall, H. J. (1921). Occupational therapy forecasts and suggestions. *Modern Hospital, 16,* 73.

Author

Kathlyn L. Reed, PhD, OTR, FAOTA, MLIS, is visiting professor at the School of Occupational Therapy at Texas Woman's University–Houston Center.

She is also chair of AOTA's Ethics Commission.

Originally copyrighted in 2006 by the American Occupational Therapy Association and published in *OT Practice,* April 17, 2006, pp. 21–25.

FIGURE 22.4. Summary of Principles Drawn From Values and Beliefs: 1904–1929

Note: The following cites only the occupational therapist, because the occupational therapy assistant position was not created until 1959.

Principles related to goals and outcomes

- The primary goal of occupational therapy is to return the person to active life and for the person to function in normal society as a whole person in body and soul.
- Additional goals may include attainment of self-control (of behavior), self-reliance and self-sufficiency (for attaining basic needs), manual skills (dexterity strength, and coordination), and good work habits (accuracy, orderliness, neatness, patience, and perseverance).
- Where disease or injury has occurred, the goal of occupational therapy is to contribute to and hasten recovery.
- The outcome of occupational therapy is to enable the person to learn to develop better, easier, or more interesting methods of performing daily occupation.
- The purpose of occupational therapy may address physical, mental, and/or social occupations.
- Occupational therapy is the making of a man (individual) stronger physically, mentally, and spiritually than he was before.
- Occupational therapy makes the patient a creator, a doer.[1]
- Occupational therapy transforms environments into more inspiring surroundings.

Principles related to the process of occupational therapy

- All persons should be regarded as unique beings.
- All persons are capable of change and improvement regardless of diagnosis or situation.
- A person should not be excluded from intervention because his/her

condition appears hopeless or unlikely to improve.

- The 24-hour cycle of time can be used successfully as a means of facilitating normal occupational behavior and organizing and structuring a person's daily occupations.
- The use of interest and motivation encourages a person to increase attention, to learn about the self and the environment, and to engage in occupations that promote self-realization.
- The person's interest in (or motivation for) occupation should always be considered and sustained.
- Interest and motivation may associate with physical, mental, or social activity.
- Appliances and assistive technology should meet the individual's needs for occupational performance and be kept to a minimum consistent with those needs.
- Appliances and assistive technology should be kept as simple as possible and still do the job.
- Occupations used in occupational therapy programs should be considered primarily for their therapeutic potential.
- Occupational therapists should focus on providing opportunities for people to practice the actual doing of occupation, not prescriptions focused on telling people which occupations to do.
- Occupational therapy should be provided in a pleasant (harmonious) environment in which useful occupations are provided and the occupational therapists act as role models.
- Occupation can be analyzed and graded along several continua including aptitude, ability, and interest. Therefore, occupation can be graded from simple

and easy or complex and hard, require low or high level of skill, require little or extensive prior experience and education, require a short or long time to complete.

- Occupation should be selected with the person's needs and abilities in mind.
- Occupational therapists need infinite patience, the ability to teach, and the power to inspire confidence in others.
- Occupational therapists need an optimistic temperament and a sense of humor.
- Occupational therapists must not become too paternal, killing personal responsibility.[1]
- Occupational therapists should always praise the attempt and use constructive and suggestive criticism.
- Occupational therapy services can be designed to meet a variety of needs and purposes.
- It takes rare gifts and personalities to be pathfinders in this work.[2]
- It requires that one be true to one's nature and teach others to do the same.[2]
- Occupational therapy is an art and a science.
- Occupational therapy must lead somewhere, and the patient must want to follow.[3]
- Occupational therapy requires understanding and give-and-take.[4]
- Occupational therapy requires spiritual vision of the end problem.[4]
- Visualizing results of therapy encourages the patient.[5]
- The use of experimental, survey, case history, and analytical methodologies can be applied to the study of therapeutic occupation and its application to patients.
- The use of systematic literature reviews can be applied to the

REFERENCE GUIDE TO THE OCCUPATIONAL THERAPY ETHICS STANDARDS

study of therapeutic occupation and its application to patients.

Principles related to personal change through occupational therapy

- Occupational therapy is a method of treatment by means of instruction and employment of productive occupation.[6]
- Occupational therapists help the person to take control of his or her life situation.
- Occupational therapists encourage the person to learn to do things for himself or herself.
- Occupational therapists encourage the person to keep life simple and simplify life.
- Occupational therapists encourage the person to engage in wholesome (healthful and moral) occupations.
- Occupational therapists increase opportunities for the person to engage in social situations.
- Occupational therapy is the science of healing by occupation.[7]

Principles related to the therapeutic application of occupation

- Focuses attention directly on the injury and uses occupation designed to promote and hasten return to function (direct approach).
- Focuses attention away from the pain of injury onto an absorbing occupation that promotes and hastens return of function through mental stimulation and doing/performing the actions required of the occupation (indirect approach).
- Keeps the mind occupied or absorbed with productive occupation and away from idleness, unreality, and self-absorbing thoughts (indirect approach).
- Keeps the mind and hands occupied so the body can rest.
- Uses a normal or familiar environment for doing/performing occupation.

- Can be graded along several criteria from bedside to workshop, diversional to work, individual to group, amusement to productive.
- Can be adjusted to fit individual needs as opposed to requiring the individual to adjust to it.
- Affords occasions for productivity and opportunity.
- Transforms environments and atmospheres.
- Aims to individualize with the temperament of each patient.
- Is a reeducation of faith and self-confidence.
- Is a scientific effort for the restoration to health of those mentally and physically ill.

Principles related to the therapeutic nature of occupation

- Occupation encourages doing and performing.
- Occupation can be goal-directed.
- Occupation is important to good health.
- Occupation is natural and familiar to people.
- Occupation can arouse interest and motivation.
- Occupation can increase contact with the environment and reality.
- Occupation can be used to increase muscle power and strength.
- Occupation can be used to increase joint function.
- Occupation can be used to improve muscle tone (physical endurance, tolerance).
- Occupation can be used to improve sensation following nerve lesion.
- Occupation and health are linked.
- Occupation can be positive, purposeful, and controlled.
- Occupational can promote a healthier lifestyle.
- Occupation has recreational, education, vocational, and therapeutic value.

- Occupations promote the resumption of natural and healthy modes of thought.
- Occupation trains and engages attention.
- Occupation develops right habit formation.
- Occupation stimulates the mind and trains interest.
- Occupation fosters dignity, competence, and health.
- Occupation reduces despair and produces hope.
- The therapeutic value of occupation can be studied by recording the response (improved, much improved, or no relief) of clients to treatment.
- Occupations can be studied based on the type of effect various occupations have on recovery from different diagnoses or symptoms (e.g., calming or exciting the patient).
- Occupations can be studied for their potential as a therapeutic agent in various settings. Factors might include cost of supplies and equipment, number of tools needed, precautions to be observed, type of work area needed, and amount of training needed.

Principles related to philosophical assumptions

- Occupational therapy is based on the idea of helping others find their way toward health (Emmanuel movement).
- Occupational therapists assume the whole is different from and more than the sum of its parts and that the person should be treated as a whole (mind, body, and soul) (Gestalt psychology). *Note:* Holism did not become a concept until 1926, but Gestalt psychology existed prior to the First World War.
- Occupational therapists believe that man learns to organize time

(continued)

and does so through doing occupation.[2]

- Occupational therapists believe that time is a person's best asset and that validation of opportunity and performance is the best measure.[2]
- The occupation (of one's hands and muscles) enables a person to achieve and attain pleasure.[2]
- Illness, especially mental illness, may be conceptualized as problems of living rather than as diseases or disorders of the bodily constitution.[2]
- Man maintains and balances in contact with reality through active involvement in life and use of time in harmony with the self and the environment surrounding the self.[2]
- Occupational therapy involves more mental action than physical.[8]
- Every human being should have both physical and mental occupation.[6]
- Sick minds, bodies, and souls can be healed through occupation.[6]

Principles related to education: The occupational therapist should

- Learn by doing.
- Learn about functional abilities.
- Learn to care for others and see oneself as a caring person.
- Learn medical (biological science) and social science.
- Learn technical training in a variety of occupations and a variety of methods of presenting or teaching the occupations.

Principles related to sociocultural influences include

- Individuals should be treated equally, regardless of political, economic, social status, or military rank (feminism and reconstruction aides).
- Occupational therapists who are women have the ability and capacity to work and interact in society.
- Occupational therapists should pay attention to urban, industrial, educational, social, and cultural issues in society.
- Occupational therapists who are women can participate in society outside the home.

- Occupational therapists facilitate the adjustment of immigrants to life and work in the new country.
- Occupational therapists can act as advocates for individuals in the neighborhood and in the nation.

References

1. Crane, B. T. (1919). Occupational therapy. *Boston Medical and Surgical Journal, 181*, 63–65.
2. Meyer, A. (1922). The philosophy of occupation therapy. *Archives of Occupational Therapy, 1*(1), 1–10.
3. Cullimore, A. R. (1921). Objectives and motivation in occupational therapy. *Modern Hospital, 17*, 537–538.
4. Slagle, E. C. (1927). To organize an "OT" department. *Occupational Therapy and Rehabilitation, 6*, 125–130.
5. Mock, H. E. (1919). Curative work. *Carry On, 1*, 12–17.
6. Dunton, W. R. (1919). *Reconstruction therapy*. Philadelphia: Saunders.
7. Upham, E. G. (1918). *Training of teachers for occupational therapy for the rehabilitation of disabled soldiers and sailors*. Washington, DC: Federal Board of Vocational Education.
8. Thom, D. A., & Singer, D. (1921). The care of neuro-psychiatric disabilities. *Public Health Reports, 36*, 2665–2677.

CHAPTER 23

Is It Possible to Be Ethical?

One common complaint about ethics is that most ethical dilemmas seem too complicated to be solved. Although it is true that ethical dilemmas can often become quite complex, especially in today's technological, global community, resolving ethical dilemmas need not be viewed as an impossible task. To claim at the outset that ethics simply cannot be accommodated is to set one's self up for failure. Even the most difficult of ethical dilemmas can be sorted through and resolved with enough time, patience, and careful reflection.

This article offers a model for ethical decision making that strives to help its users reach consensus. Although many in the public forum are fond of the claim that we can all just "agree to disagree," such an approach simply cannot work when one has entered into a therapeutic relationship, thereby making a professional promise to assist someone in the pursuit of health and optimal occupational performance. Therapy is a collaborative effort, and consensus is an implicit part of collaboration.

STRIVING FOR CONSENSUS

To clarify the need for consensus in the therapeutic relationship, we must understand what it means. Let me begin with what consensus is *not*. Consensus is not 100% total agreement. Anyone could rightly question whether, in a pluralistic society, total agreement can ever be achieved. Further, consensus cannot be completely equated with compromise. Most will recognize that compromise involves giving up something you believe or hold as a value. However, one of the foundational points of ethics is that each person must maintain personal integrity, meaning that to remain ethical there are some things that each of us should not be asked to give up. Each of us must guard the sanctity of our own conscience. Ethics never obligates one to sacrifice her or his own integrity.

What, then, does consensus entail? I would suggest that authentic consensus is achieved when all parties involved in a debate, dispute, or dilemma can accept and live with the decision being offered. By the phrase *live with* I mean that the decision under consideration does not violate one's integrity and conscience. Such a decision may not be one's top choice—to that degree, there is some give and take in arriving at consensus. But all involved must be able to accept the decision and follow through with the recommended course of action. Given this, the task of reaching a consensus must involve dialogue with all those involved.

Dialogue, of course, takes time, and so this phase is often where problems arise. Many are under the impression that ethical decisions must be made quickly and on the spur of the moment. This attitude may partly reflect the influence of capitalism on contemporary American society. The business community tells us we need to be ready to respond to the global market at any time, that opportunities only come along once and can be lost in a minute, and that in the world of business the slow always lose. And so we live in a world of overnight shipping, 24-hour stores, e-commerce, and fast food. Naturally, many assume that ethical decision making must follow the same model—be quick and responsive to the marketplace of dilemmas.

But is this presumption true? No. We all remember the story of the tortoise and the hare. Speed has its uses, but it also can breed recklessness. Remember such marketing fiascoes as New Coke and Pepsi Clear? In a hospital emergency room, decisions often need to be made quickly (although rarely as fast as a popular television drama portrays them). But for most health care and therapy, there is indeed time to carefully study and reflect before making a decision—if one but takes the time, or requests it of others. Indeed, it is even better from a business standpoint to take some time before acting instead of spending twice as much time after the fact trying to clean up whatever mess has been made. And some decisions, like the *Challenger* shuttle disaster, can never really be "cleaned up."

The first step in sound ethical decision making is to take the time to reflect on one's actions from the perspective of ethics. I often hear from people who have found themselves seemingly trapped in very complex ethical dilemmas when they never even realized that what they had been doing had ethical implications—it was just business, just billing, just legal, just personal, etc., etc., etc. Furthermore, the truly complicated ethical dilemmas that we so often hear about on newsmagazine shows rarely arise from a single action—more often, they are the result of a series of smaller, but still unethical, actions. Carefully reflecting on one's day-today actions can go a long way toward avoiding these larger dilemmas.

A MODEL FOR ETHICAL DECISION MAKING

Even the most careful people can find themselves facing an ethical dilemma—either one of their own doing or one into which they have been dragged. So how can one resolve a complex ethical dilemma? With so many different theories of ethics to choose from, how can one really figure out the best way to act? Is ethics just a crapshoot—roll the dice and take your chances? Again, my response to this is *no!* What is needed is a way to sort through the complexity of a moral dilemma. To this end, I offer the following model for ethical decision making.

This model has developed through a collaborative effort with other professionals, and I have presented it in ethics courses and workshops. I do not offer it as the only way to solve ethical dilemmas but merely as one possible guide for sorting through the complexity of some of the challenges we find ourselves facing from day to day. As such, this model is a response to the claim that ethics is often too complex to really address. Using a model can help one break the dilemma into manageable pieces, thereby reducing the complexity of the situation. It is also worth noting that using a model for thinking through a problem will not necessarily make ethics "simple." Indeed, most often the difficult part of ethics is following through upon the decision one has reached—knowing what is right and doing what is right are two different things. The goal of this model is to present an orderly way of approaching an ethical dilemma so that one can have a firmer foundation from which to make an ethical decision as well as increased confidence in following through with that action.

AM I FACING AN ETHICAL DILEMMA?

The process of ethical decision making begins, quite naturally, with the realization that one may be facing an ethical dilemma. I start the model with this question, however, because at times what may appear to be an ethical problem may actually be more of a legal matter, a personnel issue, or some other kind of dilemma (although at times laws and policies are broken and concurrently ethical principles are violated). So the first question is, Does the situation involve a violation of the American Occupational Therapy

Association (AOTA) *Occupational Therapy Code of Ethics (2000)?*[1,2] Does the problem impinge upon your personal integrity and conscience? If so, then you may be facing an ethical dilemma, and you should begin to clarify the situation.

What Are the Relevant Facts, Values, and Beliefs?

As you begin to examine the situation causing the dilemma, you should carefully examine all the pertinent facts—which also means sorting through those factors that are irrelevant. In many cases, ethical problems arise, in part, because one or both parties do not know all the facts. In such cases, getting the facts straight at the outset may lead to a quick resolution.

It is also important to try to identify the values at stake in the dilemma—both your own and those of everyone else directly involved. Values are those things we hold dear, and when values clash, ethical dilemmas arise. A misunderstanding, or outright ignoring, of others' values will only worsen the situation, putting resolution and consensus further out of reach.

Finally, what are the beliefs guiding everyone involved? Beliefs and values are both subjective, and so they will vary from person to person. But recognizing different beliefs can lead to understanding—even when disagreement over the beliefs remains.

Being clear about the facts, values, and beliefs involved in an ethical dilemma will help pave the way for dialogue among all those involved.

Who Are the Key People Involved?

Next, identify the people involved in the dilemma. It can also be helpful to prioritize each person's role. For example, in all dilemmas surrounding the therapeutic relationship, the client being served should always remain at the forefront of the dialogue.

As part of identifying the key people involved, it is also helpful to consider what might be called the "ripple effect" in ethics—those people not directly involved at that precise moment but who nonetheless will be affected (e.g., future clients, other students or faculty, other members of a clinic or hospital, other professionals, the school district).

Be thorough, so as not to leave anyone out of consideration. True dialogue cannot take place if everyone does not have a seat at the table.

State the Dilemma Clearly

As you begin to sort through the details of the situation under consideration, you must be able to bring the problem into focus. A helpful format for structuring the dilemma is to form a question identifying the possible ethical conclusions: "Is it (or *was* it) *permissible, impermissible,* or *obligatory* to_____?"[3] Stating the dilemma in this manner leaves the issue under consideration open-ended and allows for honest dialogue and debate. Being able to state the dilemma also provides direction for the dialogue. If you are in a situation that involves multiple problems, it is best to focus on the most pressing issue in need of resolution first. The other problems can be addressed at a later time. However, care should be taken not to lump too many problems together, because doing so just adds to the confusion of sorting through complex problems. It is better to sort through each problem on its own so as not to miss anything important. This kind of careful reflection can also help avoid future problems of a similar nature.

ANALYZE

What Are the Possible Courses of Action?

After it is clear that you are indeed facing an ethical dilemma, and you have identified the key factors and people involved with the problem, you can begin to search for a resolution. The first step in moving toward a consensus is to identify possible courses of action. For example, in every situation, you could always just do nothing. Even if you were in a situation in which you absolutely knew you were going to do something, it is helpful to recognize that doing nothing is always an option.

Laying out the possible actions facilitates being thorough in your reflections, and considering all the possibilities can help keep you from missing something important. People having serious dilemmas often point out that they did not realize all of their options before ending up in their present situation. We hear people say "What was I thinking?" But the problem may have been that they were not thinking—at least not thoroughly enough to avoid trouble. Taking time for reflection will add to the dialogue involved with resolving the situation at hand.

What Conflicts Could Arise From Each Action?

After the possible courses of action are identified, they must be analyzed. The task here is to consider the impact of each action as reasonably as possible. It is also important to consider the possible course of action from the vantage point of each of the key people involved with the dilemma. Granted, we cannot always predict how people will react, but the point here is not to play fortune-teller; rather, the idea is to consider the consequences of your actions—both for yourself and for everyone else involved.

Through the process of identifying the conflicts involved with certain actions, you will begin to see why certain actions are not viable—either because they are impractical, because there is something preventing them from occurring, or even because they can now be seen as unethical. With such an analysis you will be able to explain and, if necessary, defend your actions. The ultimate goal of this analysis, then, is to identify a single course of action, or a connected series of actions, that will resolve the dilemma. It is this proposed course of action that will then be evaluated for its adherence to ethical standards.

EVALUATE

The final part of the ethical decision-making process evaluates the proposed course of action. For this part of the process I am going to work backward, so to speak, beginning with

an examination of one's self-interests, to a consideration of one's social roles, then finally to a consideration of the Code and general ethical principles. This part of the model reflects the model proffered by Gregory Beabout and Daryl Wennemann in *Applied Professional Ethics*,[4] which builds on developmental psychologist Lawrence Kohlberg's ideas about moral development but also considers a critique of Kohlberg's work that incorporates notions of Carol Gilligan's "ethics of caring." The reason for this approach is that we must be careful not to justify our decisions through a simple process of rationalization. Beginning with the Code and principles may give the appearance of not being fair in our deliberations and not recognizing that at times we have a personal interest in a decision or in fulfilling a social role that is pressuring us to act. To avoid any such problems, it helps to begin with self-interest and build toward general ethical principles. That way, it will be clearer that your principles are supporting the decision at the highest levels of moral reasoning, as opposed to your own interests.

Self-Interests (Level I)

The simple fact is that each of us has personal interests at stake in the actions we perform. This alone is not necessarily a problem. We all want to give and receive good things—while at the same time we want to avoid having bad things happen to us. When a therapist creates a technically sound intervention that is also successful, it is quite natural to feel good about this accomplishment. Most people who enter the profession of occupational therapy do so because they want to help people. The problem arises when a person focuses only on his or her own interests, especially to the detriment and neglect of others. For example, spending $200 on a weekend golfing trip is not in itself unethical. But it would be if a parent did so at the expense of necessary food and clothing for his or her children. The first case is clearly an example of self-interest; the second evolves into selfishness. Therefore, it is important to recognize one's personal interests in a situation so as to recognize which interests are appropriate and which are not.

Some people believe that we should all act at the level of self-interest. This ethical theory is known as egoism and has been defended by people such as Ayn Rand. The idea behind the theory is to maximize one's personal happiness. But the problem is that our interests always conflict. I might want to speed to get home faster—but I don't want to get a ticket. If I am an egoist, and I decide to be safe and not speed, then when I get home without I ticket I think, "I could have sped and been home 20 minutes ago—there weren't any cops out tonight!" But if I speed and get a ticket, then I chastise myself, saying, "I knew this would happen—I should have been more careful!" In short, every action that holds some promise of benefit also brings with it some risk or hardship. The dieter wants to eat the doughnut, but not gain weight. The two interests are incompatible. And so, when one begins to thoroughly reflect on all the options that go into making a decision, it becomes clear that acting solely out of personal interest will not bring satisfactory results. Nor will this approach help us attain a consensus; rather, it only divides us.

Identify your interests, admit that they are there, then move on to a higher level of moral reasoning.

Social Roles (Level II)

After you move past the narrow focus of self-interest, you begin to realize that you belong to various communities. These communities are broad and include family, work, religious group, political affiliation, and friends. You will also begin to realize that the members of these groups have certain expectations of each other. These expectations establish our social roles. With our social roles come obligations. At this level, then, one moves out of the purely individualistic thinking of self-interest and begins to recognize that other people also matter. Regarding the needs and interests of others moves us to consider how our actions affect others in the groups to which we belong so as to further the interests and needs of the group over our own. It is helpful to identify your social roles in a dilemma and to clarify the expectations that may be influencing your thinking.

Clearly, social roles provide a better and more satisfactory perspective for ethics than pure self-interest. Yet this level does have its limitations because our social roles often conflict. A promotion at work that requires travel may bring added income for your family, helping to fulfill the social role of provider. But the travel required will also reduce time spent with the family, which detracts from the social roles of spouse and parent. Because each of us has so many different social roles, trying to use these roles as a basis for making a decision is often difficult—clear solutions can be hard to find.

A second problem with this level is that it is not all-inclusive. Whereas our social roles call us to consider the other members of our groups, they do not necessarily move us toward the needs and interests of those who fall outside our social groups. If I am a Democrat, do I have to care about a Republican? If I am Baptist, should I care about the Jews? Is my only priority to care for my family, or do I have any obligations toward people in other countries? At this level there is nothing that pushes us to look past our own social groups to a more global perspective. In the end, we can see that each of us has multiple social roles, and those roles tend to cause tension in our lives. Resolving these conflicts requires a higher level of moral reasoning, one that can help us prioritize our roles and bring them into harmony. This higher perspective can also draw us to a more inclusive view of humanity that challenges us to recognize the needs and rights of all.

Code of Ethics (Level II)

The highest level of moral reasoning is the level of universal moral principles, such as those embodied in the AOTA *Occupational Therapy Code of Ethics*. These are principles that apply to all occupational therapy personnel, regardless of race, gender, and creed. The spirit of the Code is not limited only to members of AOTA but extends an obligation of respect and care toward all.

As you continue to reflect on the proposed course of action, having identified personal interests and social roles, evaluating the action using the Code will bring you toward resolution. Does the Code explicitly require that the action under consideration be performed? Does the Code explicitly forbid the proposed course of action? If the Code is not explicit, what is the spirit of the Code regarding the situation? Use the Code and its principles to support your decision or to show why the decision is unethical and should not be carried out. In doing so, you will recognize how personal interests and social roles are brought into harmony through the higher, unifying perspective of the *Occupational Therapy Code of Ethics*.

Ethical Principles (Level III)

You can often further support a good decision with more general, ethical norms, such as justice, beneficence, autonomy, and so forth, which form the philosophical basis for the *Occupational Therapy Code of Ethics*. Appealing to general ethical principles is especially helpful when dealing with people who are not members of the profession and who have no specific obligations toward the Code. By pointing out the general societal norms that further support the decision at hand, you can show that action was not based solely on the role of occupational therapy (which would be Level II thinking) but rather is truly based on ethical principles. Additionally, an appeal to general ethical principles helps foster dialogue and will help further the spirit of the AOTA *Occupational Therapy Code of Ethics* in the public forum.

PROCEED: YES OR NO

In the end, the final question to ask is, "Does your proposed course of action lead to consensus?" If yes, then proceed, knowing that the decision can be supported and defended. If no, then return to the analysis portion of the model and review your evaluations. Perhaps there were more options that you did not consider or another course of action could be proposed for evaluation.

CONCLUSION

We should not be alarmed when we find that we have no consensus and that we must continue our ethical deliberations and dialogue. The process of ethical decision making can indeed be involved, especially as a situation becomes more serious. I offer the model worksheet here (see Figure 23.1) because in difficult cases it can help to sit down and organize our thoughts on paper. The worksheet can even prove useful in a group setting to foster dialogue and to help reach consensus.

If time does not allow for further consideration, then you must do the best you can and be open to reflection and critique in the future. Remember, becoming a virtuous person takes time and experience. It is a lifelong endeavor. That does not mean we can be cavalier with our decisions now and straighten up later. But it does mean that we most likely will not get everything right the first time around. Through our life experiences we all grow and develop. The same is true of our ethics. The decisions we make affect our future selves. Good decisions pave the way for more good decisions, and bad decisions must be dealt with if we are to improve ourselves and our world.

SUMMARY

In the wake of recent corporate scandals, the topic of ethics is gaining new attention. But is it possible to act ethically while meeting the needs and expectations of everyone involved in

Am I facing an ethical dilemma here?

1) What are the relevant facts, values, and beliefs? _____
_____
_____

2) Who are the key people involved? _____
_____
_____
_____

3) State the dilemma clearly. _____
_____
_____

Analysis

1) What are the possible courses of action one could take? _____
_____
_____

2) What are the conflicts that arise from each action? _____
_____
_____

Proposed Course of Action

Evaluate:

1) Ethical principles:
   Level III _____
_____
_____

2) *Code of Ethics:* _____
_____
_____
_____

3) Social roles:
   Level II _____
_____
_____

4) Self-interests:
   Level I _____
_____
_____

Does your proposed course of action lead to consensus?   If yes—then proceed . . .

If no . . .

FIGURE 23.1. Model for Ethical Decision Making.

a dilemma? The model presented here provides a step-by-step process for ethical decision making that aims at consensus among all those involved in an ethical dilemma.

REFERENCES

1. American Occupational Therapy Association. (2000). Occupational therapy code of ethics (2000). *American Journal of Occupational Therapy, 54,* 614–616. *Note:* Since this article was originally published, this reference has been updated (see American Occupational Therapy Association, 2005)
2. American Occupational Therapy Association. (2005). Occupational therapy code of ethics (2005). *American Journal of Occupational Therapy, 59,* 639–642.
3. Beabout, G. R., & Wennemann, D. J. (1994). *Applied professional ethics.* New York: University Press of America.
4. Ibid.

ACKNOWLEDGMENTS

Many thanks go to Robin Bowen, EdD, OTR, FAOTA, and Shelly Chabon, PhD, CCC-SLP. Drs. Bowen and Chabon are members of Rockhurst University and have collaborated with me on the development of this model of ethical decision making. Both have also presented this model with me at professional conferences. I especially thank them for their gracious permission to publish this model for use by members of AOTA.

Author

John F. Morris, PhD
Public Member of AOTA's Commission on Standards and Ethics.

CHAPTER 24

Unethical and Illegal:
What Is the Difference?

Members of the American Occupational Therapy Association (AOTA) often ask if something is unethical, illegal, or both. This is not a simple question with a single answer, and the answer will depend on several factors.

Ethics is a branch of applied philosophy and is the study of rules of conduct and the general nature of morals as applied to individual choice. *Law* is a body or system of rules used by an authority to impose control over a system or people. The major issue is whether the unethical action has been adopted by a legislature as being unlawful. Basically, unless the law mandates that the conduct is illegal, violations of ethical principles and standards will not result in criminal sanctions or fines. Therefore, it is best if occupational therapy practitioners check with their state's regulatory board (SRB) to inquire about the legality or illegality of an act.

Associations frequently develop codes of ethics, policies, or other guidelines that specify standards of practice or conduct that are commonly recognized and accepted to be illegal, immoral, or unacceptable in a particular profession. These codes often set forth certain rules of conduct that describe aspirational goals to be achieved by all members. The *Occupational Therapy Code of Ethics (2005)* (AOTA, 2005) is such a code. It is hoped that members aspire to do good and act in an ethically responsible manner. Members are expected to adhere to standards set forth in the Code to protect the recipients of services. While the *Oc-*

cupational Therapy Code of Ethics is a type of self-regulation within the association and profession, the *Enforcement Procedures for the Occupational Therapy Code of Ethics* (AOTA, 2007) provide a regulatory component. Violations of the Code can result in certain sanctions imposed by the Association on its members, including reprimand, censure, probation, suspension, and revocation of membership.

Not every violation of the *Code of Ethics* also is a violation of the law. An act is considered legal as long as it "conforms to law; is according to law; is required or permitted by law; is not forbidden or discountenanced by law; and is good and effectual in law" (*Black's Law Dictionary*, 1979, p. 803). An act is considered illegal if it is contrary to a law. Therefore, only if the violation prescribed by the Code also is a violation of the law will the violator be subject to criminal sanctions and penalties.

An example of an unethical and illegal practice is the following: An occupational therapy practitioner who engages in a sexual relationship with a minor or with a client who has mental impairments would be breaching Principle 2A *(nonmaleficence)* of the *Occupational Therapy Code of Ethics (2005)*. The principle states, "Occupational therapy personnel shall maintain therapeutic relationships that shall not exploit the recipient of services sexually, physically, emotionally . . . or in any other manner." It is widely acknowledged that engaging in sexual relations with a minor also is committing a criminal act.

An example of unethical behavior as defined by the *Occupational Therapy Code of Ethics (2005)*, but not necessarily illegal behavior, could be the individual violating Principle 4C *(duty)*, which states, "Occupational therapy personnel shall take responsibility for maintaining and documenting competence in practice, education, and research by participating in professional development and educational activities." An occupational therapy practitioner could fail to function within the parameters of his or her competence and not seek continuing education (CE) although the techniques that he or she was taught in school have drastically changed. New technology and emerging practice areas demand that all practitioners keep abreast of current evidence-based research and trends; however, failure to participate in CE may not be considered a criminal violation. It should be noted, however, that if the SRB requires CE to maintain one's license to practice, then failure to meet CE requirements may subject the occupational therapy practitioner to license suspension or other sanctions.

Ethics and law are indeed strange bedfellows. Ethics deals with making ethical decisions and morally good choices (not necessarily right or wrong), and law usually deals with justice, right, and wrong (not necessarily morally good choices). Occupational therapists, occupational therapy assistants, and students must gather the facts, and when an ethically appropriate course of action is unclear, seek guidance from multiple sources. These may include the SRB, the peer occupational therapy community, the state association, ethics committees, human resources personnel and policies/procedures in the workplace, AOTA, the National Board for Certification in Occupational Therapy, and legal counsel. All can provide information and different perspectives to assist in ethical decision making.

REFERENCES

American Occupational Therapy Association. (2005). Occupational therapy code of ethics. *American Journal of Occupational Therapy, 59,* 639–642.

American Occupational Therapy Association. (2007). Enforcement procedures for the occupational therapy code of ethics. *American Journal of Occupational Therapy, 61,* 679–685.

Black's Law Dictionary (5th ed.). (1979). Cincinnati, OH: West Educational.

Authors

Penny Kyler-Hutchison, MA, OT/L, FAOTA
AOTA Ethics Program Manager
Amy Mah
Paralegal, AOTA Office of General Counsel
Revised July 1998, July 2000

Deborah Yarett Slater, MS, OT/L, FAOTA
AOTA Staff Liaison to the Ethics Commission
Revised December 2005, January 2008

Originally copyrighted by the American Occupational Therapy Association in 1994 and published in *OT Week,* June 16, 1994, p. 8.

CHAPTER 25

Legal and Ethical Practice: A Professional Responsibility

If your employer asks you to provide daily maintenance for a patient's hearing aid after he or she has been instructed and is independent in its care, or to include lower-extremity lymphedema management in your treatment program until the vacant physical therapy position is filled, is it legal? Is it ethical? Is it within the occupational therapy scope of practice? Staffing patterns, emerging practice settings, alternative treatment modalities, programmatic models of care, and blurring of single-discipline supervisory models have left occupational therapists and occupational therapy assistants seeking clarification in defining their roles and their legal and ethical responsibilities. When there is divergence between legal and ethical obligations and illegal and unethical actions, where does the final authority reside?

Recently, many of the questions that come to the American Occupational Therapy Association (AOTA) share a general theme: "My supervisor is asking/demanding that I do_____ (fill in the blank with a treatment intervention). They think it's insubordination if I refuse, but I think I'm being asked to do something unethical. Or is it just unreasonable? Who is right?"

In many cases, supervisors or administrators have different expectations and understandings of "what is OT" than do occupational therapists or occupational therapy assistants themselves. Further, even if an intervention is within the legal scope of practice of occupational therapy, *should* it be done by that practitioner with that client? Questions about personal competency and doing the right thing to benefit the client must also be considered. How can practitioners understand their legal scope of practice and their responsibility to uphold the profession's ethical principles while communicating the appropriate role of occupational therapy to their consumers, colleagues, administrators, and payers?

COMMON CONCERNS

The following are samples of the types of questions relating to ethics, legal issues, and scope of practice that are often received at AOTA:

- In my facility, a PT was treating a patient for balance deficits and hit the outpatient $1,590 cap. Can I pick up the patient for OT and continue to work on balance but with OT goals?
- What can I do with respect to video fluoroscopy, functional capacity evaluations, and other particular programs or interventions?
- The PT in my facility is leaving. Can I treat lower-extremity lymphedema (I'm trained and credentialed in this area) until they hire a new PT?
- My state Practice Act does not specifically state that occupational therapists work with back-pain clients or provide back treatment. As a result, one of our major payers won't pay for back treatment. How can I prove that this is appropriate occupational therapy intervention?

- Is trachea suctioning within the occupational therapy scope of practice because I have a client who needs it? What about monitoring oxygen saturations?
- Do occupational therapists have to be certified to provide dysphagia services?
- I work in a rural area where staffing is difficult. I'm the only OT, working with several PTs. To provide continuity for my clients when I'm sick or on vacation if I can't find an OT replacement and the physician has referred for OT/PT, can I write in my evaluation that the patient will be treated by PT if indicated by the OT?
- Are lymphedema and wound care within the occupational therapy scope of practice? If so, do I need certification—what type and where do I get it?
- What are the legal and ethical implications of working in a driving program and the competency and level of training required for staff?

Other questions often arise around adding services (becoming a durable medical equipment provider; providing complementary or alternative medicine like massage, acupuncture, etc.) to an existing private practice or setting up a separate business in these areas. Is there a conflict of interest when a practitioner has access to a ready-made pool of potential patients or clients who are already in a therapeutic relationship with him or her?

For example, in these cases the practices may complement each other, but how can the business owner ensure that the clients' rights of autonomy and informed consent are safeguarded? (*Occupational Therapy Code of Ethics* [*2000*], Principle 3 and Principle 6, especially 6B[1]). As a general principle in evaluating this situation, consider that full and open disclosure of any competing businesses from which the therapist may realize financial gain is important to preserve patient rights, as are policies and procedures to avoid conflicts of interest.

Role delineation between disciplines can be another practice challenge in settings where certain referral patterns exist because of organizational history, and occupational therapy education and clinical training are not well understood. This can be a result of staffing shortages, pressure to maintain productivity within clinical departments, department leadership, and lack of confidence on the part of occupational therapy personnel in understanding and articulating the occupational therapy domain and scope of practice.

As the complexities and venues of practice grow, and new specialty areas emerge, the search for guidelines for appropriate legal and ethical practice will intensify. These questions generally do not have a direct, simple answer. Rather, a reasoning process or decision matrix for addressing these dilemmas is more appropriate and can be applied to a variety of settings and practice challenges. A number of resources are available to answer these questions.

DETERMINING SCOPE OF PRACTICE

The first step in the reasoning process is to understand what is meant by *scope of practice*. The foundation of a profession's domain has legal, professional, ethical, and educational components. Specifically, a profession's domain or scope of practice derives from three basic elements: (1) a body of knowledge historically included in the educational preparation of the disciplines; (2) a clearly established history of application in practice, as reflected in the professional literature; and (3) the legal framework created by state practice acts. It is important to understand the relationship of these elements to each other because they support our practice and are the basis for delineated scope of practice language in state law.

Education

The Accreditation Council for Occupational Therapy Education (ACOTE) standards define entry-level skills and competencies that students should acquire during the educational and fieldwork process, thereby establishing the baseline occupational therapy body of knowledge.[2] However, many practice areas, particularly as specialization and knowledge grow, require additional training (which may include hands-on practicums) to ensure competency. Competency must be documented and upgraded regularly to maintain a consistent skill level and to provide state-of-the-art care. It is also necessary to meet requirements of regulatory agencies that want proof of current competency, particularly in high-risk procedures. Principle 4 of the Code of Ethics ("Occupational therapy personnel shall achieve and continually maintain high standards of competence. [duties]"[1]) speaks specifically to this ethical obligation. In addition, an ethical mandate to "do good" or do the right thing ("Principle 1. Occupational therapy personnel shall demonstrate a concern for the well-being for the recipients of their services [beneficence]") and above all, do no harm ("Principle 2. Occupational therapy personnel shall take reasonable precautions to avoid imposing or inflicting harm upon the recipient of services or to his or her property [nonmaleficence]") reinforce the need for basic and continuing education to maintain and enhance knowledge and skills. Guideline 4.2 of *Guidelines to the Occupational Therapy Code of Ethics* provides additional support for competency in less established areas: "When generally recognized standards do not exist in emerging areas of practice, occupational therapy personnel must take responsible steps to ensure their own competence" (p. 882).[3]

Application in Practice

The second component of defining a scope of professional practice is an identifiable history of application. Although certain aspects of occupational therapy practice are well-documented in the literature, others that reflect newer or less traditional approaches to practice or atypical settings are not. Relevant literature or research studies showing the efficacy of certain interventions, combined with practitioner competency, may satisfy the test for inclusion in the occupational therapy scope of practice, especially where statutory language is very broad and nonspecific. This history may be especially important when a particular approach would not be defined as "usual and customary" practice by the average clinician.

However, a more basic consideration, particularly when an administrator or supervisor is requesting that an occupational therapist provide more medically related or maintenance-type interventions, is the appropriateness of such a request. The recipient of such services should require the skills unique to an occupational therapist or occupational therapy assistant, and the treatment plan should focus on objective, measurable goals to be met within a reasonable timeline. This guideline reflects Medicare criteria for appropriate intervention and payment but is also useful as an internal gauge of whether occupational therapy services should be provided and within what parameters.

Legal Framework

State licensure laws legally define a profession's scope of practice or domain. Although occupational therapy is regulated in all states, the District of Columbia, Puerto Rico, and Guam, several have less stringent forms of regulation, such as certification, registration, or trademark. The primary goal of all forms of regulation is to protect consumers. However, only licensure defines and legally protects the occupational therapy scope of practice so that those who are not licensed cannot call themselves occupational therapists or occupational therapy assistants and cannot provide services delineated within the occupational therapy scope of practice. Licensure for occupational therapists exists in 47 states and for occupational therapy assistants in 43 states. Certification (Indiana) and registration (Hawaii and Michigan) may contain definitions of occupational therapy but do not define a scope of practice, so others may, under some circumstances, use occupational therapy interventions if they do not call these services "occupational therapy." Colorado has a trademark law that protects the title "occupational therapist" (there is no title protection for "occupational therapy assistant") based on meeting certain educational and training requirements, but it does not define occupational therapy or delineate a scope of practice.[4]

It is every occupational therapist's and occupational therapy assistant's professional responsibility to have a copy of his or her state licensure law (or other regulatory document) and to be familiar with its contents, as well as to access updates as they occur. This is also an ethical responsibility, as per Principle 5 of the Code of Ethics ("Occupational therapy personnel shall comply with laws and Association policies guiding the profession of occupational therapy. [justice]"). About 15 states have adopted the AOTA Code of Ethics (although not always the most current version). Other states have language pertaining to ethics or ethical practice within their statutes. State licensure laws define what can legally be done by practitioners licensed in that state, so in that regard licensure laws are the final authority. However, laws can be subject to interpretation, especially because it is virtually impossible (and undesirable) to enumerate in detail every possible appropriate occupational therapy evaluation or intervention.

Members of a state licensure board may assist in clarifying what they consider to be within the occupational therapy scope of practice as defined in the licensure law. A good test is to determine whether most occupational therapy practitioners would, if called to testify in a court case, verify that the area in question is "usual and customary practice" (although this test becomes more difficult as innovative practice areas emerge that are not yet in the mainstream).

In addition to statutory language, educational criteria for accredited occupational therapy programs, support from literature and Association and other documents, as well as competency may assist practitioners in supporting their actions as within an appropriate occupational therapy scope of practice. In the case of less mainstream practice areas, these criteria, as well as align-ment with occupational therapy philosophy (as outlined later in this article) will be particularly relevant.

Practitioners also need to understand payer policies and other laws and regulations that govern their practice. This information includes Medicare rules about supervision, documentation, and coding and billing, as well as other legal information that relates to their client population or practice setting. Because these guidelines change frequently, it is important to visit the Centers for Medicare and Medicaid Services (CMS) Web site (http://www. cms.hhs.gov) frequently, as well as to use announcements and updates on the AOTA Web site (www.aota.org) from the Federal Affairs, State Policy, and Reimbursement groups. Additional resources, particularly on potential or pending legislation or other activities that affect practice and education, can be found in AOTA's monthly electronic AOTA *Scope of Practice Issues Update.* Documents such as the *Occupational Therapy Practice Framework: Domain and Process,*[5] the *Occupational Therapy Code of Ethics (2000),*[1] *Guidelines to the Occupational Therapy Code of Ethics,*[3] the *ACOTE Standards of Accreditation,*[2] *Standards for Continuing Competence,*[6] *Scope of Practice,*[7] and position papers on the specific topic can provide important guidance in supporting current and evolving practice parameters.

REASONING PROCESS

The purpose of the preceding discussion is to provide resources and foundational knowledge to understand and articulate legal and ethical occupational therapy scope of practice. However, because many of the questions posed earlier in this article do not necessarily have a straightforward, definitive answer, a framework for decision making may be useful to assist in the reasoning process. The following are some questions for self-reflection:

- Was this body of knowledge part of my educational curriculum?

- Am I competent to provide this intervention based on past education or current or continuing education?
- Is my knowledge in this area current and adequate to provide competent services?
- Is this intervention or practice usual and customary among occupational therapy practitioners, and would many of them agree? If not, is it defensible and consistent with the occupational therapy scope of practice utilizing criteria previously outlined?
- Have I sought clarification from the state licensure board in interpreting less well-defined areas of the occupational therapy scope of practice?
- Have I sought resources like AOTA position papers or official documents relating to this area of practice (or done a literature search to provide evidence for my practice interventions?)
- Is this occupational therapy? How does this relate to the philosophy of occupational therapy? Am I using occupation to promote engagement in meaningful activities and participation in life roles?

The last question may be the most critical. Despite the fact that an intervention is legal and ethical, it still may not be in line with the philosophical tenets of the occupational therapy profession. As articulated in the *Framework*, "Occupational therapy has a unique focus on occupation and daily life activities and the application of an intervention process that facilitates engagement in occupation to support participation in life" (p. 609).[5] As the profession's roles and contributions to society continue to evolve, the concepts outlined in the *Framework* can prove invaluable in facilitating the reasoning process to respond to scope of practice challenges.

CONCLUSION

The evolution of new patient populations, intervention strategies, and practice settings inevitably poses challenges to ensuring that practice is in line with legal, ethical, and philosophical guidelines and regulations. The occupational therapy profession has much to offer if occupational therapy practitioners, regardless of their roles and practice settings, have the knowledge and understanding of the underpinnings that define our profession and are able to clearly articulate it to consumers, colleagues, and outside publics.

REFERENCES

1. American Occupational Therapy Association. (2000). Occupational therapy code of ethics (2000). *American Journal of Occupational Therapy, 54,* 614–616. (*Note:* This document was updated in 2005. American Occupational Therapy Association. (2005). *American Journal of Occupational Therapy, 59,* 639–642.)
2. Accreditation Council for Occupational Therapy Education. (1999). Standards for an accredited educational program for the occupational therapist; Standards for an accredited educational program for the occupational therapy assistant. *American Journal of Occupational Therapy, 53,* 575–589. (*Note:* These documents were updated in 2007. ACOTE. (2007) Accreditation standards for a doctoral-degree-level education program for the occupational therapist; Accreditation standards for a master's-degree-level occupational therapist; Accreditation standards for an educational program for the occupational therapy assistant. *American Journal of Occupational Therapy, 61,* 641–671.)
3. American Occupational Therapy Association. (1998). Guidelines to the occupational therapy code of ethics. *American Journal of Occupational Therapy, 52,* 881–884. (*Note:* This document was updated in 2006. American Occupational Therapy Association. (2006). *American Journal of Occupational Therapy, 60,* 652–658.)
4. McCormack, G., Jaffe, E., & Goodman-Lavey, M. (Eds.). (2003). *The occupational therapy manager* (4th ed.). Bethesda, MD: AOTA Press.
5. American Occupational Therapy Association. (2002). Occupational therapy practice framework: Domain and process. *American Journal of Occupational Therapy, 56,* 609–639.
6. American Occupational Therapy Association. Standards for continuing competence. *American*

Journal of Occupational Therapy, 53, 599–600. (*Note:* This document was updated in 2005. American Occupational Therapy Association. (2005). *American Journal of Occupational Therapy, 59,* 661–662.)

7. American Occupational Therapy Association. (2004). Scope of practice. *American Journal of Occupational Therapy, 58,* 673–677.

Author

Deborah Yarett Slater, MS, OTR/L, FAOTA
AOTA Staff Liaison to the Ethics Commission

Originally published in *OT Practice,* September 6, 2004, pp. 13–16.

CHAPTER 26

Ethics in Practice: Whose Responsibility?

The resurgence in the job market for both occupational therapists and occupational therapy assistants is good news to educators, students, and practitioners alike. In some cases, sign-on bonuses and other incentives seem to be making a comeback. This would appear to be a positive sign for the profession, but is it coming at a price?

For a number of years, reimbursement in all clinical settings has generally been capitated, often at a level that barely covers costs and expenses. It is usually linked to a diagnostic category that estimates the resources required to care for the client. These resources include equipment, nursing, therapy, medical supplies, room and board, and so forth. Salaries, although increasing only in small increments, represent a significant expense against limited and fixed reimbursement. The cost of advances in technology has also added to rising expenditures. As a result of these various factors, it has become increasingly difficult for facilities to break even or to make even a modest profit. Publicly held companies, even in health care, need to show profits to their shareholders.

In an effort to earn income, given all the regulatory and other constraints, some facilities and contract staffing companies have mandated productivity requirements, documentation guidelines, and general rules about clinical management of clients that appear to be based primarily on administrative decisions to meet designated financial goals. These requirements often do not rely on the clinical judgment of

therapists or take into account the individual needs or capabilities of the client. As health care focuses on business practices and profits, there has been an "an erosion of the appropriate professional moral climate from service to self-interest in all of its forms . . . and the opposite of moral courage: indifference and apathy" (p. 215).[1]

Although this trend seems to be more prevalent in skilled-nursing facilities (SNFs) under the prospective payment system (PPS), and especially in contract staffing companies that provide employees for these facilities, it is also reported in other settings. Recently, an increasing number of questions have arisen from American Occupational Therapy Association (AOTA) members about their employers' administrative practices and directives. The questions center on ethical and legal concerns related to client safety, personal liability and licensure, and potential Medicare fraud. These situations may include

- Admitting clients who are independent, then requiring therapists to "be creative" in developing goals and treatment plans.
- Admitting clients for rehabilitation who are very acute or unstable, placing them in "high" or "ultra-high" categories to maximize reimbursement, then mandating that therapists provide the hours of therapy these categories require. This may happen in spite of the client's inability to tolerate extensive therapy and, according to some reports,

therapists are asked to record rest periods as minutes of treatment.

- Having nonclinical administrators or clinical directors in other disciplines dictate the frequency or length of treatment without input from the evaluating or treating occupational therapist.
- Asking a new therapist to "fill in" missing documentation (on clients they have not treated or who may already have been discharged), which should have been done by an occupational therapist or occupational therapy assistant at the time of treatment, so the facility can bill for those sessions after the fact.
- Not permitting clinicians to discharge clients when their goals have been met unless the discharge is "approved" by an administrator (extending length of stay and reimbursement).
- Requiring excessive group treatment and calling it "concurrent treatment" when it is not appropriate to meet the client's goals.
- Therapists and clients alike feeling like "failures" for their inability to achieve the proscribed minutes of therapy and having to provide explanations for the shortfall.

These situations can lead to loss of autonomy in clinical decision making, a potential feeling of disrespect from colleagues and, in many cases, ethical and legal unrest. The dilemmas and stress increase when therapists are told that these practices are acceptable, perhaps the industry standard, and that "others" can meet these demands. An additional source of concern is members who report that less-experienced therapists don't seem to recognize that there is a problem with these directives. Therapists may believe that when they are following a supervisor's or administrator's directive, any behavior is acceptable, and they and their licenses are protected.

In fact, each occupational therapist and occupational therapy assistant has a personal and professional responsibility to know and understand regulations that govern his or her practice. Principle 5 of the *Occupational Therapy Code of Ethics (2005)*[2] (the Code) states that "Occupational therapy personnel shall comply with laws and Association policies guiding the profession of occupational therapy." This principle includes state practice acts where applicable, Medicare and other payer regulations, and so forth. Understanding regulations is as much a part of one's job and professional role as clinical knowledge. Lack of knowledge is not an acceptable excuse and will not stand up to ethical or legal scrutiny. Therapists must provide treatment, document, and bill according to Medicare requirements for coverage of occupational therapy services (e.g., skilled services that are reasonable and necessary to meet realistic, objective goals in a specified time frame). In addition, there are clear rules about group treatment that apply to Medicare Part A in SNFs: The group may not exceed four patients and may not exceed 25% of each client's total treatment time.

The Code can provide assistance in responding to these situations. Principle 6C of the Code states that any form of communication (which includes written documentation) should not contain "false, fraudulent, deceptive, or unfair statements or claims."[2] Guideline 1.6 of the *Guidelines to the Occupational Therapy Code of Ethics* also provides relevant guidance: "Occupational therapy practitioners terminate services when the services do not meet the needs and goals of the service recipient, or when services no longer produce a measurable outcome" (p. 652).[3] These official documents, as well as relevant payer regulations, can provide support for practitioners confronting potentially unethical situations or managers who create them.

At a more fundamental level, professionals have the public's trust and operate with relative freedom and autonomy because they have a code of ethics and are generally considered altruistic. Situations like those reported directly challenge two core ethical concepts: *beneficence* and *nonmaleficence*. Principle 1 of the Code states "Occupational therapy personnel shall demonstrate a concern for the safety and well-being of the recipients of their services *(Beneficence)*."[2] Principle 2 states "Occupational therapy personnel shall take measures to ensure a recipient's safety and avoid imposing or inflicting harm *(Nonmaleficence)*." Therapy means "doing good" and a "duty to confer benefits to others." Conversely, it means "not harming or causing harm to be done . . ." and a duty to *"ensure* [emphasis added] that no harm is done."[2] Therefore, clinicians have a responsibility to provide treatment that will, in their judgment, benefit the client, not do any harm, and then to accurately document and bill for the services delivered.

Dealing with organizational pressures to use financial goals as the basis for action can be stressful and may result in negative consequences. These consequences can be severe and have both legal (fines, prison time) and ethical (reprimand, censure) implications. However, moral courage requires not only identifying ethical dilemmas and knowing what is good and right but also doing it.[1] Rather than self-serving behaviors or excuses to justify one's actions, the moral imperative to action stems from true altruism or caring about others.[1] Whistleblower laws can provide some protection from retribution, but job loss or demotion may, in some cases, be realistic deterrents. Although therapists can face difficult choices, being prepared with creative problem-solving skills and objective strategies may assist in responding to potentially unethical, and sometimes illegal, directives.

A first step may be to educate employers and colleagues. They should understand that it is in their best interest, as well as a legal requirement, to be compliant with regulations and that doing so will protect them against liability. Many resources are available from AOTA, including official documents such as the *Occupational Therapy Code of Ethics (2005);*[2] *Guidelines to the Occupational Therapy Code of Ethics;*[3] *Scope of Practice;*[4] *Standards of Practice for Occupational Therapy;*[5] and *Guidelines for Supervision, Roles, and Responsibilities During the Delivery of Occupational Therapy Services (2004).*[6] The *Reference Guide to the Occupational Therapy Ethics Standards*[7] contains advisory opinions and other articles relating to ethical challenges in practice situations. Staff in the Ethics Office at AOTA are also available to discuss ethical dilemmas and provide assistance in resolving them (e-mail ethics@aota.org). In addition, knowledge and availability of relevant Medicare and other payer regulations, as well as current written updates, are critical components of every practitioner's professional library. These are available on the AOTA Web site in the "Reimbursement" section and on the Centers for Medicare and Medicaid Services (CMS) Web site (http://www.cms.hhs.gov). CMS also maintains a hot-line in the Office of the Inspector General and provides information on how to report alleged fraud at http://oig.hhs.gov/hotline.html.

Practitioners are expected to be familiar with, make others aware of, and apply the Code to their everyday practice. Given the business-driven focus in the health care industry, practitioners are likely to encounter ethical and legal dilemmas in their workplace. It is ultimately a personal and professional responsibility not only to recognize unethical situations but to take action to expose and correct them to the extent possible.

REFERENCES

1. Davis, C. (2005). Educating adult health professionals for moral action: In search of moral courage. In R. B. Purtilo, G. M. Jensen, & C. B. Royeen (Eds.), *Educating for moral action: A sourcebook in health and rehabilitation ethics* (pp. 215, 217). Philadelphia: F. A. Davis.
2. American Occupational Therapy Association. (2005). Occupational therapy code of ethics

(2005). *American Journal of Occupational Therapy, 59,* 639–642.

3. American Occupational Therapy Association. (1998). Guidelines to the occupational therapy code of ethics. *American Journal of Occupational Therapy, 52,* 881–884. (*Note:* Since this article was originally published, this reference has been updated; see American Occupational Therapy Association. (2006). *American Journal of Occupational Therapy, 60,* 652–658.)

4. American Occupational Therapy Association. (2004). Scope of practice. *American Journal of Occupational Therapy, 58,* 673–677.

5. American Occupational Therapy Association. (2005). Standards of practice for occupational therapy. *American Journal of Occupational Therapy, 59,* 663–665.

6. American Occupational Therapy Association. (2004). Guidelines for supervision, roles, and responsibilities during the delivery of occupational therapy services (2004). *American Journal of Occupational Therapy, 58,* 663–667.

7. Scott, J. B. (Ed.). (2003). *Reference guide to the occupational therapy code of ethics.* Bethesda, MD: American Occupational Therapy Association. (*Note:* This reference is updated every two years.)

Author

Deborah Yarett Slater, MS, OT/L, FAOTA

AOTA Staff Liaison to the Ethics Commission

Originally published in *OT Practice*, October 17, 2005, pp. 13–15. References and links have been updated. Used with permission.

CHAPTER 27

The Ethics of Productivity

Productivity measures can be an effective management tracking tool, ensuring that departments are run efficiently and enabling accurate budgeting. But in the hands of overly aggressive administrators or supervisors, they sometimes are used as a tool to push the reimbursement envelope and supersede professional judgment about how clients receive occupational therapy services. In spite of organizational directives about frequency, duration, and one-on-one versus group intervention, every occupational therapist and occupational therapy assistant has a professional responsibility to ensure that they are in compliance with legal statutes and ethical principles when they provide care.

Productivity targets are frequently achieved through the use of alternatives to one-on-one intervention. These alternatives can include what Medicare defines as *concurrent therapy*, or *dovetailing*, allowing the practitioner to work with more than one client in the same treatment area. According to the *Resident Assessment Instrument (RAI) User's Manual*[1] (an instrument developed by the Centers for Medicare & Medicaid Services [CMS] for the Minimum Data Set [MDS] in Nursing Homes), the total time of concurrent therapy may be counted when

A licensed therapist starts work directly with one resident beginning a specific task. After the resident can proceed with supervision, the licensed therapist works directly with a second resident to get him/her started on a different task, while continuing to supervise the first resident (p. 187).[1]

In this situation the total therapy time, including when the therapist is supervising client activity, may be counted for each client. The example provided in the RAI clarifies CMS's expectation that the client is receiving a substantial amount of true one-on-one therapy in addition to the therapy provided concurrently. In addition, CMS has stated that the decision of whether concurrent therapy is to be used should be made at the treating therapist's discretion and should not be concerns.[2]

Group therapy is another method of providing care to multiple clients at the same time. Skilled nursing facility Part A rules require that group therapy be limited to 25% of the patient's time spent in therapy (as defined by the 7-day lookback during MDS assessments) and that there be only 4 clients per group per supervising therapist or therapy assistant.[2] Medicare rules emphasize that, although concurrent therapy is allowable, the decision to use it must be based on the therapist's judgment when clinically appropriate and documented as part of the client's plan of treatment.

The *Standards of Practice for Occupational Therapy*[3] outline the appropriate components of the service delivery process. With support from the "Ethics Standards" and relevant legal statutes, they also define best practice. These documents can assist practitioners in making appropriate decisions about how to render care.

After evaluation, occupational therapists develop plans of care, including frequency, duration, and types of intervention that best match the collaborative goals set by therapists with their clients. The plan of care may incorporate not only one-on-one direct service but, where appropriate, may reflect the use of group or concurrent therapy as elements of the intervention plan. However, individualized, one-on-one intervention should be part of every client's plan of care for the following reasons:

- The collaboration between the client and the therapist to identify meaningful goals and the strategies to attain them is, by nature, an individualized, developmental process.
- The treatment plan should be reassessed and revised at different points in the course of rehabilitation based on the client's response to intervention.
- Group or concurrent therapy does not allow for the therapist, who is overseeing multiple patients, to adapt the activity to provide the "just-right" challenge based on individual performance or response.

"Reductionist" therapy interventions, such as basic exercises, are easily adapted to group or concurrent therapy but often are not occupation based. Therapists should consider the following questions when deciding whether to use group or concurrent therapy:

- Am I choosing to provide treatment concurrently or in a group because that form of treatment is the most effective method of providing the necessary intervention and is, therefore, in the client's best interests?
  or
- Am I selecting group or concurrent therapy because these interventions are easiest and result in the ability to "treat" many more clients than a labor-intensive, one-on-one service delivery model?

Organizations may mandate that all clients be treated in groups or that several will be treated concurrently. This mandate is clearly designed to maximize billable hours and extend staff as much as possible. Staff at these organizations report that administrators also claim that this practice is perfectly legal. It is true that there is nothing inherently unethical or illegal with using these service delivery models as part of an overall occupational therapy plan of care. However, an ethical issue can arise when these models make up the bulk of the occupational therapy intervention or when the client's needs are not appropriate for this model.

It is the role of the occupational therapist, using clinical judgment, to determine an appropriate mix of group, concurrent, and individual interventions as supported by the goals and outcomes that he or she has identified with the client. It is also the role and ethical responsibility of the therapist to personally know, understand, and interpret payer and other rules and regulations that govern the delivery of services. Copies of the relevant statutes, program transmittals, and so forth should be available in clinical departments for reference and support if challenged. It is not acceptable for practitioners to permit external, sometimes nonclinical, staff or administrators to supersede their own clinical judgment. That said, it is also a professional responsibility to incorporate a mix of service delivery models that will most efficiently meet the therapy goals, so limited staffing resources can be allocated appropriately and fairly. Again, the key is that the decisions must be clinically based.

Occupational therapy practitioners sometimes have a unique challenge in that our focus on occupational performance may present an even greater challenge to productivity. The nature of much of our profession is based on occupation-based evaluation and collaborative goal setting to ensure that therapeutic interventions are leading to performance of meaningful activities for that client. Hopefully these interventions will ultimately facilitate greater engagement and participation, both internally and in larger society.

CASE EXAMPLE

An occupational therapist is hired to work 8 hours of PRN coverage in a local skilled nursing facility over the weekend. Upon arrival, he finds coverage notes indicating that he is to complete 20 Medicare Part A treatments and 3 occupational therapy evaluations. Overwhelmed, he contacts the facility rehabilitation director to ask for clarification. The director advises him to "dovetail" or provide concurrent therapy for 5 clients at a time, seeing each cluster of clients for a 1-hour period. This approach will allow the therapist to complete all 20 treatments in 4 hours and will leave the other half of his workday free to complete the evaluations. In examining the goals and clinical issues of some of the clients on his caseload, the occupational therapist suggests that one-on-one therapy visits may be more appropriate for some of the treatments. The director replies that this is the facility "protocol" and if the occupational therapist cannot fulfill the demands of the policy, then perhaps he should find another place to work. The therapist is torn between doing what he clinically believes to be the right thing and satisfying the expectations of the work site. *(Case example submitted by Pam Toto, MS, OTR/L, BCG, FAOTA)*

DISCUSSION

So how do intervention models that use group therapy or concurrent therapy fit with the client-centered approach we all promote? Are we working to increase employer reimbursement or to benefit our clients? Can both of these mandates be satisfied? Are we using intervention models that maximize the number of clients who can be "treated" at once so staff numbers can be kept unrealistically low and re-

imbursement can be kept relatively high? These questions can present true ethical dilemmas because an organization must be financially viable, yet our clients trust us to provide only the services we believe will be effective for their particular clinical situations and for only as long as they benefit from them. The American Occupational Therapy Association frequently gets inquiries from members who are challenged to meet productivity requirements that seem arbitrary (or are based on the number needed to hit reimbursement targets), while providing what they consider to be ethical treatment in line with the philosophy of occupational therapy.

How should practice decisions be made, and what constitutes "best practice"? In addition to the *Standards of Practice for Occupational Therapy*,[3] the *Occupational Therapy Code of Ethics (2005) (Code)*[4] and the *Guidelines to the Occupational Therapy Code of Ethics* (Guidelines)[5] provide guidance that ensures that the best interests of the client are served. They also can serve as support for practitioners' right to autonomy in making clinical decisions based on their knowledge, competence, and status as a professional. Several principles of the Code are particularly relevant. Clearly, Principle 1: "Occupational therapy personnel shall demonstrate a concern for the safety and well-being of the recipients of their services *(beneficence)*" (p. 639) and the related Principle 1C: "Occupational therapy personnel shall make every effort to advocate for recipients to obtain needed services through available means" (p. 639) are central concepts.[4] We have an ethical obligation to "do good" for our clients and provide what we believe is in their best interests to address their performance and other needs. An equally central principle of ethical treatment is to prevent harm *(nonmaleficence)*. Principle 2C requires that occupational therapy personnel "refrain from any undue influences that may compromise provision of service" (p. 240).[4] Likewise, Principle 2D requires that we "exercise professional judgment and critically analyze directives that could result in potential harm before implementation" (p. 240).[4] This principle applies to physician orders that may conflict with what we believe will benefit the client or are counter to current best practice and evidence. It also applies to administrative mandates that violate clinical judgment about what will benefit our clients. Principles 5 *(procedural justice)* and 6 *(veracity)* of the Code also speak to ethical imperatives that are relevant to practice. Principle 5 requires us to be knowledgeable about and compliant with laws, rules, policies, and so forth, whether they are local, state, federal, or institutional, that are applicable to delivering occupational therapy services, including payer regulations. This Principle obligates us to ensure that our employers are also aware of the ethical requirements of our profession. Further, Principle 6C prohibits the use of "false, fraudulent, deceptive, or unfair statements or claims" (p. 641).[4] Therefore, practitioners cannot document for group or concurrent therapy services as if one-on-one, individual services were actually provided, and they should not allow their employers to do so either.

Guideline 2.10 of the *Guidelines to the Occupational Therapy Code of Ethics*[5] is also particularly relevant to this issue: "Occupational therapy personnel who provide information through oral and written means shall emphasize that ethical and appropriate service delivery for clients cannot be done without proper individualized evaluations and plans of care." This guideline also addresses facility administrators who may direct practitioners to just put all clients into groups or provide treatment when no physician referral or evaluation has been done first, as is required. Of course, services should be terminated "when they do not meet the needs and goals of the recipient or when services no longer produce a measurable outcome" (Guideline 1.6).[5] Therefore, all aspects of the service delivery process, from the initial evaluation, to the plan of care, to discharge, must be provided with the client's goals and benefit in mind, supported by the practitioner's clinical judgment and objective documentation. This process is also necessary to meet coding and billing regulations for legitimate payment for services.

Guideline 3.4 emphasizes that occupational therapy personnel need to work with their employers to develop policies and procedures to ensure that they are legal, in compliance with regulations, and consistent with the Code. Lastly, when conflict or potential ethical violations do occur within an organization, occupational therapy personnel should first attempt to resolve them internally. If that is not successful or appropriate, action may be "taken by consultation with or referral to institutional, local, district, territorial, state, or national groups who have jurisdiction over occupational therapy practice."[5] This guideline implies an obligation not only to ensure that one's facility is in compliance with legal and ethical mandates but that one's clinical colleagues are as well.

A challenging reimbursement environment has the potential to give rise to unrealistic productivity requirements that are potentially illegal or unethical. Occupational therapy practitioners should remember that they have an obligation to exercise their professional judgment in making clinical decisions, and to be in compliance with the *Standards of Practice*,[3] *Code of Ethics*,[4] and applicable laws, regardless of organizational, supervisory, or peer pressure.

REFERENCES

1. Centers for Medicare & Medicaid Services. (2002, December). *Revised long term care Resident Assessment Instrument (RAI) user's manual for the minimum data set (MDS)* (Version 2.0). Retrieved August 8, 2006, from http://www.cms. hhs.gov /nursinghomequalityinits/20_nhqimds20.asp

2. Prospective Payment System and Consolidated Billing for SNF for FY 2006. Final Rule. (2005, August 4). *Federal Register, 70,* 45026–45125.

3. American Occupational Therapy Association. (2005). Standards of practice for occupational therapy. *American Journal of Occupational Therapy, 59,* 663–665.

4. American Occupational Therapy Association. (2005). Occupational therapy code of ethics (2005). *American Journal of Occupational Therapy, 59,* 639–642.

5. American Occupational Therapy Association. (2006). Guidelines to the occupational therapy code of ethics. *American Journal of Occupational Therapy, 60,* 652–658.

FOR MORE INFORMATION

- **AOTA Web Site**—Medicare rules about concurrent therapy (dovetailing) and group therapy can be found with clinical interpretations in question-and-answer format in the Reimbursement section of the AOTA Web site (http://www.aota.org/members/area5/links/link25.asp?PLACE=/members/area5/links/link25.asp)

- *Resident Assessment Instrument User's Manual*—Get more information about Medicare rules for correctly documenting therapy minutes on the CMS Web site (http://www.cms.hhs.gov/)

- *Explanation of Medicare Rules for Concurrent Therapy*—American Occupational Therapy Association. (2006). Retrieved August 7, 2006, from http://www.aota.org/members/area5/links/link25.asp

If you suspect that a facility is intentionally disregarding Medicare rules to the detriment of clients, reports can be made through official channels. More information can be found at http://www.medicare.gov/FraudAbuse/HowToReport.asp

Author

Deborah Yarett Slater, MS, OT/L, FAOTA, is a practice associate and staff liaison to the Ethics Commission for the American Occupational Therapy Association.

Originally published and copyrighted in 2006 by the American Occupational Therapy Association in *OT Practice,* October 23, 2006, pp. 17–20.

CHAPTER 28

To Err Is Human!

To err is human. As with other health care professionals, occupational therapy practitioners sometimes make errors and even cause harm to clients as well as to themselves.[1–3] Although errors are inevitable, the costs of human tragedy for clients, practitioners, and others highlight the urgent need for error reduction and prevention.

A first step in error reduction and prevention is to describe and understand common errors that occupational therapy practitioners make in practice. This understanding will allow practitioners to select appropriate prevention strategies.

Since 2000, the authors of this article have conducted a series of research projects on occupational therapy practice errors, supported by the Health Future Foundation and the National Patient Safety Foundation. Specifically, we examined the types, root causes, and impact of practice errors and preventive strategies in physical rehabilitation and geriatrics practice settings.[3] In this article, we synthesize our findings and discuss their implications.

COMMON OCCUPATIONAL THERAPY PRACTICE ERRORS

Practice errors can be categorized in different ways (see Table 28.1). One is to consider the severity, from minor to severe. Examples of minor errors include ripping fingernails, causing a client unnecessary fatigue, scratching a client's skin, or fabricating unit splints. More severe errors consist of a client falling during a transfer and being injured, rupturing tendons, fracturing bones, pulling out catheters during transfers, treating the wrong client or the wrong site, burning the client when applying a hot pack, causing urine backflow, and even contributing to client's death.

Errors also can be categorized as *technical* or *moral*. Technical errors, which concern certain methods, skills, or approaches within the scope of practice, often cause physical harm to clients. Technical errors include things like causing damage by using improper passive range of motion techniques, exceeding client limitations after a hip replacement, equipment malfunction, and so forth. Moral errors concern behaviors that (a) undercut the basic fabric of the professional–client relationship, or (b) are inconsistent with the *Occupational Therapy Code of Ethics (2005)*[4] and *Standards of Practice for Occupational Therapy*.[5] Examples of moral errors consist of failing to refer clients to the most appropriate provider or for the most appropriate services, providing unneeded service to obtain payment or reimbursement, being unable to provide needed services due to impairments or lack of knowledge and skills, and creating unrealistic expectations about a client's prognosis.

Errors can be further classified based on the occupational therapy process as delineated in the *Occupational Therapy Practice Framework: Domain and Process* (i.e., evaluation, interven-

TABLE 28.1. Classifications of Occupational Therapy Practice Errors

CLASSIFICATION	CATEGORIES	EXAMPLES
Severity	Minor	The therapist was transferring a client and had a poor grip on the gait belt when the client began to fall. The therapist readjusted his hold and ripped off his own thumbnail while simultaneously hitting the client.
	Severe	The therapist left a client unattended on a commode chair. The client tried to get up and fell off, hitting his head, which eventually led to his death.
Domain	Technical	A client requested a home evaluation after a hip replacement surgery. The therapist transported the client to her home. While the therapist was getting a walker for the client, the client independently got out of the car and popped the affected hip.
	Moral	The therapist conducted an evaluation, and the intervention was provided by an occupational therapy assistant who did not follow the treatment plan written by the therapist. The occupational therapy assistant required the client to use adaptive equipment that was inappropriate to the level of functioning. The client began to think negatively and felt disabled as a result of the adaptive equipment, which he did not need to use.
Occupational therapy process	Referral	The therapist failed to read the physician's orders.
	Evaluation	While establishing the client's occupational profile, which includes taking the medical history, the therapist failed to clarify the client's weight-bearing status.
	Intervention planning	The therapist failed to consider the layout of the client's bathroom when ordering a transfer bench, and it did not fit.
	Intervention	While the therapist was working on cooking activities with the client standing, the client lost her balance and fell.
	Discontinuation of service	The therapist discontinued a splint for a client recovering from a fracture without a physician's order.
Act	Omissions	The therapist failed to perform a driving evaluation for a client who stated his intentions to resume driving.
	Commission	The therapist underestimated the strength required to independently transfer a client, resulting in a client fall.
Scope	Individual	The therapist allowed the client to do tasks independently without direct supervision, when it was unsafe.
	Systemic	During a room exchange, the therapist failed to transfer all of the client's name-marked items, leading to future confusion.

tion, outcomes).[6] We found that the vast majority of practitioners' errors occur during the intervention phase.[3]

Errors can also occur as a result of an act of omission or an act of commission. *Omission* is the failure to do something one can and ought to do, or the failure to do the right thing. For example, failing to communicate the deteriorating mental status or disorientation of a client to other health care professionals, which results in the client falling, is an error of omission. An act of *commission* is a direct action that is wrong or incorrect, such as performing the wrong procedure on a client.

Furthermore, errors can be classified as individual (active) or systemic (latent). Individual errors are those for which a particular person is clearly responsible. Systemic errors are removed from the direct control of the person and frequently remain unnoticed or dormant until the resultant error occurs.

ROOT CAUSES

When an error occurs, most practitioners are extremely concerned and want to identify the underlying causes to understand how it could have happened and to prevent it from occurring again. However, the root causes of errors are multidimensional. They may involve human factors, equipment factors, controllable or uncontrollable environmental factors, and poorly structured organizations. The Joint Commission of Accreditation of Healthcare Organizations reported that many errors in health care are due to inadequate orientation, training, and education; communication failure; insufficient staffing; or distraction.[7] The major reported causes of error in occupational therapy are similar: misjudgment of the situation, inadequate preparation, lack of experience, inadequate training and knowledge, miscommunication among professionals, lack of attention, heavy workload, and others.[8]

Many of these causes of errors can be viewed as the result of problematic systems or process failures, to which there can be contributing factors. For example, inadequate preparation may

involve a lack of necessary training, the quality of the training program, and the level of competence or proficiency testing following the training.[9] Miscommunication may occur when there is a hierarchical culture that inadvertently creates barriers to sharing information. In fact, some reported practice errors in occupational therapy are caused by the practitioner's reluctance to raise concerns or question the physician or other health care professionals involved with the client's care.[3] This example raises further concerns since preventing, alleviating, or eliminating harm is an ethical concern as well. Many errors in occupational therapy are due to inadequate supervision of staff or unrealistic workloads. Heavy workload is a human resource and a supervisor issue and not just an individual occupational therapy practitioner problem.

Furthermore, when occupational therapy practitioners cause errors, it is assumed that, if they pay more attention or are more careful in the future, these errors will not occur again. Again, this approach points only to the individual as the source of error. In a complex system such as health care delivery, however, errors are inevitable regardless of how skilled, well-intentioned, or careful the individual practitioner may be. The potential for disastrous outcomes to occur in complex systems is well-documented.[10] Rarely is there just one isolated cause of error; rather, a series of events occur that ultimately result in the error.

Reason uses a Swiss cheese model to illustrate how the random chance of multiple errors can create organizational accidents or system errors.[10] In this model, latent conditions lie dormant in a system and become evident when they combine with other factors, thus wreaking havoc and posing a threat to the system. In hindsight, we often refer to these as *accidents waiting to happen.* On the other hand, unsafe acts that are committed by practitioners who are in direct contact with the client or system are referred to as *active errors* and "are felt almost immediately" (p. 173).[10] These active errors "nibble away at the cheese," thus making more holes in a system's defense. To illustrate, it would normally be impossible to place a stick straight through a block of Swiss cheese via the holes, because they do not line up. But when latent conditions combine with active errors, the system (or cheese) is "eaten away," creating more holes. The eventual alignment of holes is a perfect trajectory of opportunity for error and harm.[9] Most adverse events that result in harm to clients involve this combination of active and latent conditions.[10]

ERROR PREVENTION AND IMPLICATIONS

Fortunately, there are effective strategies to prevent or reduce errors. The most significant is to take a proactive, rather than a reactive, approach. Examples of proactive preventive approaches include, but are not limited to, establishing policies and procedures related to client safety, modifying existing safety protocols, cultivating a nonpunitive work culture, and critically considering the client mix to determine the most appropriate error prevention approaches. These strategies involve an administrative focus on safety and error prevention. For example, a facility manager may establish specific safety protocols for splint application. But for these protocols to work, the manager must also create a nonpunitive work environment where practitioners feel comfortable reporting and learning from errors. Policies and procedures must also be developed to address problems, and compliance must be mandated. A nonpunitive atmosphere promotes open and honest sharing and discussion to encourage practitioners to learn from errors. In fact, research suggests that practitioners value the learning opportunity when errors occur, and as a result they make constructive changes to their future practice.[3,8] Critically examining the client mix is another proactive approach. An example of this would be to establish a skin care program to help prevent skin breakdown after determining from an elder's medical history the potential for that problem.

A number of specific and discrete strategies can also be used by administrators and practitioners to prevent and reduce errors. For instance, administrators can strengthen the orientation process for new occupational therapists, occupational therapy assistants, and students. During the orientation, participants can be informed of situations in which errors have occurred or are prone to occur, the procedures that need to be followed when errors do occur, and the processes that need to be undertaken to ensure that staff members learn from the situation.

Providing frequent in-service training can improve practitioners' clinical competence. In-service training is a proactive approach to preventing and decreasing practice errors that occur due to lack of knowledge or lack of experience. It may also be instituted to generate ideas, strategies, and standards to reduce errors if a quality assurance review suggests particular trends. This training should also address areas identified as causative factors, based on facility data. For example, our research findings identified a lack of therapist assertiveness with physicians as a causative factor for client errors. Providing an in-service program focused on assertiveness training was one approach for reducing these errors. Another is creating a culture that supports assertiveness under certain conditions. In situations where therapists' poor judgment is a factor, in-service training could review case studies and potential interventions to hone clinical decision-making skills.

Professional educational programs should enhance their curriculum content pertaining to error reduction and client safety. Professional training should also teach future occupational therapy practitioners to be assertive in encouraging communication and collaboration among other health care professionals through an interdisciplinary care management process.[11] Offering an interprofessional course that focuses on client safety and error prevention is one way to promote effective communication and team building with other health care professionals. It is also important for educational programs to require critical analysis and active learning components to prepare students for the ambiguity of the practice environment. Students learn through activity by doing, including

REFERENCE GUIDE TO THE OCCUPATIONAL THERAPY ETHICS STANDARDS

the practice environment. Students learn through activity by doing, including continual exploration and interaction with others. An example of active learning is to role-play the handling of certain error scenarios.

Another major error preventive mechanism, recommended by the National Institute of Medicine, is to establish a comprehensive client safety program in individual health care settings.[12] For example, a nursing home could establish a splint safety program in which precautions and wearing schedules are clearly communicated to all staff. In any facility, the operations manager can make sure that the equipment is in good repair.

Error prevention and reduction should target the particular causes of the errors (see Table 28.2). For example, if a client fall was caused by poor judgment by the occupational therapist, a suggested preventive strategy is to teach therapists when it is appropriate to secure additional

TABLE 28.2. Error Examples, Possible Causes, and Preventive Strategies

ERROR EXAMPLES	POSSIBLE CAUSES	PREVENTIVE STRATEGIES (Select those most appropriate to the setting)
Falls	Distraction, lack of attention, misjudgment, insufficient staffing, inadequate training	▦ Cultivate a nonpunitive work culture to encourage reporting and learning from errors
Skin breakdown as a result of a splint being on too long	Insufficient staffing, poor communication, inexperience, insufficient monitoring	▦ Create policies and procedures and require staff to follow them
Not reviewing and verifying chart information	Poor communication, heavy workload, unavailability of chart	▦ Conduct a critical review of client mix
Treating the wrong client	Poor verification and communication, lack of attention	▦ Hold department orientation and training for all new staff
Hot pack on too long, resulting in burn	Lack of attention, heavy workload, inadequate knowledge	▦ Provide frequent in-services ▦ Establish department/institution programs for areas of concern (e.g., falls prevention plan)
Ruptured tendon	Lack of attention, misjudgment, inexperience, inadequate knowledge	
Not involving the client in the care plan	Misjudgment, inexperience	▦ Provide staff in-services on how to generally work with different treatment approaches (e.g., with a splint program)
Applying a serial cast on a person with poor sensation, resulting in pressure sores	Lack of attention, misjudgment, inexperience, inadequate knowledge	▦ Maintain appropriate staff levels ▦ Verify clients before beginning intervention
Making assumptions about an elder, such as cognitive impairment	Misjudgment, poor communication, inexperience	▦ Secure assistance when needed
False documentation	Inexperience, lack of assertiveness, inadequate knowledge, or unethical behavior	▦ Provide assertiveness training

help with transfers and to create a trigger list of criteria that might warrant help (e.g., client weighs more than 200 pounds). If the error involves treating the wrong client, a suggested prevention strategy is to have all clients wear, and practitioners verify, identification bracelets.

CONCLUSION

Although researchers have been studying practice errors by physicians, nurses, and pharmacists for some time, there is still much to be learned about occupational therapy errors. There is a need to continue to establish baseline data on errors and to implement changes and evaluate improvement. There is also a need to create a learning culture in which errors are not "swept under the carpet," so that authentic learning can take place. Client safety and error-reduction education and training should be made available to all occupational therapy practitioners. Knowledge is power, and learning from errors gives the practitioner and other health care professionals the tools necessary to improve client safety.

REFERENCES

1. American Occupational Therapy Association. (2001). *Ethics officer report: Comparison of occupational therapy insurance claims and ethics complaints.* Bethesda, MD: Author.
2. National Board for Certification in Occupational Therapy. (2000). *Investigations program manager report, NBCOT cases (complaints) broken down by state in the past 5 years (1995–1999).* Gaithersburg, MD: Author.
3. Scheirton, L., Mu, K., & Lohman, H. (2003). *Occupational therapists' responses to practice errors in physical rehabilitation settings.*
4. American Occupational Therapy Association. (2005). Occupational therapy code of ethics (2005). *American Journal of Occupational Therapy, 59,* 638–642.
5. American Occupational Therapy Association. (2005). Standards of practice for occupational therapy. *American Journal of Occupational Therapy, 59,* 663-665
6. American Occupational Therapy Association. (2002). Occupational therapy practice framework: Domain and process. *American Journal of Occupational Therapy, 56,* 609–639.
7. Joint Commission on Accreditation of Healthcare Organizations. (2003). *Root cause analysis in health care: Tools and techniques* (2nd ed.). Oakbrook Terrace, IL: Author.
8. Lohman, H., Mu, K., & Scheirton, L. (2003). Occupational therapists' perspectives on practice errors in geriatric practice settings. *Occupational Therapy in Geriatrics, 21*(4), 21–39.
9. Joint Commission on Accreditation of Healthcare Organizations. (2002). *Failure mode and effects analysis in health care: Proactive risk reduction.* Oakbrook Terrace, IL: Author.
10. Reason, J. (1990). *Human error.* New York: Cambridge University Press.
11. Joint Commission on Accreditation of Health-care Organizations. (2005). *Essentials for health care: Patient safety* (3rd ed.). Oakbrook Terrace, IL: Author.
12. Aspden, P., Corrigan, J. M., Wolcott, J., & Erickson, S. M. (Eds.). (2004). *Patient safety: Achieving a new standard for care.* Washington, DC: National Academies Press.

Authors

Keli Mu, PhD, OTR/L
Assistant Professor, Department of Occupational Therapy, Creighton University Medical Center, Omaha, NE

Helene Lohman, OTD, OTR/L
Associate Professor, Department of Occupational Therapy, Creighton University Medical Center, Omaha, NE

Linda Scheirton, PhD
Associate Dean, Academic Affairs, Associate Professor, Department of Occupational Therapy, Creighton University Medical Center, Omaha, NE

Originally published in *American Journal of Occupational Therapy, 58,* 109–112.

APPENDIXES

AOTA Position Statement on Occupational Therapy's Commitment to Nondiscrimination and Inclusion

The occupational therapy profession affirms the right of every individual to access and full participation within society. This paper states the profession's stance on nondiscrimination and inclusion.

Nondiscrimination exists when we accept and treat all people equally. In doing so, we avoid differentiating between people because of biases or prejudices. We value individuals and respect their culture, ethnicity, race, age, religion, gender, sexual orientation, and capacities. Nondiscrimination is a necessary prerequisite for inclusion. Inclusion requires that we ensure not only that everyone is treated fairly and equitably but also that all individuals have the same opportunities to participate in the naturally occurring activities of society, such as attending social events, having access to public transportation, and participating in professional organizations. We also believe that when we do not discriminate against others and when we include all members of society in our daily lives, we reap the benefits of being with individuals who have different perspectives, opinions, and talents from our own.

We support nondiscrimination and inclusion throughout our profession. Our concerns are twofold—for the persons who receive occupational therapy services and for our professional colleagues. In professional practice, our evaluations and interventions are designed to facilitate our clients' engagement in occupations to support participation in the various contexts of their lives, including their social and cultural contexts. As occupational therapists and occupational therapy assistants, we assume a collaborative partnership with clients and their significant others to support the individual's right to self-direction.

We believe that inclusion is achieved through the combined efforts of clients, their families, and significant others; health, education, and social service professionals; legislators; community members; and others. We support all individuals and their significant others' rights to fully participate in making decisions that concern their daily occupations: activities of daily living, instrumental activities of daily living, work, education, play, leisure, and social participation.

The American Occupational Therapy Association and its members recognize the legal mandates concerning nondiscriminatory practices. However, the concept of nondiscrimination is not limited to that which is dictated by law. This professional association, through its members, boards, commissions, committees, officers, and staff, supports the belief that all members of the occupational therapy professional community are entitled to maximum opportunities to develop and use their abilities. These individuals also have the right to achieve productive and satisfying professional and personal lives.

We are committed to nondiscrimination and inclusion as an affirmation of our belief that the interests of all members of the profession are best served when the inherent worth of every individual is recognized and valued. We maintain that society has an obligation to provide the reasonable accommodations necessary to allow individuals access to social, educational, recreational, and vocational opportunities. By embracing the concepts of nondiscrimination and inclusion, we will all benefit from the opportunities afforded in a diverse society.

Authors

Ruth H. Hansen, PhD, FAOTA
Jim Hinojosa, PhD, OT, FAOTA

for

The Commission on Practice
Mary Jane Youngstrom, MS, OTR—
Chairperson

Adopted by the Representative Assembly 1999M4

Edited by the Commission on Practice 2004

Received by the Representative Assembly 2004C28

Note: This document replaces the 1995 Position Paper *Occupational Therapy: A Profession in Support of Full Inclusion,* and accompanying 1996 White Paper *The Role of the Occupational Therapy Practitioner in the Implementation of Full Inclusion,* and the 1999 Position Paper *Occupational Therapy's Commitment to Nondiscrimination and Inclusion.*

Originally published in *American Journal of Occupational Therapy, 58,* p. 668.

Successful OT–OTA Partnerships
Staying Afloat in a Sea of Ethical Challenges

Your employer reduces the occupational therapist's hours to part-time status for "evaluations only" while increasing the use of occupational therapy assistants to provide all direct patient treatment in efforts to reduce costs. . . .

The occupational therapist, who also serves as the department head, regularly reduces the hours of the occupational therapy assistant when productivity and census are low so that she can maintain her own full-time status. . . .

Your employer no longer reimburses you for time not spent providing direct patient care; OT–OTA supervision must be completed on your own time and at your own expense. . . .

Do any of these scenarios sound familiar? If so, you are not alone. Dramatic changes in our health care system, especially those related to reduced reimbursement, have perpetuated unanticipated conflicts and issues among teams at all levels in the health care field. Since the surge of practitioners entering the profession, and perhaps even earlier, occupational therapy leaders have struggled to define specific roles for occupational therapists and occupational therapy assistants in traditional health care models. Emerging and expanding practice areas, as well as new holistic approaches to existing health care programs, further challenge one's ability to define this unique partnership. For many occupational therapy practitioners, these changes in practice have affected relationships, communication, and even ethics. In her book *Occupational Therapy Leadership*, Grace Gilkeson, EdD,

OTR, FAOTA, wrote, "Change is inevitable, but how you handle it makes all the difference between success and failure, satisfaction and disappointment" (p. 158).[1]

OT–OTA collaboration can be powerful when both parties embrace ethical and legal decision-making and problem-solving processes. This affirmative partnership can be successful as long as all practitioners have a common set of values in their therapeutic relationships and use of self. The American Occupational Therapy Association (AOTA) provides practitioners with guidelines for ethical practice through the AOTA *Occupational Therapy Code of Ethics (2000)*.[2] This document, combined with specific state regulations, provides a framework through which effective OT–OTA partnerships can be established and maintained. The following examples are common situations that may challenge professional ethics and the relationship of OT–OTA teams in practice. Solutions and strategies for maintaining strong and healthy OT–OTA partnerships also are offered.

SUPERVISION CHALLENGES

An occupational therapist has regularly been traveling among her company's inpatient, outpatient, and home health departments to complete evaluations and discharges. In each of these settings, occupational therapy assistants regularly provide all treatment. Because of limited time and scheduling conflicts, the occupational therapist rarely performs her supervisory role; she frequently cosigns notes without reading them, does not provide input on changes to the treatment plan, and relies on the occupational therapy assistants to determine independently when discharge is appropriate.

This situation addresses ethical and legal supervision issues, role delineation, and whether current practice patterns facilitate the best and most efficient patient care (*Occupational Therapy Code of Ethics,* Principle 5). Overriding these issues is the certainty that this OT–OTA team lacks, at the very least, effective communication.

Communication is one of the most critical variables for effective OT–OTA relationships, yet current practice trends offer significantly reduced opportunities for traditional methods of sharing information. One of the simplest ways for occupational therapists and occupational therapy assistants to communicate efficiently is through hands-on client care opportunities. If a picture is worth a thousand words, a treatment session is worth a million words!

Establish systems to ensure that the occupational therapist provides hands-on treatment at least once a week or on a regular basis for each client. In environments where the clients do not change quickly, such as long-term-care settings, consider switching caseloads 1 day per week or rotating workdays or work times for part-time employees. If the occupational therapist has time constraints that prohibit caseload changes, consider splitting the client's treatment session between the occupational therapist and the occupational therapy assistant, with the occupational therapist addressing those issues that most significantly affect goal changes and treatment plan upgrades. Providing opportunities for the occupational therapist to actually observe changes in function instead of relying on second-hand information for documentation and discharge planning can foster efficient communication between team members.

The pressure to maintain productivity standards sometimes seems to "force" practitioners to choose between direct client care and indirect, yet vital, communication. Practitioners should try to maintain more constant productivity percentages by managing and monitoring treatment caseloads throughout the week, thus allowing consistent productivity with adequate time for nonbillable necessities. It is also prudent to explore the many different modes of communication readily available as alternatives to face-to-face discussion. For example, storing information in a central, secure area or a communication book allows efficient access by all team members. Checklist notes and communication boards further increase efficiency by providing easy visual status of both direct and indirect client information. OT–OTA teams may also choose to create checklist forms to manage documentation and billing details or to ensure that all goals and performance areas and components are being addressed. (Not doing so is a common error when multiple clinicians are managing caseloads.) Laminated, wall-mounted communication boards can provide interdisciplinary team members with valuable information regarding evaluation and discharge dates, day and treatment minutes, and caseload assignments. E-mail and voicemail allow clinicians to exchange clinical information at their convenience. These alternatives, as well as regularly scheduled telephone conferences, reduce wasted time from playing "telephone tag" and interruptions during valuable direct client care.

SCOPE OF PRACTICE CHALLENGES

The occupational therapy assistant is the only full-time therapy practitioner providing services in one specific school-based setting. As such, he serves as the occupational therapy representative at family meetings and interdisciplinary team conferences. Often, due to their lack of knowledge, parents and faculty members refer to the assistant as the "occupational therapist" and seek his judgment on issues that affect the entire operation of occupational therapy services at the school. Because of time factors and the need for others to have immediate information, the occupational therapy assistant feels obligated to address all issues as they arise. As a result, the occupational therapist, who travels to sev-

eral schools and, thus, spends limited time in any single setting, feels as though she is "out of the loop" and is angry that the assistant is assuming roles that she believes are beyond the scope of practice for an occupational therapy assistant.

Ethics can be challenged when practitioners assume roles not representative of their credentials (*Occupational Therapy Code of Ethics,* Principle 6A). Conversely, practitioners must acknowledge and permit fellow team members to explore all opportunities that are within their scope of practice as defined by AOTA[3] and state regulations.

The complex elements required for effective teamwork can challenge even the strongest OT–OTA partnerships. The best way to resolve conflict is to anticipate issues and avoid problems through clearly established roles and responsibilities. In a 1999 *OT Practice* article, Barbara Hanft, MA, OTR, FAOTA, and Barbara Banks, COTA, identified expectations of occupational therapists and occupational therapy assistants that must be met for success in teamwork.[4] Occupational therapy assistants expected occupational therapists to share professional knowledge, help link interventions to meaningful outcomes, provide feedback that the occupational therapy assistant has value, be dependable, and provide tangible supervision. Conversely, the occupational therapist requested that the occupational therapy assistant ask questions, follow the treatment plan, and provide feedback for modifications. It is critical that OT–OTA teams take the time to recognize and address each other's needs.

If conflict arises, assertive communication and negotiation are generally the most effective way of addressing it. Both parties should attempt to keep an open mind, remain relaxed, and agree at the outset to seek a resolution. According to Pat Crist, PhD, OTR, FAOTA, conflict is first noted as a "*trigger*—any action or word that causes a negative response. Triggers can include body language or gestures (rolling of eyes); a loud stressed voice; physical actions; or even not taking action when it is expected" (p. 5).[5]

Passive or aggressive behavior can result from triggers or from any situation that causes one to perceive a threat of rejection or disapproval. When dealing with conflict, remain aware of others' trigger points and focus on the issues at hand rather than on negative emotions. Along with respect and active listening, Crist noted that using summary and reflection, incorporating "I" statements to describe the situation (e.g., "I feel. . ."), expressing your feelings, and noting the change you desire and the expected consequence are advantageous. Conflict is resolved in one of three ways—through authority, compromise, or consensual integration of the disagreeing parties' ideas. Consensus is the best choice in terms of team satisfaction but, unfortunately, is also the most difficult and time consuming. The sooner conflicts are managed, the easier the resolution. In this example, the occupational therapist and occupational therapy assistant should work together to identify the various job responsibilities crucial to success in this setting. Keeping their respective scopes of practice in mind, they should determine which roles are best suited for each. They will need to communicate this information to the school administrators and establish strategies to meet the needs of parents, students, and fellow professionals in a timely fashion. Lastly, the occupational therapist and occupational therapy assistant should establish a system to improve communication within their department, with an additional commitment to remain open-minded and address issues as they arise.

NOVICE PRACTITIONER CHALLENGES

An occupational therapy department in an acute-care hospital recently increased service availability from 5 days per week to 7 days per week. The department supervisor has left the task of determining work schedules up to the staff. Occupational therapists and occupational therapy assistants with the most seniority have exerted their influence in this decision-making process, and as a consequence, the new graduate therapist and entry-level assistant regularly are left to work alone on the weekends. Al-

though these novice clinicians have expressed their concern over a lack of guidance and mentorship, as well as frustration with permanent weekend duties, their complaints have not been answered.

This situation presents several concerns. From an ethical standpoint, the practitioners who are forced to work weekends regularly do not believe that they are receiving adequate supervision (*Occupational Therapy Code of Ethics,* Principle 4F). Additionally, respect for fellow team members has been replaced by personal working preferences. For OT–OTA teams and departments to develop and maintain healthy relationships, a commitment to flexibility is crucial. At a minimum, flexibility must be examined from the two key aspects of *scheduling* and *work hours.* Scheduling considerations include seeing clients at the best time of the day to meet the client's goals (e.g., seeing a client in the morning for activities of daily living [ADL] retraining) and allowing opportunities to share caseloads. Depending on the work setting, opportunities may arise to develop creative schedules that meet clients' needs more effectively. For example, when providing therapy in a skilled-nursing facility, the most valuable treatment interventions may require practitioners to alternate disciplines and treatment days, save their minutes, or barter for minutes with other disciplines to provide a complete occupation-based treatment session. One comprehensive session that addresses a specific performance area in an appropriate context may meet client-centered goals more effectively than several short sessions that only allow enough time to focus on limited performance components.

Often, the distribution of duties is lopsided, with the occupational therapy assistant performing most or all of the direct client care. By caseload sharing, an OT–OTA team commits to establishing a balance of duties involved with daily practice at a given site. This balance results in improved communication and enables both the occupational therapist and the occupational therapy assistant to enjoy other aspects of the job, such as program development, interdisciplinary team participation, and administrative functions.

For many veteran clinicians, the end of the traditional work schedule has been one of the hardest new trends to accept. OT–OTA teams must continuously analyze admission patterns and schedule workdays and hours to provide the best treatment at the best time to meet their clients' goals. Some facilities may regularly schedule admissions in late afternoon, which might mean that the occupational therapist needs to start the workday later. A caseload may be heavy with clients who require ADL retraining, and thus, the occupational therapy assistant may need to start work earlier than usual. Weekend and evening services should be rotated, or positions should be established and marketed as permanent off-hours assignments. Occupational therapy practitioners should also remain cognizant of legal and ethical obligations regarding entry-level practitioners. Teaming new clinicians with more experienced therapists and assistants not only will minimize supervision issues, but also will facilitate learning opportunities for both parties. As new graduates "learn the ropes" from their counterparts, senior clinicians may gain exposure to the current theories, new assessment techniques, and emerging trends in occupational therapy education. Flexibility demonstrates commitment to the profession and respect for colleagues. Remember, it is better to bend than to break.

MAINTAINING COMPETENCY CHALLENGES

The occupational therapy department staff in a local skilled-nursing facility has been reduced from six practitioners to one full-time occupational therapist and one full-time occupational therapy assistant. They consider themselves to be "survivors," having maintained employment and a commitment to their profession in spite of the many changes in reimbursement, documentation, supervision, and service delivery as a result of implementation of the prospective payment system (PPS). After the turmoil associated with PPS, they welcomed the renewed sense of normalcy and routine. However, this OT–OTA team now finds itself in somewhat of a rut. Each day seems remarkably the same as the pattern of meetings, documentation procedures, and treatment regimes is repeated; the budget no longer provides for continuing education; the employer does not reimburse for membership in professional associations; and there never seems to be time for program development. A profession that once offered novelty and excitement to these practitioners now seems monotonous.

As with an optimist who sees the glass half-full, so too can practitioners embrace change as an opportunity for improvement. In the March 1999 issue of the AOTA *Gerontology Special Interest Section Quarterly,* Pamela Lindstrom, MS, OTR/L, and Jennifer Westropp, MS, OTR/L, provided an explicit example of using change as a catalyst for revitalization.[6] They challenged practitioners to change their work environment to make it easier to engage in meaningful occupation-based treatment interventions. As part of their transformation, they rearranged supplies and physical space for activities and secured items such as clothing, horticulture materials, golfing equipment, and board games to help clients participate in meaningful tasks. They also created kits with supplies already assembled for occupation-based activities, such as grooming. These kits greatly reduced the time needed to set up activities. By facilitating a more occupation-based work environment, these authors improved service delivery and job satisfaction.

A commitment to excellence in occupational therapy requires us to examine our skills, practice patterns, and relationships continuously to define ways to maintain competency (*Occupational Therapy Code of Ethics,* Principles 4C and 4D). The value of new learning through continuing education or networking opportunities through membership in professional organizations may far outweigh their financial costs. OT–OTA teamwork presents an advantage to those seeking meaning and excellence in their practice through the sharing of knowledge and ideas. As the saying goes, "Two heads are better than one!"

CONCLUSION

Despite the challenges, OT–OTA teamwork is more critical than ever for advocacy and success in today's health care environment. As scrutiny increases over the efficacy of rehabilitation, including occupational therapy, occupational therapists and occupational therapy assistants must maintain healthy partnerships that enable the team to demonstrate the necessity of occupation to well-being. As our state and national professional associations work to improve OT–OTA role delineations and guides to practice, so too must we commit to engaging in team practice patterns that promote excellence in care and ensure viability of this essential partnership.

REFERENCES

1. Gilkeson, G. (1997). *Occupational therapy leadership.* Philadelphia: F. A. Davis.
2. American Occupational Therapy Association. (2000). Occupational therapy code of ethics (2000). *American Journal of Occupational Therapy, 54,* 614–616.
3. American Occupational Therapy Association. (1993). Occupational therapy roles. *American Journal of Occupational Therapy, 47,* 1087–1099.
4. Hanft, B., & Banks, B. (1999). Competent supervision: A collaborative process. *OT Practice, 4*(5), 31–34.
5. Crist, P. (1998, February 16). Hearing, understanding, resolving. *Advance for Occupational Therapists,* 5.
6. Lindstrom, P. R., & Westropp, J. (1999). Renewed energy following an epiphany at Annual Conference. *Gerontology Special Interest Section Quarterly, 22*(1), 1–3.

Authors

Pam Toto, MS, OTR/L, BCG
Diane M. Hill, COTA/L, AP

Pam Toto, MS, OTR/L, BCG, is an adjunct instructor at the University of Pittsburgh and Philadelphia University. She also provides occupational therapy services as a direct care provider in home health care and completes functional assessments as part of a National Institutes of Health–funded research project through the Mind–Body Research Center at the University of Pittsburgh Medical Center. Pam is the current editor of the *Gerontology Special Interest Section Quarterly* and the state secretary of the Pennsylvania Occupational Therapy Association.

Diane M. Hill, COTA/L, AP, is a direct care provider at an adult living community, Longwood at Oakmont, in a suburb of Pittsburgh, Pennsylvania. She is a member of the AOTA Standards and Ethics Commission and Advance Practice Program Committee. She has 14 years of experience as a practitioner and has earned the AOTA AP (advanced practitioner) credential in the specified area of geriatrics.

The authors co-wrote the article "OT/OTA Team Building in the SNF Environment: Meeting the Challenge" for the June 2001 issue of the *Gerontology Special Interest Section Quarterly*.

Originally published as *OT Practice,* July 2, 2001, pp. 9–12.

Glossary of Ethics Terms

altruism The promotion of good for others and the consideration of the consequences of the action for everyone except oneself.

autonomy (*auto = self, nomos = law*) The right of an individual to self-determination; the ability to independently act on one's decisions for his or her own well-being (Beauchamp & Childress, 2001).

beneficence (*bene faceae = to do well*) Doing good for others or bringing about good for them; the *duty* to confer benefits on others.

bioethics A type of *normative ethics* involving the application of ethical principles in health care delivery, medical treatment, and research.

care ethics An ethical concept found primarily in nursing and feminist literature that states that the attitude of being a moral person is based on the concepts of receptivity, relatedness, and responsiveness by the caregiver to the one being cared for.

casuistry Ethical decision making based on the understanding of a specific situation in relation to past events and historical records of similar cases; particular features of a case versus the broad overarching principles are studied.

categorical imperative A maxim described by Immanuel Kant as a "command" that has three components: universality, respect, and *autonomy*. Together they establish that an action is properly called "morally good" only if we can will all persons to do it, it enables us

to treat other persons as ends and not merely as the means to our own selfish ends, and it allows us to see other persons as mutual law-makers. Arguments are grounded in reason as opposed to tradition, emotion, or intuition.

confidentiality Not disclosing data or information that should be kept private to prevent harm and to abide by policies, regulations, and *laws*.

deontological (*deon = duty*) A classical ethical theory that states that the concept of *duty* is independent of the concept of good or consequences of the action. The nature of a person's actions are assessed by their ability to follow such things as religious codes, *laws*, and professional codes of ethics.

dilemma A situation in which one moral conviction or right action conflicts with another; exists because there is no one, clear-cut, right answer.

duty Actions required of professionals by society or actions that are self-imposed.

ethical relativism Moral judgments that depend on subjective or cultural acceptance.

ethics A systematic view of rules of conduct that is grounded in philosophical principles and theory; character and customs of societal values and norms that are assumed in a given cultural, professional, or institutional setting as ways of determining right and wrong.

fidelity Faithfully fulfilling vows and promises, agreements, and discharging *fiduciary* responsibilities.

fiduciary One often in a position of authority who obligates himself or herself to act on behalf of another (as in managing money or property) and assumes a *duty* to act in good faith and with care, candor, and loyalty in fulfilling the obligation; one (as an agent) having a fiduciary duty to another.

impairment Impairments are problems in body function or structure as a significant deviation or loss (World Health Organization, 2001, p. 12).

justice The act of distributing goods and burdens among members of society. Three types include

    compensatory justice The making of reparations for wrongs that have been done.

    distributive justice Comparative treatment or allocation of benefits and burdens to groups or individuals.

    procedural justice The assurance that processes are organized in a fair manner.

law A body or system of rules used by an authority to impose control over a system or humans.

meta-ethics A branch of philosophy that studies the underlying reasons for setting and making moral judgments.

morals Personal beliefs regarding values, rules, and principles of what is right or wrong; may be culture-based or culture-driven (see *ethical relativism*).

morality Personal beliefs regarding values, rules, and principles of what is right or wrong; may be culture-based or culture-driven.

nonmaleficence Not harming or causing harm to be done to oneself or others; the *duty* to ensure that no harm is done.

normative ethics The study of right and wrong from a societal perspective; the goal is the harmonious function of society and welfare of the individual member of society.

paternalism An action taken by one person in the best interests of another without his or her consent.

strong paternalism Action taken that is exercised against the competent wishes of another.

weak paternalism Action taken that is presumed to be according to the wishes of the person, usually done because of the individual's age or mental status.

rights Specific legal, moral, and social claims humans possess that require others to act in specific ways toward us. With all rights is the implied obligation or duty on the part of the other person.

situational ethics The consideration of circumstances and situations are used along with ethical principles and rules in the decision-making process.

social contract ethics An ethical theory that promotes the concept that each individual as a member of society adheres to moral norms in their relationships with each other and that the larger community has special responsibilities to protect the more vulnerable members of society.

teleological (*telos = end*) An *ethics* theory that focuses on outcomes or consequences. This classical theory states that the morally right action is determined by the outcome it produces; frequently stated as "the ends justify the means."

utilitarianism An ethical theory that states right actions are those that maximize utility (the greatest good for the greatest number); results in the best consequences for all involved.

veracity A duty to tell the truth.

virtue ethics A form of philosophy that emphasizes character and personal integrity; about deliberation and the quality of choice and how someone responds to his or her poor choices.

REFERENCE

World Health Organization. (2001). *International classification of functioning, disability, and health.* Geneva, Switzerland: Author.

Resources

ASSOCIATIONS AND ORGANIZATIONS

American Society for Bioethics and Humanities
(formerly Society for Health and
Human Values)
4700 W. Lake Avenue
Glenview, IL 60025-1485
Phone: 847-375-4745
Fax: 847-375-6345
Web: http://www.asbh.org
E-mail: info@asbh.org

American Society of Law, Medicine, & Ethics
765 Commonwealth Avenue, 16th Floor
Boston, MA 02215
Phone: 617-262-4990
Fax: 617-437-7596
Web: http://www.aslme.org
E-mail: info@aslme.org

American Occupational Therapy Association
4720 Montgomery Lane
PO Box 31220
Bethesda, MD 20824-1220
Phone: 301-652-6611, ext. 2930
Fax: 301-652-7711
Web:
    http://www.aota.org/Consumers/Ethics.aspx
    (Consumers/non-members)
    http://www.aota.org/Practitioners/Ethics.aspx
    (Members-additional resources)
E-mail: ethics@aota.org

Association for Practical and Professional Ethics
Indiana University
618 E. Third Street
Bloomington, IN 47405
Phone: 812-855-6450
Fax: 812-855-3315
Web: http://www.indiana.edu/~appe/
E-mail: appe@indiana.edu

National Center for Ethics in Healthcare
Veterans Health Administration
810 Vermont Avenue, NW
Washington, DC 20420
Phone: 202-501-0364
Fax: 202-501-2238
Web: http://www.ethics.va.gov/
E-mail: vhaethics@hq.med.va.gov

The Hastings Center
21 Malcolm Gordon Drive
Garrison, NY 10524-5555
Phone: 845-424-4040
Fax: 845-424-4545
Web: http://www.thehastingscenter.org/
E-mail: mail@thehastingscenter.org

The Joseph and Rose Kennedy
  Institute of Ethics
Georgetown University
Healy, 4th Floor
Washington, DC 20057
Phone: 202-687-8099
Fax: 202-687-8089
Web:
  http://kennedyinstitute.georgetown.edu/
  index.htm
E-mail: kicourse@georgetown.edu

ETHICS RESOURCES FOR EDUCATORS

Bioethics Discussion Pages
Host: Maurice Bernstein, MD
Web: http://www-hsc.usc.edu/?mbernste/
A variety of issues and information ranging from
  information for the ethics novice to provoca-
  tive and insightful discussions of substantive
  clinical issues.

Bioethics for Beginners
Internet Bioethics Project at the University of
  Pennsylvania Center for Bioethics
Web: http://www.bioethics.upenn.edu/bioethics/
Contains educational tools to help people inter-
  ested in bioethics learn more about what
  bioethics means, how it is studied, and where
  it can take you.

Bioethics for Clinicians
Canadian Medical Association Journal
Web:
  http://www.cmaj.ca/misc/bioethics_e.shtml
A Canadian series intended to clarify key concepts in bioethics and help integrate bioethics
  knowledge into daily practice.

The Ethics Connection
Markkula Center for Applied Ethics at
  Santa Clara University
Web: http://www.scu.edu/ethics/
The center's goal is to heighten ethical aware-
  ness and improve ethical decision-making.
  Topics include student issues, character de-

velopment, diversity, hospice, and other
  clinical issues.

National Reference Center for
  Bioethics Literature
Georgetown University/Kennedy Institute
  on Bioethics
Web: http://bioethics.georgetown.edu/nrc/
A specialized collection of books, journals, news-
  paper articles, legal materials, regulations, codes,
  government publications, and other relevant
  documents about issues in biomedical and professional ethics. The library holdings represent
  the world's largest collection related to ethical
  issues in medicine and biomedical research.

OTHER INTERNET RESOURCES

The following Internet sites have been selected to
  inform readers rather than to persuade or ad-
  vertise. These sites offer multiple links to other
  information sites and are updated frequently.

Association for Practical and
  Professional Ethics
http://www.indiana.edu/~appe/

American Society of Law, Medicine, & Ethics
http://www.aslme.org/

American Speech–Language–Hearing
  Association
http://www.asha.org/about/ethics/roundtable/

Bioethics for Beginners (on Bioethics.net)
http://www.bioethics.net/articles.php?
  viewCat=3&articleId=1

BIOETHICSLINE®
The Joseph P. and Rose F. Kennedy Institute
  of Ethics, Georgetown University
http://wings.buffalo.edu/faculty/research/
  bioethics/bio-line.html

Center for Academic Integrity
http://www.academicintegrity.org

The Center for Bioethics
http://www.bioethics.upenn.edu/

Center for Ethics and Social Justice,
    Loyola University
www.luc.edu/depts/ethics/

Center for Practical Bioethics
http://www.practicalbioethics.org/

Center for the Study of Ethics
    in the Professions
http://www.iit.edu/departments/csep/

Complete Guide to Ethics Management:
    An Ethics Toolkit for Managers
www.mapnp.org/library/ethics/ethxgde.htm

The Consortium Ethics Program,
    University of Pittsburgh
http://www.pitt.edu/~cep/

The Ethics Connection
http://www.scu.edu/ethics/links/

Ethics Update
http://ethics.sandiego.edu/

Health Insurance Portability and
    Accountability Act of 1996 (HIPAA)
http://www.hipaa.org/

Hoffberger Center for Professional Ethics,
    University of Baltimore
http://www.ubalt.edu/template.cfm?page=1882
Offers resources to increase ethical awareness
    and assist with ethical decision making and
    codes of ethics

The Institute for Global Ethics
http://www.globalethics.org/index.htm

Legal Information Institute,
    American Legal Ethics Library
http://www.law.cornell.edu/ethics/

National Bioethics Advisory Commission
www.bioethics.gov/

National Board for Certification in
    Occupational Therapy (NBCOT)
http://www.nbcot.org/

National Center for Ethics in Health Care
    Veteran Health Administration
http://www.ethics.va.gov/

National Institutes of Health;
    Bioethics on the Web
http://bioethics.od.nih.gov/
Resources related to research/IRB in bioethics.

National Reference Center for
    Bioethics Literature
http://www.georgetown.edu/research/nrcbl/

U.S. Office of Government Ethics
http://www.usoge.gov

Werner Institute for Negotiation
    and Dispute Resolution Creighton
    University School of Law
http://culaw.creighton.edu/wernerInstitute/
    index.aspx?p=2

Annotated Bibliography

Beauchamp, T. L., & Childress, J. F. (2001). *Principles of biomedical ethics* (5th ed.). New York: Oxford University Press.

Beauchamp, the author or coauthor of many books over about 40 years, is with the Kennedy Institute of Ethics and the Department of Philosophy at Georgetown University, a major center for bioethics nationally. Childress is with the Department of Religious Studies at the University of Virginia and also is a well-known author. This book was first published in 1977 and is one of the earliest texts to focus on bioethics. Each of the subsequent four revisions has been well-researched and expanded. This book is considered by many to be a standard for the field. It describes traditional bioethics theory and application. One criticism of past editions was that newer ethics theories and approaches, such as ethic of care or relationship-based approaches and virtue ethics, were given little attention. The 5th edition expands somewhat on virtue theory but does not go into much detail on ethic of care or narrative approaches to ethics.

According to the authors, "*ethics* is a generic term for various ways of understanding and examining the moral life" (p. 1, italics added). The book starts with chapters on moral norms and character and then devotes a chapter to each of four basic groups of principles, respect for autonomy, nonmaleficence, beneficence, and justice. The next chapter "examines the moral rules of veracity, privacy, confidentiality, and fidelity in the context of relationships between health care professionals and patients and between researchers and participants in research" (p. vii). The remaining two chapters examine moral theories and such as utilitarianism and duty-based theory and models of theory and application. Finally, 10 case studies are provided and analyzed.

The book assumes that readers have some knowledge of philosophy and may be a somewhat difficult read as a first book in bioethics. However, *Principles of Biomedical Ethics* is one of the most often referred to and cited texts by major authors in bioethics, and it is considered a standard and authoritative text in the field.

Beauchamp, T. L., & Walters, L. (2003). *Contemporary issues in bioethics* (6th ed.). Belmont, CA: Thomson/Wadsworth.

A collection of essays and court opinions on ethical issues in medicine. Includes information on ethical theories and ethics in relation to the law and public policy. Appropriate for graduate students.

Boss, J. A. (2008). *Ethics for life: A text with readings* (4th ed.). Boston: McGraw-Hill.

Covers a variety of ethnic and religious groups' ethical philosophies. Uses cases and personal reflection exercises throughout the chapters. Appropriate for all levels of students.

Bowie, G. L., Higgins, K. M., & Michaels, M. W. (1998). *Thirteen questions in ethics and social philosophy* (2nd ed.). New York: Harcourt Brace Jovanovich.

Ideal for introductory courses in ethics, applied ethics, or moral problems. In response to rising student interest in multiculturalism and to reflect the current issues of today, this edition has been updated with new articles and discussions on a variety of topics from sexual harassment to medical ethics. Appropriate for graduate students.

Jonsen, A. R., Siegler, M., & Winslade, W. J. (2006). *Clinical ethics: A practical approach to ethical decisions in clinical medicine* (6th ed.). New York: McGraw-Hill.

Offers advice about the often-difficult decisions health professionals encounter daily concerning ethics and medical issues. Provides a broad knowledge base as well as different perspectives so the best solution can emerge. A physician, lawyer, and ethicist combine expertise and supply invaluable insight on AIDS, economics of care, and more. Clinical cases coupled with counseling instruction highlight the material. Appropriate for graduate students.

Monagle, J. F., & Thomasma, D. C. (1998). *Health care ethics: Critical issues for the 21st century.* Gaithersburg, MD: Aspen.
Provides readers with an array of ethical dilemmas that they may see professionally and personally. Chapters focus on the plight of the reinstitutionalized person with chronic mental disorders, domestic violence, genetics, elderly people living in nursing homes, HIV/AIDS, the business of health care, and advanced directives.

Percesepe, G. (1995). *Introduction to ethics: Personal and social responsibility in a diverse world.* Englewood Cliff, NJ: Prentice Hall.
A comprehensive overview of ethics. Includes discussion of theory and reading groups as well as chapters related to race and power, sex and power, community, and more. Each chapter includes additional readings. Appropriate for all levels.

Purtilo, R. (2004). *Ethical dimensions in the health professions* (4th ed.). Philadelphia: W. B. Saunders.
An introductory textbook for students in the health care professions. There are sets of learning objectives at the beginning of each chapter and questions interspersed in the text to allow readers time to reflect on particular issues or points. Includes new chapters on organizational ethics, diversity, and assisted suicide. Each chapter uses case examples to illustrate and explain key points. Appropriate for all levels.

Purtilo, R. B., Jensen, G. M, & Royeen, C. B. (Eds.). (2005). *Educating for moral action: A sourcebook in health and rehabilitation ethics.* Philadelphia: F. A. Davis.
The book, the result of a 3-day working conference on Leadership in Ethics Education for Physical Therapy and Occupational Therapy at the Center for Health Policy and Ethics at Creighton University in September

2003, is divided into three major sections. Section 1, "Broadening Our Worldview of Ethics," includes chapters on topics such as respect, empathy, competence (client-centered and cultural), ethics of social responsibility and leadership, and the ethic of care as illustrated in the moral dimensions of a chronic illness. Section 2 centers on the health care environment, with chapters discussing moral agency; neuroethics; the impact of institutional practices and policies; roles of professional organization ethics committees; a process model for ethical decision making; and a discussion of what John Glaser referred to as the three realms of ethics: (1) individual, (2) organizational, and (3) societal. The editors note that "currently the individual realm has a hold on our moral thinking and action" (p. x), and Glaser and other authors in this text argue convincingly that occupational and physical therapists must broaden their view of what is right, moral, and ethical beyond the individual patient. Section 3 is devoted specifically to ethics education in physical and occupational therapy. Topics include mindfulness, exploring a link between spiritual self-awareness and ethical behavior, adult education models and ethics curricula, clinical education, research ethics, ethics of teaching, and the application of the scholarship of teaching and learning to critical inquiry about ethics education in the health professions.

While the book will be of interest to ethics educators, it is not intended to be used as another ethics textbook for the classroom. Rather, it is intended to be both a resource and a springboard for further discussion and comment.

Scott, R. (1998). *Professional ethics: A guide for rehabilitation professionals.* Philadelphia: Mosby.
Has a multidisciplinary focus. Addresses issues of informed consent, professional business arrangements, and more. Very appropriate for all levels of occupational and physical therapy students and clinical educators.

Sieber, J. E. (1992). *Planning ethically responsible research: A guide for students and internal review boards.* Newbury Park, CA: Sage.

Excellent small text that addresses practical issues and concerns for those doing research in an academic or clinical environment. Appropriate for graduate students.

Veatch, R. M., & Flack, H. E. (1997). *Case studies in allied health ethics.* Upper Saddle River, NJ: Brady/Prentice Hall.

Includes more than 80 cases from the areas of occupational therapy, physical therapy, clinical laboratory sciences, dietetics, and other allied health professions.

Helps to answer the question, "Do all allied health professions impose ethical standards and obligations on their practitioners?" Appropriate for all levels of students.

Weiss, J. W. (2006). *Business ethics: A stakeholder and issues management approach* (4th ed.). Mason, OH: Thomson South-Western

Integrating current and emerging issues rom today's complex workplace, this comprehensive text spotlights major contemporary and international topics in business ethics. Following the premise that, though ethical issues change, ethical principles remain constant, the text equips readers with practical guidelines to apply to the ethical dilemmas they will ultimately face in their world of work.

Originally compiled February 1995
Revised July 1998, November 2000,
December 2005, February 2008

Index

leaders of, 97–99

nondiscrimination and inclusion position statement from, 163–164

Professional and Technical Role Analysis Study, 11

Representative Assembly, 3, 4, 25, 114, 122

Standards and Ethics Commission, 11

Standards of Practice, 3–4

Web site resources of, 4, 47, 66, 114, 153, 173

Americans with Disabilities Act, 85–86, 87, 90

AOTA. See American Occupational Therapy Association

Appeal Panel, 26, 36–37

composition of, 36

decisions of, 36–37

Appeal process, 26, 36–37

Aspirational codes, 113, 114, 115, 137

Assertiveness

in conflict resolution, 167

in error prevention and reduction, 158, 159

Attitudes

definition of, 11

in occupational therapy practice, 11–13

Autonomy

in business transactions with clients, 73, 140

in competency of professionals, 18, 81

cultural issues in, 78, 79, 81

definition of, 8, 171

and freedom as core value, 12

in honesty of professionals, 15

Occupational Therapy Code of Ethics principle on, 6–7, 113

in organizational ethics, 103, 104, 105, 106

in payment for services, 49, 50, 51, 146

in professional education of students with disabilities, 88, 89

in value conflicts, 94, 95

B

Bartering for services, 20

Beneficence principle

in communication, 16

in competency of professionals, 18

cultural, 80, 81

definition of, 8, 171

in financial arrangements, 6, 20, 49, 50, 147

in honesty of professionals, 15

in leadership, 98

Occupational Therapy Code of Ethics on, 6, 113

in organizational ethics, 106

in productivity requirements, 151

in scope of practice, 141

Bias, cultural, 81

Billing practices, 20, 115–116

fraudulent, 20, 115–116, 147

and payment for services, 49–53. *See also* Payment for services

in productivity measures, 149–153

professional responsibilities in, 145–147

Bioethics, definition of, 171

Burnette, Norman L., 122, 123

Business transactions with clients, 71–75, 140

C

Capitated payment systems, 50, 145

Care ethics, definition of, 171

Caring of leaders, 97, 98

Casuistry, definition of, 171

Categorical imperative, definition of, 171

Censure, 28, 43

in credential and licensure violations, 68

by National Board for Certification in Occupational Therapy, 44

by state regulatory boards, 45

Centers for Medicare and Medicaid Services, 142, 147, 153

Certification, 3

loss of, 116

by National Board for Certification in Occupational Therapy, 43–44, 116

of occupational therapy assistants, 44

by state regulatory boards, 45

Citizenship of leaders, 97, 98

Commission errors, 156, 157

Common good

in professional education of students with disabilities, 89

social responsibility for, 17

Communication

competency of professionals in, 18

confidentiality of, 18
cultural issues in, 79, 81
ethical principles in, 16, 18
with occupational therapy assistant, 166,
167
plagiarism in, 61–63
practice errors related to, 157, 158
Compensatory justice, definition of, 8, 172
Competency, professional
challenges in maintenance of, 168–169
complaints on
in impaired practitioner, 19
to National Board for Certification
in Occupational Therapy, 44
to state regulatory boards, 44
cultural, 18, 77–82
as duty, 7, 17–18, 66, 80, 138
and duty to treat, 58
of novice practitioners, 167–168
Occupational Therapy Code of Ethics on, 113
and payment for services, 50, 51–52
and scope of practice, 140–141, 142, 143
and state licensure, 65–69
Complaints, 25–26, 28–38
confidentiality and disclosure of, 25, 28–29
disciplinary actions in. *See* Disciplinary
actions
dismissal of, 31
on educational programs, 116
formal statement of, 30, 38
jurisdiction in handling of, 114–117
NBCOT procedures in, 44
respondent's response to charges in, 33
review and investigation of, 26, 30–32,
115–116
sources of
from Ethics Commission, 30
from interested party, 29–30
time limits in filing of, 31
on unlicensed practitioners, 66
Complementary and alternative interventions,
payment for services in, 50
Compliance with code of ethics, enforcement
of, 25–38. *See also* Enforcement procedures
Concurrent therapy, legal and ethical issues
in, 149–153

Confidentiality, 18
in business transactions with clients, 73
in compliant and enforcement procedures,
25, 28–29
definition of, 8, 171
of disability-related information, 87, 88, 89
fidelity in, 8
Occupational Therapy Code of Ethics
principle on, 7, 113
Conflicts
abandonment of patient in, 55–57
decision-making process in, 129–136
of interest, 8, 18–19
in business transactions with clients,
71, 72, 74
in compliant investigation, 31
in Disciplinary Council, 34
of leaders, 97, 98
between patient rights and practitioner
values, 55–57, 93–95
resolution of, 8, 21, 25–26, 29–30
with occupational therapy assistant,
167
on productivity requirements, 152
Consensus in ethical decisions, 126–130
Consent, informed, 6, 15
in business transactions with clients, 140
cultural issues in, 79
payment for services in, 50, 51
Consultations, duty in, 7
Contracts
employee job description in, 115
for occupational therapy services, 16
Copyright laws, 62
*Core Values and Attitudes of Occupational
Therapy Practice* of AOTA, 3, 4, 5, 11–13,
27, 114, 119
Credentials, 65–69
state licensure in. See State licensure
Cultural competency, 18, 77–82
Cultural values of practitioner, 56–57

D

De jure complaints, 30
Decision making process, 129–136
of Appeal Panel, 36–37

in business transactions with clients, 140
common concerns in, 139–140
in comparison of illegal and unethical
        actions, 111, 137–138, 139
in copyright protection and plagiarism, 62
definition of, 137, 172
in Disciplinary Council hearings, 35
Family Education Rights and Privacy Act,
        85, 87
in occupational therapy assistants, 165, 166
in payments for services, 139, 145–147
        in productivity measures, 150, 152
in professional education of students with
        disabilities, 85–87, 90
in scope of practice, 139, 140–143
in state regulation of occupational therapy,
        3, 44–45, 65–69
violations of, 137–138
Leadership qualities, 97–99
Learning disability, 87–88
Liability issues in business transactions, 72
Licensure by states, 45, 65–69. *See also* State
        licensure

M
Marketing and advertising, veracity in, 15
Medicare and Medicaid
    on business transactions with clients, 72, 74
    payments from, 49, 53, 142, 145, 146, 147
        in group or concurrent therapy, 149,
            153
    on usual and customary practices, 141
Meta-ethics, definition of, 172
Moral errors, 155, 156
Morality, definition of, 8, 172
Morals, definition of, 172

N
National Board for Certification in Occupational
    Therapy, 3, 28, 66
    alleged violations reported to, 115
    certification by, 43–44, 116
    disciplinary actions of, 44
    jurisdiction of, 3, 31, 32, 41, 43–44, 115, 120
NBCOT. *See* National Board for Certification
    in Occupational Therapy

Noncompliance of patient
    discontinuation of services in, 57
    value conflicts in, 93
Nondiscrimination, AOTA position statement
    on, 163–164
Nonmaleficence principle
    in business transactions with clients, 73, 75
    in communication, 16
    in competency of professionals, 18
        cultural, 81
    in conflicts of interest, 18
    definition of, 8, 172
    in impaired practitioner, 19
    Occupational Therapy Code of Ethics on, 6,
        113
    in payments for services, 147
    in productivity requirements, 151
    in scope of practice, 141
    in sexual relationships, 19–20
Normative ethics, definition of, 172
Notifications in complaint and enforcement
    process, 37
    on Disciplinary Council hearings, 34
    on Ethics Commission charges, 32–33

O
Occupational Therapist Registered, 43–44
Occupational therapy, definition of, 5, 143
Occupational therapy assistants, 165–169
    certification of, 44
    scope of practice, 166–167
    supervision of, 165–166
Occupational Therapy Code of Ethics, 4, 5–9
    application of, 5–6
    as aspirational code, 114, 115, 137
    enforcement of, 25–38, 114–117
    and Ethics Commission functions, 119–120
    as factor in ethical decisions, 134
    and function of professional ethics, 113–117
    guidelines to, 15–21, 114, 119
    Preamble to, 5–6, 58
    principles of, 6–8, 113
    purpose of, 6
    review and revision of, 114
Office of Disability Accommodations, 86,
    87–88

Omission errors, 156, 157
Organizational ethics, 101–106

P

Paternalism, 103
    definition of, 172
PATRA (Professional and Technical Role
    Analysis Study), 11
Payment for services, 20, 49–53
    beneficence principle in, 6, 20, 49, 50, 147
    in fraudulent billing, 20, 115–116, 147
    in group or concurrent therapy, 149–152
    legal issues in, 139, 145, 146
        in productivity measures, 150, 152
    of occupational therapy assistant, 165
    in pro bono services, 20, 51
    in productivity measures, 149–153
    professional responsibilities in, 145–147
    in reduced-fee services, 20, 51
    in scope of practice, 141, 142
Plagiarism, 61–63
    definition of, 61
    forms of, 61, 62–63
Power issues, cultural differences in, 79
Practice errors, 155–160
Practitioner values balanced with patient
    rights, 55–57, 93–95
Pro bono services, 20, 51
Probation, 29, 43
    in credential and licensure violations, 68
    by NBCOT, 44
Procedural justice
    in communications, 16
    in conflict resolution, 21
    in conflicts of interest, 19
    definition of, 8, 172
    in ensuring common good, 17
    in financial arrangements, 20
    in honesty, 15
    in leadership, 98
    Occupational Therapy Code of Ethics principle
        on, 7, 113
    in productivity requirements, 152
    in professional education of students with
        disabilities, 88, 89

Product sales to clients, 71–75
Productivity measures, 111, 145, 149–153
    occupational therapy assistants in, 166
    practice errors in, 157
Professional and Technical Role Analysis
    Study of AOTA, 11
Professional behaviors
    guidelines to ethical principles in, 15–21
    responsibilities in, 27–28, 145–147
Prospective payment systems, 145
Prudence
    as core value, 12–13, 68
    in credentials and licensure, 68
    in leadership, 97
Psychological abandonment of patient, 59

R

Reason and prudence
    as core value, 12–13, 68
    in credentials and licensure, 68
    in leadership, 97
Record-keeping. *See* Documentation
Referrals
    of complaints to other authorities, 32
    of service recipients
        duty in, 7
        honesty in, 15
Refusal of services by client, 7
    cultural issues in, 78
    organizational ethics in, 103–106
Refusal to treat by health care professional
    patient abandonment in, 55–59
    in unsafe environment, 93–94, 95
    in value conflicts, 93, 94
Regulatory codes, 113–114, 137
Rehabilitation Act of 1973, Section 504, 85,
    86, 90
Reimbursement for services. *See* Payment for
    services
Relativism, ethical, definition of, 171
Religious values of practitioners, 56–57
Representative Assembly of AOTA, 3, 4, 25,
    114, 122
Reprimands, 28, 43
    in credential and licensure violations, 68

by NBCOT, 44

Research, procedural justice and common
good in, 17

Resident Assessment Instrument User's Manual,
149, 153

Resource allocation decisions, 50

Respect
in cultural competency, 81
in leadership, 97, 98
in organizational ethics, 104, 105
in value conflicts, 94

Revocation, 29, 43, 116
in credential and licensure violations, 68
by NBCOT, 44
by state regulatory boards, 45

Rights, definition of, 172

Root cause analysis of practice errors,
157–158

Roster of Fellows, 29

Roster of Honor, 29

Russell, William L., 122, 123

S

Safety issues in treatment environment,
93–94, 95
complaints on, 116
in error prevention, 158–160

Sanctions, 28, 30, 116
disclosure of, 29

Scheduling of work hours, 167–168

Scope of practice
legal issues in, 139, 140–143
for occupational therapy assistants,
166–167
reasoning process on, 142–143
usual and customary practices in, 141,
142, 143

Section 504 of 1973 Rehabilitation Act, 85,
86, 90

Self-care, cultural issues in, 79

Self-dealing in business transactions, 74

Self-interests
in business transactions, 74
in ethical decisions, 132–133

Sexual relationships

misconduct in, 19–20
as unethical and illegal, 137
withdrawal of services in, 56

Situational ethics, definition of, 172

Skilled nursing facilities
competency of practitioners in, 168–169
payment for services in, 145, 169
in concurrent or group therapy, 149,
151

Skin problems in practice errors, 155, 159

Slagle, Eleanor Clarke, 122, 123

Social contract ethics, definition of, 172

Social roles as factor in ethical decisions,
133–134

Standards and Ethics Commission of AOTA,
11

Standards of Practice of AOTA, 3–4

State licensure, 65–69
regulatory boards in, 45
requirements for, 138
scope of practice in, 141–142, 143
suspension or revocation of, 116

State regulatory boards, 3
alleged violations reported to, 115
disciplinary actions of, 45
ethical codes of, 114
jurisdiction of, 3, 31, 32, 41, 44–45, 115,
120
on legality of actions, 137
licensure requirements, 138

Sua sponte complaint, 30

Supervision
of novice practitioners, 167–168
of occupational therapy assistants,
165–166

Suspension, 29, 43
in credential and licensure violations, 68
by NBCOT, 44
by state regulatory boards, 45

Systemic errors, 156, 157

T

Technical errors, 155, 156

Teleological theory, 172

Termination of services, 15

abandonment of patient in, 55–59
guidelines on, 146, 152
Timeline
in appeal process, 36, 37
in Disciplinary Council decisions, 36
in filing of complaints, 31
in investigation of complaints, 32
Trust in leaders, 97, 98
Truth
in business transactions with clients, 74
as core value, 12, 67–68
in credentials and licensure, 67–68
cultural issues in, 78
in leadership, 97
and plagiarism prohibition, 61–63
and veracity. *See* Veracity

U
Unethical actions compared to illegal actions,
111, 137–138, 139
Upham, Elizabeth Greene, 121
Utilitarianism, definition of, 172

V
Values
core, in occupational therapy practice, 11–13
definition of, 11
of practitioner, balanced with patient
rights, 55–57, 93–95
Veracity
in business transactions with clients, 73, 74
in communication, 16
in conflicts of interest, 19
as core value, 12

in credentials and licensure, 67
in cultural competency, 81
definition of, 9, 172
in honesty, 15–16
in leadership, 97
Occupational Therapy Code of Ethics principle
on, 7–8, 113
and plagiarism prohibition, 61–63
in productivity requirements, 152
in professional education of students with
disabilities, 89
Violence
in abusive relationships, 94, 95
of patient, withdrawal of services in, 56
Virtue ethics, definition of, 172
Volunteer activities, 20

W
Web site resources, 173–175
of American Occupational Therapy
Association, 4, 47, 66, 114, 153, 173
of Centers for Medicare and Medicaid
Services, 142, 147, 153
Witnesses in Disciplinary Council hearings,
34–35
Work environment
productivity requirements in, 149–152
role of occupational therapy assistants in,
165–169
safety of, 93–94, 95
complaints on, 116
in error prevention, 158–160
scheduling and work hours in, 167–168

About the Editor

Deborah Yarett Slater, MS, OT/L, FAOTA, is a practice associate and staff liaison to the Ethics Commission and the Special Interest Sections at the American Occupational Therapy Association (AOTA.) She has over 30 years of experience in administration and management within diverse health care organizations, including oversight of large single and multi-disciplinary departments in both inpatient and outpatient settings. She has developed start-up off-site satellite clinics for several organizations, including new program development, and has extensive experience in financial management as well as reimbursement.

Ms. Slater also has been active in a variety of volunteer leadership positions for her state occupational therapy association, and prior to working at AOTA, served as AMSIS (Administration and Management Special Interest Section) committee member and chair, SISSC (Special Interest Section Steering Committee) chair, practice representative to the Ethics Commission (EC), and chair of the EC from 2000-2001, as well as being a member of the AOTA Board of Directors and chair of the ad hoc committee on scope of practice.

She has done numerous presentations on ethical issues and their application to clinical practice at state and national conferences. She also has published articles and an advisory opinion on topics related to ethics, most recently co-authoring a chapter on "Ethical Reasoning" in the text *Clinical and Professional Reasoning in Occupational Therapy* published in 2008. In addition, she co-edits the AOTA *Scope of Practice Issues Update* newsletter and has done conference workshops and an AOTA Insight continuing education presentation on "Understanding and Asserting the Occupational Therapy Scope of Practice" with AOTA colleagues.

Ms. Slater is an AOTA Fellow and has received numerous service awards for volunteer leadership positions. In May 2005 she received the Distinguished Alumna Award from Columbia University in New York City.